MATHEMATICAL TOOLS FOR ECONOMICS

MATHEMATICAL TOOLS FOR ECONOMICS

DARRELL A. TURKINGTON

Blackwell
Publishing

© 2007 by Darrell A. Turkington

BLACKWELL PUBLISHING
350 Main Street, Malden, MA 02148-5020, USA
9600 Garsington Road, Oxford OX4 2DQ, UK
550 Swanston Street, Carlton, Victoria 3053, Australia

The right of Darrell A. Turkington to be identified as the Author of this Work has been asserted in accordance with the UK Copyright, Designs, and Patents Act 1988.

First published 2007 by Blackwell Publishing Ltd

2   2009

Library of Congress Cataloging-in-Publication Data

Turkington, Darrell A.
  Mathematical tools for economics / Darrell A. Turkington.
    p. cm.
  Includes bibliographical references and index.
  ISBN: 978-1-4051-3380-7 (hardback)
  ISBN: 978-1-4051-3381-4 (pbk.)
  1. Economics, Mathematical. 2. Economics—Mathematical Models. I. Title.

HB135.T85 2007
330.01'5195—dc22

                                    2006026293

A catalogue record for this title is available from the British Library.

Set in 10/12pt Times
by Newgen Imaging Systems (P) Ltd., Chennai, India

The publisher's policy is to use permanent paper from mills that operate a sustainable forestry policy, and which has been manufactured from pulp processed using acid-free and elementary chlorine-free practices. Furthermore, the publisher ensures that the text paper and cover board used have met acceptable environmental accreditation standards.

For further information on
Blackwell Publishing, visit our website:
www.blackwellpublishing.com

For Josh and Niki

Contents

Preface

Books on mathematics for economists abound. Most of them are, at least for the student, dauntingly large, containing every bit of mathematics one could possibly need in economics. This book is far less ambiguous. What it purports to present is the material needed for a second course in mathematics for students of economics. Such a course is typically taught in a semester, in second or third year undergraduate courses in British universities and in upper division courses in American universities. In terms of subject matter, it fits somewhere between that of S. Glaister's *Mathematical Methods for Economists* and P. Lambert's *Advanced Mathematics for Economists* – two very good books already published by Blackwell. For the vast majority of students of economics, this will be the last course they do in mathematics or quantitative methods.

Having said this, there are a few sections in the book which may be considered too advanced or too specialized for such a course. These sections are marked with asterisks.

This book also differs in the way the material has been presented. The pedagogical approach taken is to stress the teaching of the mathematics first and follow this by illustrating how the mathematics has been used in economics. The examples taken from quantitative economics are not necessarily the latest applications in economics of the mathematical technique. Instead I have chosen what I regard to be the classic applications.

The text is aimed at students of economics rather than students of mathematics and in this respect, some compromises have been made. I have included some proofs of theorems to give students a flavor of mathematical reasoning but I have left others out so as not to overwhelm them. I have also included many worked out examples, believing that such examples are needed to illustrate and reinforce the rather abstract concepts and methods dealt with in the main text. Exercises are given at the end of each chapter section and these are specifically chosen to highlight the material covered in that section. Students are urged to work through these exercises, as for most of us, mathematics is learnt by doing mathematics.

Finally, the book contains some mathematics which may be new to economists. For example, I have included a section on matrix calculus. I believe that this subject matter will prove very useful for quantitative economists in the future and it is easily mastered once one is familiar with the usual techniques of multivariate calculus and the rules of matrix algebra with respect to vecs and traces.

Several people deserve to be thanked with regard to the production of this book: my colleagues Juerg Weber and Michael McAleer for their help and encouragement, Helen Reidy and Linda Barbour for their patience and skills in typing the manuscripts, my student Giri Parameswaren for his proof reading ability, and my wife Sonia for putting up with it all.

Part I

Matrix Algebra and Linear
Economic Models

Chapter 1

Matrix Algebra

1.1 Basic Concepts

Introduction

The vast majority of economic analysis is done in terms of linear economic models. In mathematical terms, such models are nothing more than systems of simultaneous linear equations. Matrix Algebra is a branch of mathematics that grew out of the study of such systems, so it is a convenient starting point for our work.

There are pedagogical reasons as well, for beginning our study with matrix algebra. Certain concepts from this body of knowledge, such as determinants and positive definite matrices, are a necessary prerequisite for the full understanding of optimization problems, which will occupy us in the second part of this book.

Without further ado, we commence our work with the mathematics of matrix algebra, leaving economic applications of this study to the end of this section.

The emphasis is on understanding the concepts used in this branch of mathematics. Proofs are given sparingly. Formal proofs of all the theorems presented in this Chapter can be found in Hadley, G. (1964) "Linear Algebra."

A **matrix** is a rectangular array of elements. We represent a matrix by a capital letter, sometimes with subscripts signifying the number of rows and columns in the array. Elements are represented by little letters. For example,

$$
A_{m \times n} = \begin{pmatrix}
a_{11} & a_{12} & \cdots & a_{1n} \\
a_{21} & a_{22} & \cdots & a_{2n} \\
\vdots & \vdots & & \vdots \\
a_{m1} & a_{m2} & \cdots & a_{mn}
\end{pmatrix}.
$$

Notice that each element also has two subscripts. The first signifies the row the element is in and the second signifies the column the element is in. In general

a_{ij} = the element in the ith row and jth column, the (i,j)th element. In our course, all the elements of a matrix will be real numbers. Often we represent a matrix more succinctly by $A = \{a_{ij}\}$, that is a bracket surrounding the (i,j)th element of the matrix.

Basic matrix operations

1   Equality

Two matrices are equal if they are of the **same order** (same numbers of rows and same number of columns), and if corresponding elements are equal.

That is, let $A_{m \times n} = \{a_{ij}\}$ and $B_{m \times n} = \{b_{ij}\}$. Then $A = B$ if and only if $a_{ij} = b_{ij}$.

2   Addition

Again let $A_{m \times n} = \{a_{ij}\}$ and $B_{m \times n} = \{b_{ij}\}$. Then $A + B = \{a_{ij} + b_{ij}\}$.

Example

Let

$$A = \begin{pmatrix} 2 & 5 & 7 \\ 8 & 9 & 1 \end{pmatrix}, \quad \text{and} \quad B = \begin{pmatrix} -1 & 6 & 4 \\ 5 & 2 & 0 \end{pmatrix}.$$

Then

$$A + B = \begin{pmatrix} 1 & 11 & 11 \\ 13 & 11 & 1 \end{pmatrix}.$$

3   Scalar multiplication

A **scalar** in matrix terminology is a real number. Suppose $A = \{a_{ij}\}$ and λ is a scalar.

Then

$$\lambda A = \{\lambda a_{ij}\}.$$

Example

Let

$$A = \begin{pmatrix} -2 & 0 \\ -7 & 4 \end{pmatrix}.$$

Then

$$-3A = \begin{pmatrix} 6 & 0 \\ 21 & -12 \end{pmatrix}.$$

4   Matrix multiplication

Let $A_{m \times n} = \{a_{ij}\}$ and $B_{n \times p} = \{b_{ij}\}$. Then $C = AB$ is a $m \times p$ matrix where (i, j)th element is given by $c_{ij} = \sum_{k=1}^{n} a_{ik} b_{kj} = a_{i1} b_{1j} + a_{i2} b_{2j} + \cdots + a_{in} b_{nj}$.

That is the (i, j)th element of the **product** matrix AB is formed by taking the ith row of A and the jth column of B, multiplying corresponding elements together, and summing.

Example

Let

$$A_{3 \times 2} = \begin{pmatrix} 3 & 0 \\ 1 & 2 \\ -1 & 6 \end{pmatrix} \quad \text{and} \quad B_{2 \times 2} = \begin{pmatrix} 2 & 1 \\ 1 & 1 \end{pmatrix}.$$

Then

$$C_{3 \times 2} = AB = \begin{pmatrix} 3.2 & + & 0.1 & 3.1 & + & 0.1 \\ 1.2 & + & 2.1 & 1.1 & + & 2.1 \\ -1.2 & + & 6.1 & -1.1 & + & 6.1 \end{pmatrix} = \begin{pmatrix} 6 & 3 \\ 4 & 3 \\ 4 & 5 \end{pmatrix}.$$

Note

(i)   For AB to exist, the number of columns of A must be equal to the number of rows of B. If this is the case we say A and B are **conformable** by multiplication.

(ii) The order of AB is found as follows:

$$\underset{m \times \not{n} \; \not{n} \times p}{AB}.$$

Example

In our example $C_{3 \times 2} = AB_{3 \times \not{2} \, \not{2} \times 2}$.

(iii) Matrix multiplication does not obey the **commutative law**. That is $AB \neq BA$ in general. In our above example AB is a 3×2 matrix but BA does not exist. Even if both AB and BA exist they will not be equal in general.

Example

Let

$$A_{3 \times 2} = \begin{pmatrix} 3 & 2 \\ -1 & 4 \\ 5 & 0 \end{pmatrix} \quad \text{and} \quad B_{2 \times 3} = \begin{pmatrix} -1 & 0 & 1 \\ 5 & 2 & 4 \end{pmatrix}.$$

Then

$$AB = \begin{pmatrix} 7 & 4 & 11 \\ 21 & 8 & 15 \\ -5 & 0 & 5 \end{pmatrix} \quad \text{and} \quad BA = \begin{pmatrix} 2 & -2 \\ 33 & 18 \end{pmatrix}.$$

Because AB and BA are of different orders, AB being 3×3 and BA being 2×2, they cannot possibly be equal.

Even if AB and BA are of the same order, generally $AB \neq BA$.

Example

Let

$$A = \begin{pmatrix} 2 & 1 \\ -1 & 0 \end{pmatrix} \quad \text{and} \quad B = \begin{pmatrix} 3 & 4 \\ 0 & 5 \end{pmatrix}.$$

Then

$$AB = \begin{pmatrix} 6 & 13 \\ -3 & -4 \end{pmatrix}$$

but

$$BA = \begin{pmatrix} 2 & 3 \\ -5 & 0 \end{pmatrix}.$$

Again $AB \neq BA$.

If both AB and BA exist for the former we say A **premultiplies** B, and for the latter we say A **postmultiplies** B.

(iv) Although matrix multiplication does not obey the commutative law, matrix multiplication and addition obey the **distributive law**. That is,

$$A(B + C) = AB + AC$$
$$(B + C)A = BA + CA.$$

5 The trace of a matrix

Suppose A is $n \times n$. That is the number of rows of A equals the number of columns of A. We say A is a **square** matrix. If this is the case, then the **trace** of A, denoted by $\operatorname{tr} A$, is the sum of the **main diagonal** elements. That is,

$$\operatorname{tr} A = \sum_{i=1}^{n} a_{ii}.$$

Example

Let

$$A = \begin{pmatrix} 3 & 7 & 5 \\ 6 & -1 & 0 \\ 0 & 0 & 4 \end{pmatrix}.$$

Then

$$\text{tr}\, A = 3 + (-1) + 4 = 6.$$

An important property of the trace operator is $\text{tr}\, AB = \text{tr}\, BA$ and $\text{tr}\, ABC = \text{tr}\, BCA = \text{tr}\, CAB$.

6 The transpose of a matrix

The **transpose** of $A_{m \times n} = \{a_{ij}\}$, denoted by A' is the $n \times m$ matrix where the (i, j)th element is a_{ji}. That is to get A' we interchange rows and columns of A.

Example

$$A_{3 \times 2} = \begin{pmatrix} 4 & 5 \\ 8 & 9 \\ 1 & 2 \end{pmatrix}, \quad A'_{2 \times 3} = \begin{pmatrix} 4 & 8 & 1 \\ 5 & 9 & 2 \end{pmatrix}.$$

If $A' = A$, then A is **symmetric**.

Example

Let

$$A = \begin{pmatrix} 3 & 4 & 5 \\ 4 & 2 & -1 \\ 5 & -1 & 0 \end{pmatrix}.$$

Then

$$A' = A.$$

Notice that for A to be symmetric it must be square.

Rules regarding transposes

(i) $(A')' = A$

(ii) $(A + B)' = A' + B'$

(iii) $(AB)' = B'A'$

(iv) AA' and $A'A$ are symmetric.

To satisfy ourselves that the last rule holds consider

$$(AA')' = (A')'A' \quad \text{by rule (iii)}$$
$$= AA' \quad\quad \text{by rule (i)}$$

Special matrices

1   The identity matrix

The **identity matrix** is a square matrix with ones in the main diagonal positions and zeros elsewhere.

Example

$$I_{2\times2} = \begin{pmatrix} 1 & 0 \\ 0 & 1 \end{pmatrix}, \quad I_{3\times3} = \begin{pmatrix} 1 & 0 & 0 \\ 0 & 1 & 0 \\ 0 & 0 & 1 \end{pmatrix}.$$

A neat way of representing the $n \times n$ identity matrix is $I_{n\times n} = \{\delta_{ij}\}$, where δ_{ij} is the **Kronecker delta** defined by

$$\delta_{ij} = 1 \quad i = j$$
$$= 0 \quad i \neq j.$$

The identity matrix plays the same role in matrix algebra as the number 1 does in the real number system. For any real number a,

$$1.a = a.1 = a.$$

Thus for any $m \times n$ matrix A

$$I_{m\times m}A = AI_{n\times n} = A.$$

Notice that to get conformability we have to use identity matrices of different orders.

2   *A scalar matrix*
A **scalar matrix** is $\lambda I_{n \times n}$ where λ is scalar. That is

$$\lambda I = \{\lambda \delta_{ij}\} = \begin{pmatrix} \lambda & & 0 \\ & \ddots & \\ 0 & & \lambda \end{pmatrix}.$$

The two big zeros signify that zeros fill up all the nondiagonal positions.

3   *A diagonal matrix*
A **diagonal matrix** is

$$D = \{\lambda_i \delta_{ij}\} = \begin{pmatrix} \lambda_1 & & 0 \\ & \ddots & \\ 0 & & \lambda_n \end{pmatrix}.$$

4   *The null matrix*
A **null matrix** is one all of whose elements are zeros. We represent the null matrix by a big zero.

Thus

$$0_{3 \times 2} = \begin{pmatrix} 0 & 0 \\ 0 & 0 \\ 0 & 0 \end{pmatrix}.$$

The null matrix plays the same role in matrix algebra as zero does in the real number system. For any real number a,

$$a + 0 = 0 + a = a$$

and

$$a.0 = 0.a = 0.$$

Thus for any $m \times n$ matrix A

$$A_{m \times n} + 0_{m \times n} = 0_{m \times n} + A_{m \times n} = A,$$
$$A_{m \times n} 0_{n \times n} = 0_{m \times m} A_{m \times n} = 0_{m \times n}.$$

5   An idempotent matrix

A square matrix is **idempotent** if $AA = A$. For example

$$A = \begin{pmatrix} \dfrac{1}{2} & \dfrac{1}{2} \\[2mm] \dfrac{1}{2} & \dfrac{1}{2} \end{pmatrix}.$$

6   Vectors

A **row vector** is a $1 \times n$ matrix whereas a **column vector** is a $m \times 1$ matrix. We represent a column vector thus:

$$a = \begin{pmatrix} a_1 \\ \vdots \\ a_n \end{pmatrix}.$$

The bold lettering reminds us this is a vector we are dealing with not a scalar. A row vector is then written a'. Notice that we can now look at an $m \times n$ matrix A as being made up of a series of vectors. First we can regard A as being made up of n $m \times 1$ column vectors, namely the n columns of A. Second we can regard A as being made up of m $1 \times n$ row vectors, namely the m rows of A. This is important when we come to deal with the rank of A.

The set of all $n \times 1$ column vectors (or $1 \times n$ row vectors) whose elements are real numbers has a special symbol namely $\mathbf{R}^n$. The nth Euclidean space, denoted by $\mathbf{E}^n$ is simply R^n with some notion of distance between two vectors defined on R^n. The usual concept of distance used is Euclidean distance which is defined as follows. The **distance** between vector x and vector y is

$$d(x,y) = \sqrt{(x_1 - y_1)^2 + (x_2 - y_2)^2 + \cdots + (x_n - y_n)^2}.$$

Exercises for 1.1

1. Consider the following matrices:

$$A = \begin{pmatrix} 2 & -5 \\ 6 & 1 \end{pmatrix}, \quad B = \begin{pmatrix} 2 & 3 \\ -2 & 7 \end{pmatrix}, \quad C = \begin{pmatrix} 0 & 1 \\ 5 & 8 \end{pmatrix}.$$

   (i)   Work out $A + B, -3A, C(A + B), CA + CB, (A + B)C$.
   (ii) Work out AB, BA, ABC, BCA, and CAB. Are AB and BA the same?
   (iii) Work out tr AB, tr BA, tr ABC, tr BCA, and tr CAB.

2. Let

$$A = \begin{pmatrix} 1 & 3 & 7 \\ 5 & 0 & 8 \end{pmatrix} \quad \text{and} \quad B = \begin{pmatrix} 1 & 4 & 2 \\ -2 & 5 & -1 \\ 3 & -1 & 6 \end{pmatrix}.$$

   (i) Work out AB. Does BA exist?
   (ii) Work out $(AB)'$ and $B'A'$.
   (iii) Show that AA' is symmetric.
3. Consider the following matrices:

$$A = \begin{pmatrix} 2 & -3 & -5 \\ -1 & 4 & 5 \\ 1 & -3 & -4 \end{pmatrix}, \quad B = \begin{pmatrix} -1 & 3 & 5 \\ 1 & -3 & -5 \\ -1 & 3 & 5 \end{pmatrix}, \quad \text{and}$$

$$C = \begin{pmatrix} 2 & -2 & -4 \\ -1 & 3 & 4 \\ 1 & -2 & -3 \end{pmatrix}.$$

   (i) Show that $AB = BA$. What is this product?
   (ii) Show that $AC = A$ and $CA = C$.
   (iii) Show that $A^2 = A$ and $C^2 = C$.
   (iv) Using the results of (i) and (ii) prove that
      (a) $A'ACB = 0$.
      (b) $(A - B)^2 = A^2 + B^2$.
4. Define a symmetric idempotent matrix. Let I be the $n \times n$ identity matrix and i be an $n \times 1$ vector whose elements are all 1. Let x be an $n \times 1$ vector whose jth element is x_j.
   (i) Prove that $A = i\,i'/n$ and $B = I - A$ are symmetric idempotent matrices. What are their traces?
      Hint: $i'i$ is a scalar and recall that tr $AB = $ tr BA.
   (ii) Describe the vectors Ax and Bx.

1.2   Determinants

Introduction

Associated with any square matrix A is a real number formed from the elements of A called the **determinant** of A.

Notation

$$|A|, \ \det A$$

1   2 × 2 Case

$$A = \begin{pmatrix} a_{11} & a_{12} \\ a_{21} & a_{22} \end{pmatrix}$$

$$|A| = a_{11}a_{22} - a_{12}a_{21}.$$

Example

$$\begin{vmatrix} 7 & 4 \\ -2 & 1 \end{vmatrix} = 7.1 - 4.(-2) = 15.$$

2   3 × 3 Case
Consider

$$A = \begin{pmatrix} a_{11} & a_{12} & a_{13} \\ a_{21} & a_{22} & a_{23} \\ a_{31} & a_{32} & a_{33} \end{pmatrix}.$$

Then

$$|A| = a_{11}a_{22}a_{33} - a_{12}a_{21}a_{33} + a_{12}a_{23}a_{31} - a_{13}a_{22}a_{31} + a_{13}a_{21}a_{32}$$
$$- a_{11}a_{23}a_{32}.$$

Example

$$\begin{vmatrix} 1 & 0 & 5 \\ 8 & -2 & 3 \\ 6 & 7 & 1 \end{vmatrix} = 1.(-2).1 - 0.8.1 + 0.3.6 - 5.(-2).6 + 5.8.7 - 1.3.7$$
$$= -2 + 60 + 280 - 21$$
$$= 317.$$

Note

(i) Each term in the expansion of these determinants has the same number of elements as the order of the square matrix concerned.

Example

$$2 \times 2 \quad 2$$
$$3 \times 3 \quad 3.$$

(ii) Each term has one and only one element from each row and one and only one element from each column.

(iii) The first subscripts on the elements of each term appear in natural order. The second subscripts appear in some rearrangement or permutation of the natural order.

Expansion of a determinant using cofactors

Consider A, an $n \times n$ matrix.

Definition

If we delete a row of A and a column of A we get an $n - 1 \times n - 1$ **submatrix** of A. If we take the determinant of this submatrix we get a **minor** of A.

Notation

Let $|A_{ij}|$ denote the minor of A when we delete row i and column j.

Example

$$A = \begin{pmatrix} 2 & 4 & 6 \\ 3 & 2 & 3 \\ 1 & 4 & 9 \end{pmatrix}$$

$$|A_{11}| = \begin{vmatrix} 2 & 3 \\ 4 & 9 \end{vmatrix} = 18 - 12 = 6$$

$$|A_{12}| = \begin{vmatrix} 3 & 3 \\ 1 & 9 \end{vmatrix} = 27 - 3 = 24$$

$$|A_{13}| = \begin{vmatrix} 3 & 2 \\ 1 & 4 \end{vmatrix} = 12 - 2 = 10$$

$$|A_{32}| = \begin{vmatrix} 2 & 6 \\ 3 & 3 \end{vmatrix} = 6 - 18 = -12.$$

Definition

The **cofactor** of a_{ij} denoted by c_{ij} is $c_{ij} = (-1)^{i+j}|A_{ij}|$.

Example

Above example

$$c_{11} = (-1)^{1+1}|A_{11}| = 1.6 = 6$$

$$c_{12} = (-1)^{1+2}|A_{12}| = (-1)24 = -24$$

$$c_{13} = (-1)^{1+3}|A_{13}| = 1.10 = 10$$

$$c_{32} = (-1)^{3+2}|A_{32}| = (-1)(-12) = 12.$$

The expansion

Theorem

Let A be an $n \times n$ matrix. Then

$$|A| = \sum_{j=1}^{n} a_{ij}c_{ij} \quad \text{for any } i, \text{ (expansion by the } i\text{th row), and} \qquad (1.1)$$

$$= \sum_{i=1}^{n} a_{ij}c_{ij} \quad \text{for any } j, \text{ (expansion by the } j\text{th column).} \qquad (1.2)$$

Writing (1.1) out in full we have

$$|A| = a_{i1}c_{i1} + a_{i2}c_{i2} + \cdots + a_{in}c_{in}.$$

That is, take the elements of the ith row, multiply each element by its cofactor and sum. This is true for any row.

Writing (1.2) out in full we have

$$|A| = a_{1j}c_{1j} + a_{2j}c_{2j} + \cdots + a_{nj}c_{nj}.$$

That is, take all elements of the jth column, multiply each element by its cofactor and sum. This is true for any column.

Above Example

Suppose we expand the determinant using the first row, then

$$|A| = a_{11}c_{11} + a_{12}c_{12} + a_{13}c_{13}$$
$$= 2(6) + 4(-24) + 6(10)$$
$$= 12 - 96 + 60$$
$$= -24.$$

Exercise

Choose any other row or column and obtain $|A|$.

Example

$$|A| = \begin{vmatrix} 0 & 2 & 0 & 3 \\ 5 & 4 & 0 & 7 \\ 6 & 2 & 1 & 3 \\ 0 & 1 & 0 & 1 \end{vmatrix}.$$

Notice that the third column has a lot of zeros in it. When these elements are multiplied by their cofactors we still get zero. Hence we would expand $|A|$ using the third column:

$$|A| = 1(-1)^{3+3} \begin{vmatrix} 0 & 2 & 3 \\ 5 & 4 & 7 \\ 0 & 1 & 1 \end{vmatrix} = \begin{vmatrix} 0 & 2 & 3 \\ 5 & 4 & 7 \\ 0 & 1 & 1 \end{vmatrix}.$$

Now we have to evaluate a 3×3 determinant. Again the first column has zeros in it. Therefore expanding this determinant using this column, we have

$$|A| = 5(-1)^{2+1} \begin{vmatrix} 2 & 3 \\ 1 & 1 \end{vmatrix} = -5(2 - 3) = 5.$$

Procedure

If a matrix has a row or a column with a lot of zeros in it, expand the determinant using that row or that column.

Question

What happens if a matrix has no zeros in it? To answer this question we first need to look at the properties of determinants.

Properties of determinants

The proofs for these properties can be found in Hadley, G. (1964) "Linear Algebra," pp. 87–95.

1. $|A'| = |A|$

Example

$$A = \begin{pmatrix} 3 & 7 & 1 \\ 2 & 0 & 6 \\ -1 & 4 & 1 \end{pmatrix} \quad A' = \begin{pmatrix} 3 & 2 & -1 \\ 7 & 0 & 4 \\ 1 & 6 & 1 \end{pmatrix}$$

$$\begin{vmatrix} 3 & 2 & -1 \\ 7 & 0 & 4 \\ 1 & 6 & 1 \end{vmatrix} = \begin{vmatrix} 3 & 7 & 1 \\ 2 & 0 & 6 \\ -1 & 4 & 1 \end{vmatrix}.$$

2. Interchanging any 2 rows (columns) of A changes the sign of the determinant.

Example

$$A = \begin{pmatrix} 3 & 7 & 1 \\ 2 & 0 & 6 \\ -1 & 4 & 1 \end{pmatrix}$$

$$B = \begin{pmatrix} -1 & 4 & 1 \\ 2 & 0 & 6 \\ 3 & 7 & 1 \end{pmatrix}.$$

Then $|B| = -|A|$.

3. If each element of a row (column) of A is multiplied by a real number λ to get B say

$$|B| = \lambda |A|.$$

Example

$$A = \begin{pmatrix} 3 & 7 & 1 \\ 2 & 0 & 6 \\ -1 & 4 & 1 \end{pmatrix}$$

$$B = \begin{pmatrix} 3 & 7 & 1 \\ -4 & 0 & -12 \\ -1 & 4 & 1 \end{pmatrix}.$$

Then $|B| = -2|A|$.

4. $|\lambda A_{n \times n}| = \lambda^n |A|$.

Example

$$A = \begin{pmatrix} 3 & 7 & 1 \\ 2 & 0 & 6 \\ -1 & 4 & 1 \end{pmatrix}$$

$$C = \begin{pmatrix} 6 & 14 & 2 \\ 4 & 0 & 12 \\ -2 & 8 & 2 \end{pmatrix} = 2A.$$

Then

$$|C| = 2^3|A|$$
$$= 8|A|.$$

5. If A and B are $n \times n$,

$$|AB| = |BA| = |A|.|B|.$$

6. Adding a multiple of one row (column) to another row (column) leaves the determinant unaltered.

It is property (6) that allows us to answer the question posed earlier in this section.

Procedure
If no zeros are in A, add a multiple of one row (column) to another to get as many zeros appearing as possible in a given row or column.

Example 1

$$\begin{vmatrix} 1 & 2 & 3 \\ 5 & 4 & 7 \\ 4 & 1 & 1 \end{vmatrix} \begin{matrix} \\ r_1' = r_1 - 2r_3 \\ r_2' = r_2 - 4r_3 \end{matrix} = \begin{vmatrix} -7 & 0 & 1 \\ -11 & 0 & 3 \\ 4 & 1 & 1 \end{vmatrix}$$

$$= 1(-1)^{3+2} \begin{pmatrix} -7 & 1 \\ -11 & 3 \end{pmatrix}$$

$$= -1(-21 + 11) = 10.$$

Example 2

$$
\begin{vmatrix} 2 & 4 & 6 & 8 \\ 3 & 2 & 3 & 4 \\ 1 & 4 & 9 & 3 \\ 2 & 2 & 3 & 4 \end{vmatrix} \underset{r_1' = r_1 - 2r_4}{=} \begin{vmatrix} -2 & 0 & 0 & 0 \\ 3 & 2 & 3 & 4 \\ 1 & 4 & 9 & 3 \\ 2 & 2 & 3 & 4 \end{vmatrix}
$$

$$
= -2(-1)^{1+1} \begin{vmatrix} 2 & 3 & 4 \\ 4 & 9 & 3 \\ 2 & 3 & 4 \end{vmatrix} \underset{r_1' = r_1 - r_3}{\overset{= -2}{=}} \begin{vmatrix} 0 & 0 & 0 \\ 4 & 9 & 3 \\ 2 & 3 & 4 \end{vmatrix} = 0.
$$

Before leaving this section we should note another interesting result to do with cofactors.

Theorem

Let $A = \{a_{ij}\}$ be an $n \times n$ matrix and c_{ij} be the cofactor of a_{ij}. Then

$$
\sum_j a_{ij} c_{kj} = 0 \quad i \neq k
$$

$$
\sum_i a_{ij} c_{ik} = 0 \quad j \neq k.
$$

This result is often referred to as the "expansion using alien cofactors."

Exercises for 1.2

1. Consider the square matrices

$$
A = \begin{pmatrix} -1 & 0 \\ 5 & 6 \end{pmatrix} \quad \text{and} \quad B = \begin{pmatrix} 2 & 4 \\ -1 & 9 \end{pmatrix}.
$$

Compute $|A|$, $|B|$, $|AB|$, $|BA|$, $|A'|$, and $|B'|$.

2. By actual computation show that $|A| = |A'|$ where

$$
A = \begin{pmatrix} 4 & 1 & 6 \\ 7 & 2 & 9 \\ 3 & 0 & 8 \end{pmatrix}.
$$

3. Evaluate the determinants of the following matrices:

$$
A = \begin{pmatrix} 1 & 2 & 3 & 2.5 \\ 1 & 2 & 3 & 4 \\ 1 & 2 & 3 & -3 \\ 3 & -1 & 1 & -2 \end{pmatrix} \quad \text{and} \quad B = \begin{pmatrix} 2 & 1 & 3 & 3 \\ 3 & 2 & 1 & 6 \\ 1 & 3 & 0 & 9 \\ 2 & 4 & 1 & 12 \end{pmatrix}.
$$

1.3　The Inverse of a Matrix

Introduction

Consider for a moment the real number system. Given any real number $a \neq 0$, there exists a number a^{-1}, the inverse of a, such that $a.a^{-1} = a.^{-1}a = 1$.

In fact $a^{-1} = 1/a$. Does this inverse property carry over to matrices? For a given matrix A does a matrix A^{-1} exist such that

$$AA^{-1} = A^{-1}A = I?$$

$$\uparrow$$

Identity matrix.

Note

(i) A can only have an inverse if A is square $n \times n$.

$$A_{m \times n}A_{n \times m}^{-1} = A_{n \times m}^{-1}A_{m \times n} \text{ only works if } m = n.$$

(ii) $A^{-1} \neq 1/A$ or $A^{-1} \neq I/A$.

We have no rules for dividing by a matrix!

Definition

Let A be a square $n \times n$ matrix. If there exists a square $n \times n$ matrix A^{-1} such that

$$A^{-1}A = AA^{-1} = I_{n \times n}$$

then A^{-1} is called the **inverse** of A.

Example

$$A = \begin{pmatrix} 1 & 2 & 1 \\ 0 & -1 & 1 \\ 2 & 1 & 4 \end{pmatrix}.$$

Consider

$$B = \begin{pmatrix} -5 & -7 & 3 \\ 2 & 2 & -1 \\ 2 & 3 & -1 \end{pmatrix}$$

$$AB = \begin{pmatrix} 1 & 2 & 1 \\ 0 & -1 & 1 \\ 2 & 1 & 4 \end{pmatrix} \begin{pmatrix} -5 & -7 & 3 \\ 2 & 2 & -1 \\ 2 & 3 & -1 \end{pmatrix} = \begin{pmatrix} 1 & 0 & 0 \\ 0 & 1 & 0 \\ 0 & 0 & 1 \end{pmatrix}.$$

Exercise
Show

$$BA = \begin{pmatrix} 1 & 0 & 0 \\ 0 & 1 & 0 \\ 0 & 0 & 1 \end{pmatrix}.$$

Hence, $B = A.^{-1}$

Not all square matrices have an inverse as the following theorem demonstrates.

Theorem
A square matrix A has an inverse if and only if $|A| \neq 0$.

Example
For A above we have

$$|A| = \begin{vmatrix} 1 & 2 & 1 \\ 0 & -1 & 1 \\ 2 & 1 & 4 \end{vmatrix} \underset{r_3' = r_3 - 2r_1}{=} \begin{vmatrix} 1 & 2 & 1 \\ 0 & -1 & 1 \\ 0 & -3 & 2 \end{vmatrix}$$

$$= 1(-1)^{1+1} \begin{vmatrix} -1 & 1 \\ -3 & 2 \end{vmatrix} = 1(-2+3) = 1 \neq 0.$$

Hence this matrix has an inverse.

Example

$$A = \begin{pmatrix} 1 & 7 & 5 \\ 3 & 21 & 15 \\ -2 & 8 & 17 \end{pmatrix}$$

$$|A| = \begin{vmatrix} 1 & 7 & 5 \\ 0 & 0 & 0 \\ -2 & 8 & 17 \end{vmatrix} = 0.$$

A has no inverse.

Definition

If a square matrix *A* has an inverse it is **nonsingular**. If a square matrix *A* has no inverse it is **singular**.

Properties of inverses

  (i) If *A* has an inverse then its inverse is unique.
 (ii) $(AB)^{-1} = B^{-1}A^{-1}$ provided *A* and *B* are nonsingular.
(iii) $(A^{-1})^{-1} = A$.
(iv) $(A')^{-1} = (A^{-1})'$.

Proof

  (i) Suppose *A* has two inverses *B* and *C* so $AB = BA = I$ and $AC = CA = I$. Now

$$B = BAC = IC = C.$$

 (ii) Consider

$$(AB)(B^{-1}A^{-1}) = ABB^{-1}A^{-1} = AIA^{-1} = AA^{-1} = I,$$

so $B^{-1}A^{-1}$ must be the inverse as the inverse is unique.
(iii) Consider $AA^{-1} = A^{-1}A = I$. It follows immediately that $A = (A^{-1})^{-1}$ as the inverse is unique.
(iv) Now as

$$AA^{-1} = A^{-1}A = I,$$

we have

$$(A^{-1})'A' = A'(A^{-1})' = I,$$

so

$$(A^{-1})' = (A')^{-1}.$$

Finding the inverse using cofactors

Definition

Let $A_{n \times n} = \{a_{ij}\}$. Suppose that we form a new matrix by replacing all the elements of A by their cofactors. The **adjoint** of A, denoted by Adj A is the transpose of this new matrix.

That is, let $c_{ij} =$ the cofactor of a_{ij} . Then

$$\text{Adj } A = \begin{pmatrix} c_{11} & c_{12} & \cdots & c_{1n} \\ c_{21} & c_{22} & \cdots & c_{2n} \\ \vdots & \vdots & & \vdots \\ c_{n1} & c_{n2} & \cdots & c_{nn} \end{pmatrix}' = \begin{pmatrix} c_{11} & c_{21} & \cdots & c_{n1} \\ c_{12} & c_{22} & \cdots & c_{n2} \\ \vdots & \vdots & & \vdots \\ c_{1n} & c_{2n} & \cdots & c_{nn} \end{pmatrix}.$$

Example

$$A = \begin{pmatrix} 1 & 2 & 3 \\ 1 & 3 & 5 \\ 1 & 5 & 12 \end{pmatrix}$$

$$\text{Adj } A = \begin{pmatrix} \begin{vmatrix} 3 & 5 \\ 5 & 12 \end{vmatrix} & -\begin{vmatrix} 1 & 5 \\ 1 & 12 \end{vmatrix} & \begin{vmatrix} 1 & 3 \\ 1 & 5 \end{vmatrix} \\ -\begin{vmatrix} 2 & 3 \\ 5 & 12 \end{vmatrix} & \begin{vmatrix} 1 & 3 \\ 1 & 12 \end{vmatrix} & -\begin{vmatrix} 1 & 2 \\ 1 & 5 \end{vmatrix} \\ \begin{vmatrix} 2 & 3 \\ 3 & 5 \end{vmatrix} & -\begin{vmatrix} 1 & 3 \\ 1 & 5 \end{vmatrix} & \begin{vmatrix} 1 & 2 \\ 1 & 3 \end{vmatrix} \end{pmatrix}'$$

$$= \begin{pmatrix} 11 & -7 & 2 \\ -9 & 9 & -3 \\ 1 & -2 & 1 \end{pmatrix}' = \begin{pmatrix} 11 & -9 & 1 \\ -7 & 9 & -2 \\ 2 & -3 & 1 \end{pmatrix}.$$

Theorem

Let A be a square matrix that is nonsingular. Then

$$A^{-1} = \text{Adj } A / |A|.$$

Proof

Consider the (i, j)th element of A Adj A which is given by

$$(A \text{ Adj } A)_{ij} = \sum_k a_{ik} c_{kj}.$$

If $i = j$ this is equal to $|A|$ and if $i \neq j$ this is equal to zero. Hence

$$A \operatorname{Adj} A = |A|I.$$

Similarly,

$$\operatorname{Adj} A \, A = |A|I.$$

It follows that $A^{-1} = \operatorname{Adj} A / |A|$.

Above Example

$$|A| = \begin{vmatrix} 1 & 2 & 3 \\ 0 & 1 & 2 \\ 0 & 3 & 9 \end{vmatrix} = (-1)^{1+1} \begin{vmatrix} 1 & 2 \\ 3 & 9 \end{vmatrix} = 3.$$

Hence

$$A^{-1} = \frac{1}{3} \begin{pmatrix} 11 & -9 & 1 \\ -7 & 9 & -2 \\ 2 & -3 & 1 \end{pmatrix} = \begin{pmatrix} \dfrac{11}{3} & -3 & \dfrac{1}{3} \\[2mm] -\dfrac{7}{3} & 3 & -\dfrac{2}{3} \\[2mm] \dfrac{2}{3} & -1 & \dfrac{1}{3} \end{pmatrix}.$$

Check
As an exercise show that $AA^{-1} = A^{-1}A = I_{3 \times 3}$.

Note
From our theorem we can clearly see that A^{-1} only exists if $|A| \neq 0$.

Finding the inverse using elementary row (column) operations

A second method for finding the inverse of a matrix involves the use of elementary row or elementary column operations. An **elementary row operation** is one of the following:

  (i) Interchanging any two rows of a matrix.
 (ii) Multiplying any row of a matrix by a nonzero scalar.
(iii) Adding a multiple of one row to another.

Similar definitions apply for **elementary column** operations.

The first thing to note about elementary row operations is that each operation can be achieved by premultiplying the matrix in question by a given matrix. The latter is called, naturally enough, an **elementary matrix**.

Example
Consider

$$A = \begin{pmatrix} 1 & 2 & 3 \\ 0 & 4 & 2 \\ 3 & 1 & 4 \end{pmatrix}.$$

(i) Suppose we interchange row 1 and 3 to achieve

$$B = \begin{pmatrix} 3 & 1 & 4 \\ 0 & 4 & 2 \\ 1 & 2 & 3 \end{pmatrix}.$$

Then

$$\begin{pmatrix} 0 & 0 & 1 \\ 0 & 1 & 0 \\ 1 & 0 & 0 \end{pmatrix} \begin{pmatrix} 1 & 2 & 3 \\ 0 & 4 & 2 \\ 3 & 1 & 4 \end{pmatrix} = B.$$

(ii) Suppose we multiply row 2 by -3 to achieve

$$C = \begin{pmatrix} 1 & 2 & 3 \\ 0 & -12 & -6 \\ 3 & 1 & 4 \end{pmatrix}.$$

Then

$$\begin{pmatrix} 1 & 0 & 0 \\ 0 & -3 & 0 \\ 0 & 0 & 1 \end{pmatrix} \begin{pmatrix} 1 & 2 & 3 \\ 0 & 4 & 2 \\ 3 & 1 & 4 \end{pmatrix} = C.$$

(iii) Suppose onto row 2 we add 7 times row 3 to achieve

$$D = \begin{pmatrix} 1 & 2 & 3 \\ 21 & 11 & 30 \\ 3 & 1 & 4 \end{pmatrix}.$$

Then

$$\begin{pmatrix} 1 & 0 & 0 \\ 0 & 1 & 7 \\ 0 & 0 & 1 \end{pmatrix} \begin{pmatrix} 1 & 2 & 3 \\ 0 & 4 & 2 \\ 3 & 1 & 4 \end{pmatrix} = D.$$

Similarly every elementary column operation can be achieved by post-multiplying a matrix by a suitable elementary matrix.

Example

Suppose for the above A, we subtract twice column 3 from column 2 to achieve

$$E = \begin{pmatrix} 1 & -4 & 3 \\ 0 & 0 & 2 \\ 3 & -7 & 4 \end{pmatrix}.$$

Then

$$E = \begin{pmatrix} 1 & 2 & 3 \\ 0 & 4 & 2 \\ 3 & 1 & 4 \end{pmatrix} \begin{pmatrix} 1 & 0 & 0 \\ 0 & 1 & 0 \\ 0 & -2 & 1 \end{pmatrix}.$$

As a point of interest it should be noted that all elementary matrices themselves are nonsingular.

Suppose now that we use elementary row operations to transform a non-singular matrix A to the identity matrix and suppose that that we need t such operations to do this. Suppose the first operation can be achieved by premultiplying A by the elementary matrix R_1 say, the next by premultiplying the new matrix by R_2 and so on. Then clearly we have $R_t R_{t-1} \ldots R_1 A = I$.

Now letting $R = R_t R_{t-1} \ldots R_1$ we have $RA = I$.

But as the inverse of a matrix is unique we must have $R = A^{-1}$. But $R = RI$. Thus we have

$$A^{-1} = RI = R_t R_{t-1} \ldots R_1 I.$$

Putting the last equality in words gives us our method. We perform elementary row operations on A to transform A to the identity matrix. The same set of elementary row operations will transform the identity matrix to the inverse of A.

Example

Find the inverse of

$$A = \begin{pmatrix} 1 & 2 & 1 \\ 0 & -1 & 1 \\ 2 & 1 & 4 \end{pmatrix}.$$

Note that before we start we should satisfy ourselves that A is nonsingular. As an exercise show that $|A| \neq 0$. Now in what follows we use the following notation:

$$A \cong B$$

means that B was achieved by applying elementary row (column) operations to A.

Using this notation consider

$$(A:I) = \begin{pmatrix} 1 & 2 & 1 & . & 1 & 0 & 0 \\ 0 & -1 & 1 & . & 0 & 1 & 0 \\ 2 & 1 & 4 & . & 0 & 0 & 1 \end{pmatrix}$$

$$\underset{r_3' = r_3 - 2r_1}{\cong} \begin{pmatrix} 1 & 2 & 1 & . & 1 & 0 & 0 \\ 0 & -1 & 1 & . & 0 & 1 & 0 \\ 0 & -3 & 2 & . & -2 & 0 & 1 \end{pmatrix}$$

$$\underset{\substack{r_1' = r_1 + 2r_2 \\ r_3' = r_3 - 3r_2 \\ r_2' = -r_2}}{\cong} \begin{pmatrix} 1 & 0 & 3 & . & 1 & 2 & 0 \\ 0 & 1 & -1 & . & 0 & -1 & 0 \\ 0 & 0 & -1 & . & -2 & -3 & 1 \end{pmatrix}$$

$$\underset{\substack{r_1' = r_1 + 3r_3 \\ r_2' = r_2 - r_3 \\ r_3' = -r_3}}{\cong} \begin{pmatrix} 1 & 0 & 0 & . & -5 & -7 & 3 \\ 0 & 1 & 0 & . & 2 & 2 & -1 \\ 0 & 0 & 1 & . & 2 & 3 & -1 \end{pmatrix}.$$

It follows then that

$$A^{-1} = \begin{pmatrix} -5 & -7 & 3 \\ 2 & 2 & -1 \\ 2 & 3 & -1 \end{pmatrix}.$$

We finish this section by noting that the inverse could also be achieved by using elementary column operations. Suppose that s elementary column operations are needed to transform A to the identity matrix I. Recalling that an elementary column operation can be achieved by postmultiplying the matrix by an appropriate elementary matrix we have

$$AC_1 \dots C_s = I.$$

Hence $A^{-1} = C_1 C_2 \dots C_s = IC_1 C_2 \dots C_s$.

That is the same elementary column operations that transform A to I, transform I to A^{-1}.

Finally in using this method we have the choice of working with elementary row operations or elementary column operations. What we cannot do, however, is mix them up.

Exercises for 1.3

1. Consider the matrices

$$A = \begin{pmatrix} 1 & -1 \\ 2 & 4 \end{pmatrix} \quad \text{and} \quad B = \begin{pmatrix} -2 & 0 \\ 5 & 8 \end{pmatrix}.$$

   Using cofactors compute A^{-1}, B^{-1}, and $(AB)^{-1}$.
2. Determine whether the following matrices are singular or nonsingular and if nonsingular, find their inverse:

$$A = \begin{pmatrix} 2 & 1 & 0 \\ 6 & 2 & 6 \\ -4 & -3 & 9 \end{pmatrix}, \quad B = \begin{pmatrix} 1 & 3 & 3 \\ 1 & 3 & 4 \\ 1 & 4 & 3 \end{pmatrix}.$$

3. Using elementary row operations find the inverse of

$$A = \begin{pmatrix} 2 & 4 & 5 \\ 0 & 3 & 0 \\ 1 & 0 & 1 \end{pmatrix}.$$

   Using elementary column operations find the inverse of

$$B = \begin{pmatrix} 1 & 2 & 1 \\ 0 & -1 & 1 \\ 2 & 1 & 4 \end{pmatrix}.$$

4. Show that A is nonsingular and find its inverse using cofactors where

$$A = \begin{pmatrix} 1 & -1 & 0 \\ 3 & 2 & 1 \\ 2 & 1 & 1 \end{pmatrix}.$$

1.4   Linear Dependence of Vectors and the Rank of a Matrix

Earlier we saw that an $m \times n$ matrix $A_{m \times n}$ can be regarded as made up of m row vectors or n column vectors.

Example

$$A = \begin{pmatrix} 4 & 5 & 7 \\ 8 & 6 & 2 \\ 5 & 0 & 1 \\ 6 & -1 & 7 \end{pmatrix}.$$

A can be regarded as made up of 3 4×1 column vectors

$$\begin{pmatrix} 4 \\ 8 \\ 5 \\ 6 \end{pmatrix}, \begin{pmatrix} 5 \\ 6 \\ 0 \\ -1 \end{pmatrix}, \begin{pmatrix} 7 \\ 2 \\ 1 \\ 7 \end{pmatrix}$$

or 4 1×3 row vectors

$$\begin{pmatrix} 4 & 5 & 7 \end{pmatrix},$$
$$\begin{pmatrix} 8 & 6 & 2 \end{pmatrix},$$
$$\begin{pmatrix} 5 & 0 & 1 \end{pmatrix},$$
$$\begin{pmatrix} 6 & -1 & 7 \end{pmatrix}.$$

The rank of a matrix has to do with the linear dependence of these vectors.

Definition
A set of m column vectors of order $n \times 1, a_1, a_2, \ldots, a_m$ are **linearly dependent** if there exist scalars $\lambda_1, \ldots, \lambda_m$ not all equal to zero, such that

$$\lambda_1 a_1 + \lambda_2 a_2 + \cdots + \lambda_m a_m = \underset{n \times 1}{\mathbf{0}}.$$

Example

$$a_1 = \begin{pmatrix} 2 \\ 1 \\ 5 \end{pmatrix}, \quad a_2 = \begin{pmatrix} 10 \\ 5 \\ 25 \end{pmatrix}.$$

Clearly

$$5a_1 - a_2 = \begin{pmatrix} 0 \\ 0 \\ 0 \end{pmatrix} = 0_{3 \times 1}.$$

Note

A similar definition holds for row vectors. Suppose $b'_1, \ldots, b'_m$ are m, $1 \times n$ row vectors. These are linearly dependent if there exist scalars, $\lambda_1, \ldots, \lambda_m$ not all equal to zero, such that $\lambda_1 b'_1 + \cdots + \lambda_m b'_m = 0'$.

Example

$$b'_1 = \begin{pmatrix} 4 & 6 & 8 \end{pmatrix} \quad b'_2 = \begin{pmatrix} 2 & 3 & 4 \end{pmatrix}$$
$$b'_1 - 2b'_2 = \begin{pmatrix} 0 & 0 & 0 \end{pmatrix}.$$

Definition

A vector **b** is a **linear combination** of vectors $a_1, \ldots, a_r$ if there exist scalars $\mu_1, \ldots, \mu_r$ such that $b = \mu_1 a_1 + \mu_2 a_2 + \cdots + \mu_r a_r$.

Note

Vectors being linearly dependent mean that at least one of these vectors can be written as a linear combination of the others.

Example

$$a_1 = \begin{pmatrix} 4 \\ 8 \\ 11 \end{pmatrix}, \quad a_2 = \begin{pmatrix} 1 \\ 2 \\ 2 \end{pmatrix}, \quad a_3 = \begin{pmatrix} 2 \\ 4 \\ 5 \end{pmatrix}.$$

Clearly $a_1 + 2a_2 - 3a_3 = 0$.
  Hence $a_2 = \frac{1}{2}a_1 + \frac{3}{2}a_3$.

Definition

A set of m column vectors $a_1, \ldots, a_m$ are **linearly independent** if

$$\lambda_1 a_1 + \lambda_2 a_2, \ldots, \lambda_m a_m = 0$$
$$\Rightarrow \lambda_1 = \lambda_2 = \cdots = \lambda_m = 0.$$

That is, the only linear combination of $a_1, \ldots, a_m$ that gives the null vector is the one with all scalars set equal to zero.

Example

$$e_1 = \begin{pmatrix} 1 \\ 0 \\ 0 \end{pmatrix}, \quad e_2 = \begin{pmatrix} 0 \\ 1 \\ 0 \end{pmatrix}, \quad e_3 = \begin{pmatrix} 0 \\ 0 \\ 1 \end{pmatrix},$$

are linearly independent.

A similar definition exists for row vectors.

Example

$$a'_1 = \begin{pmatrix} 1 & 3 & 5 & 6 \end{pmatrix}, \quad a'_2 = \begin{pmatrix} 0 & 4 & 3 & 2 \end{pmatrix}, \quad a'_3 = \begin{pmatrix} 0 & 0 & 4 & 5 \end{pmatrix},$$

are linearly independent.

Note

If a set of vectors contains the null vector, then the vectors in this set are linearly dependent.

Example

$$a_1 = \begin{pmatrix} 5 \\ 6 \\ 7 \end{pmatrix}, \quad a_2 = \begin{pmatrix} -3 \\ -1 \\ 8 \end{pmatrix}, \quad a_3 = \begin{pmatrix} 0 \\ 0 \\ 0 \end{pmatrix}.$$

Then $0a_1 + 0a_2 + \lambda a_3 = 0$ with $\lambda \neq 0$, so the vectors are linearly dependent.

The rank of a matrix

Once we have understood what constitutes a set of linearly independent vectors we are in a position to define the rank of a matrix. Recall from our section on vectors, that we can regard a matrix as being made up of a series of column vectors or a series of row vectors. The rank of a matrix is concerned with the linear dependence (or otherwise) of these vectors.

Definition

The **rank** of a matrix A, denoted by $r(A)$ is the maximum number of linearly independent rows of the matrix.

Clearly in this definition we are regarding the matrix as being made up of a series of row vectors. What happens if we view it as made up of column vectors? The following theorem provides the answer.

Theorem

The rank of a matrix A is also the maximum number of linearly independent columns of A.

Clearly from the definition and this theorem the rank of a matrix is less than or equal to the minimum of its number of rows and its number of columns.

That is, $r(A_{m \times n}) \leq \min(m, n)$.

Examples

$$A = \begin{pmatrix} 2 & 10 \\ 1 & 5 \\ 5 & 25 \end{pmatrix}, \text{ clearly has rank one.}$$

$$B = \begin{pmatrix} 2 & 10 \\ 1 & 5 \\ 5 & 20 \end{pmatrix}, \text{ clearly has rank two.}$$

$$I_3 = \begin{pmatrix} 1 & 0 & 0 \\ 0 & 1 & 0 \\ 0 & 0 & 1 \end{pmatrix}, \text{ clearly has rank three.}$$

$$C = \begin{pmatrix} 1 & 3 & 5 & 6 \\ 0 & 4 & 3 & 2 \\ 0 & 0 & 4 & 5 \\ 0 & 0 & 0 & 0 \end{pmatrix}, \text{ clearly has rank three.}$$

Methods for finding the rank of a matrix

In the above examples the rank is immediately obvious but for most matrices this is not the case. Two methods for determining the rank of a matrix involve the use of determinants and the use of elementary row or column operations.

1 Finding the rank using determinants

Recall that a minor of A is obtained by first crossing out a certain number of rows and/or columns of A to achieve a square submatrix of A, and then taking the determinant of this square submatrix. We have the following theorem.

Theorem
The rank of A is K if and only if every minor of submatrices of A, of order $(K + 1) \times (K + 1)$ or higher is zero, while there is at least one minor of a $K \times K$ submatrix which is nonzero.

Notice that if A is square, the largest submatrix we can get from A is A itself, so in applying this theorem we would start with $|A|$.

Example
Find the rank of

$$A = \begin{pmatrix} 1 & 7 & 5 \\ 3 & 21 & 15 \\ -2 & 8 & 17 \end{pmatrix}.$$

$$|A| = \begin{vmatrix} 1 & 7 & 5 \\ 0 & 0 & 0 \\ -2 & 8 & 17 \end{vmatrix} = 0.$$

$$\begin{vmatrix} 1 & 7 \\ 3 & 21 \end{vmatrix} = 0.$$

But

$$\begin{vmatrix} 3 & 21 \\ -2 & 8 \end{vmatrix} = 66, \text{ so } r(A) = 2.$$

2   Finding the rank using elementary row or column operations
An important theorem concerning rank is the following.

Theorem
For any two matrices A and B,

$$r(AB) \leq \min(r(A), r(B)).$$

Even more important for us is the following corollary of this theorem:

Corollary
The rank of a matrix A is unaltered when A is premultiplied or postmultiplied by a nonsingular matrix.

Recall that performing an elementary row or column operation on A is equivalent to premultiplying or postmultiplying A by an elementary matrix, and that all elementary matrices are nonsingular. Hence applying any elementary row or column operation to A leaves the rank of A unaltered. This forms the basis of our method. We apply elementary row or column operations to A to reduce

A to a matrix whose rank is immediately obvious. In general, for any matrix A, elementary row and column operations exist that will transform A into the form

$$\begin{pmatrix} I_K & 0 \\ 0 & 0 \end{pmatrix},$$

and then the $r(A) = K$.

Example
A trivial example is finding the rank of

$$A = \begin{pmatrix} 2 & 10 \\ 1 & 5 \\ 5 & 20 \end{pmatrix}.$$

As an exercise spot the elementary row operations needed to achieve the following transformations:

$$A \cong \begin{pmatrix} 5 & 20 \\ 1 & 5 \\ 2 & 10 \end{pmatrix}$$

$$\cong \begin{pmatrix} 5 & 20 \\ 1 & 5 \\ 0 & 0 \end{pmatrix}$$

$$\cong \begin{pmatrix} 1 & 4 \\ 1 & 5 \\ 0 & 0 \end{pmatrix}$$

$$\cong \begin{pmatrix} 1 & 4 \\ 0 & 1 \\ 0 & 0 \end{pmatrix}$$

$$\cong \begin{pmatrix} 1 & 0 \\ 0 & 1 \\ 0 & 0 \end{pmatrix}.$$

Hence $r(A) = 2$.

However we need not go as far as this to find the rank of a given matrix. Instead we apply elementary row and/or column operations on A to reduce A to its echelon form.

Definition

The **echelon form** of a matrix A is obtained by applying elementary row and/or column operations to A to reduce A to a series of steps proceeding from the upper left hand corner to the lower right hand corner with zeros below each step.

Example

The following matrices are in echelon form.

$$\begin{pmatrix} 1 & 4 \\ 0 & 1 \\ 0 & 0 \end{pmatrix}, \begin{pmatrix} 1 & -1 & 1 & 3 & 7 \\ 0 & 1 & 0 & -2 & 9 \\ 0 & 0 & 0 & 1 & 4 \\ 0 & 0 & 0 & 0 & 0 \end{pmatrix}.$$

Notice that the steps need not be of uniform length.

Theorem

The rank of A is the number of non-null rows in its echelon form.

Although we do not give a proof of this theorem, the result is obvious. Clearly we cannot obtain a linear combination of the non-null rows of the echelon form that will reduce the entries above the steps to zero. That is, the only linear combination of the non-null row vectors that gives the null vector, is the one with all the scalars in it set equal to zero. If we then introduce one of the null rows of the echelon form, the set of vectors automatically become linearly dependent.

Example

Use the above method to find the rank of

$$A = \begin{pmatrix} 1 & 7 & 5 \\ 3 & 21 & 15 \\ -2 & 8 & 17 \end{pmatrix}.$$

$$A \cong \begin{pmatrix} 1 & 7 & 5 \\ -2 & 8 & 17 \\ 3 & 21 & 15 \end{pmatrix}$$

$$\cong \begin{pmatrix} 1 & 7 & 5 \\ 0 & 22 & 27 \\ 0 & 0 & 0 \end{pmatrix}.$$

Therefore, $r(A) = 2$.

The next chapter represents an area in which we can apply the results of matrix algebra which we have obtained to date.

Exercises for 1.4

1. (i) Define a set of linearly dependent vectors.

   (ii) Show that the following vectors are linearly dependent:

$$x_1 = \begin{pmatrix} 2 \\ -7 \\ 1 \end{pmatrix}, \quad x_2 = \begin{pmatrix} 2 \\ 4 \\ -1 \end{pmatrix}, \quad x_3 = \begin{pmatrix} 14 \\ -27 \\ 3 \end{pmatrix}$$

   (iii) Show that the following vectors are linearly independent:

$$x_1 = \begin{pmatrix} 9 \\ -3 \\ -1 \end{pmatrix}, \quad x_2 = \begin{pmatrix} 2 \\ 0 \\ 2 \end{pmatrix}, \quad x_3 = \begin{pmatrix} -4 \\ 0 \\ 8 \end{pmatrix}$$

2. (i) Using elementary row or column operations, reduce A to its echelon form and hence find the rank of A where

$$A = \begin{pmatrix} 1 & -3 & -2 & 11 \\ 2 & -5 & 7 & -11 \\ -1 & 2 & -3 & 4 \\ 1 & 2 & -1 & 8 \end{pmatrix}.$$

   (ii) Using determinants, find the rank of

$$B = \begin{pmatrix} 1 & -1 & 2 & 2 \\ 2 & -1 & 4 & 2 \\ -1 & 1 & -1 & -1 \\ 2 & -1 & 2 & 1 \end{pmatrix}.$$

3. For all values of x determine the rank of A where

$$A = \begin{pmatrix} 5-x & 2 & 1 \\ 2 & 1-x & 0 \\ 1 & 0 & 1-x \end{pmatrix}.$$

4. Let X be an $n \times K$ matrix.

   (i) Prove that $N = X(X'X)^{-1}X'$ and $M = I - N$ are symmetric idempotent and that $MN = 0$.

   (ii) A theorem states that if C is a symmetric idempotent matrix, then the rank of C is equal to the trace of C. Use this theorem to find $r(N)$ and $r(M)$.

*1.5   Kronecker Products and Vecs of Matrices

In the previous section we showed that it is often convenient to regard an $m \times n$ matrix A as being made up of n $m \times 1$ column vectors. Suppose now that we want to make a large column vector out of the elements of A by stacking the columns of A under each other. The operator that does this is called the vec operator and its uses abound in econometrics and statistics. In these fields too, we sometimes have occasions to form very large matrices, in a certain manner, out of existing matrices. An operator that does this is the Kronecker product operator. It turns out that these two operators – the vec operator and the Kronecker product operator – are intimately connected. In this section, we introduce these operators and study some of their properties. In Section 6.5 of Chapter 6 we see how these concepts are used in matrix calculus.

Definition
Let A be an $m \times n$ matrix and suppose we partition A into its columns

$$A = (a_1 a_2 \ldots a_n)$$

where a_j is the jth column of A. Then **vec** A is the $mn \times 1$ column vector defined by

$$\mathbf{vec}\, A = \begin{pmatrix} a_1 \\ \vdots \\ a_n \end{pmatrix}.$$

Example
Suppose

$$A = \begin{pmatrix} 3 & 5 \\ -2 & 0 \\ 1 & 7 \end{pmatrix}.$$

Then

$$\text{vec}\, A = \begin{pmatrix} 3 \\ -2 \\ 1 \\ 5 \\ 0 \\ 7 \end{pmatrix}.$$

Definition

Let $A = \{a_{ij}\}$ be an $m \times n$ matrix and B be a $p \times q$ matrix. The $mp \times nq$ matrix given by

$$\begin{pmatrix} a_{11}B & \cdots & a_{1n}B \\ \vdots & & \vdots \\ a_{m1}B & \cdots & a_{mn}B \end{pmatrix}$$

is called the **Kronecker product** of A and B, denoted by $A \otimes B$.

Example

Let

$$A = \begin{pmatrix} 2 & 0 \\ 1 & 9 \end{pmatrix}, \quad B = \begin{pmatrix} -1 & 5 \\ 8 & 4 \end{pmatrix}.$$

Then

$$A \otimes B = \begin{pmatrix} 2\begin{pmatrix} -1 & 5 \\ 8 & 4 \end{pmatrix} & 0\begin{pmatrix} -1 & 5 \\ 8 & 4 \end{pmatrix} \\ 1\begin{pmatrix} -1 & 5 \\ 8 & 4 \end{pmatrix} & 9\begin{pmatrix} -1 & 5 \\ 8 & 4 \end{pmatrix} \end{pmatrix}$$

$$= \begin{pmatrix} -2 & 10 & 0 & 0 \\ 16 & 8 & 0 & 0 \\ -1 & 5 & -9 & 45 \\ 8 & 4 & 72 & 36 \end{pmatrix}.$$

Notice that for this example

$$B \otimes A = \begin{pmatrix} -1\begin{pmatrix} 2 & 0 \\ 1 & 9 \end{pmatrix} & 5\begin{pmatrix} 2 & 0 \\ 1 & 9 \end{pmatrix} \\ 8\begin{pmatrix} 2 & 0 \\ 1 & 9 \end{pmatrix} & 4\begin{pmatrix} 2 & 0 \\ 1 & 9 \end{pmatrix} \end{pmatrix}$$

$$= \begin{pmatrix} -2 & 0 & 10 & 0 \\ -1 & -9 & 5 & 45 \\ 16 & 0 & 8 & 0 \\ 8 & 72 & 4 & 36 \end{pmatrix}.$$

So the Kronecker product does not obey the commutative law. That is,

$$A \otimes B \neq B \otimes A.$$

Useful properties concerning Kronecker products are listed here:

(i) $A \otimes (B \otimes C) = (A \otimes B) \otimes C = A \otimes B \otimes C,$

(ii) $(A + B) \otimes (C + D) = A \otimes C + A \otimes D + B \otimes C + B \otimes D,$

(iii) $(A \otimes B)(C \otimes D) = AC \otimes BD$ provided AC and BD exist,

(iv) $(A \otimes B)' = A' \otimes B',$

(v) $r(A \otimes B) = r(A)r(B).$

Additionally if A is a square $n \times n$ matrix and B is a square $p \times p$ matrix then

(vi) $\text{tr} (A \otimes B) = \text{tr} A \, \text{tr} B,$

(vii) $|A \otimes B| = |A|^p |B|^n,$

and if A and B are nonsingular then

(viii) $(A \otimes B)^{-1} = A^{-1} \otimes B^{-1}.$

There is nothing stopping us taking the vec of a product of matrices and if we do this we find that the vec operator and the Kronecker product operator are connected as the following property shows:

$$\text{vec } ABC = (C' \otimes A)\text{vec } B. \tag{1.3}$$

The vec operator is also connected to the trace operator by the following property:

$$\text{tr } AB = (\text{vec } A')'\text{vec } B. \tag{1.4}$$

When we take the trace of a product of three matrices, the Kronecker product also enters the picture by using equations (1.3) and (1.4). For example,

$$\text{tr } ABC = (\text{vec } A')'\text{vec } BC$$
$$= (\text{vec } A')'(I \otimes B)\text{vec } C$$
$$= (\text{vec } A')'(C' \otimes I)\text{vec } B,$$

and numerous other such expressions can be obtained when we recall that $\text{tr } AB = \text{tr } BA$ and that $\text{tr } ABC = \text{tr } BCA = \text{tr } CAB.$

Exercises for 1.5

1. Let

$$A = \begin{pmatrix} -1 & 2 \\ 3 & 4 \end{pmatrix}, \quad B = \begin{pmatrix} 0 & 7 \\ 8 & 5 \end{pmatrix}, \quad C = \begin{pmatrix} 3 & 4 \\ 2 & -1 \end{pmatrix}.$$

(i) Find $A \otimes B$, $B \otimes A$, $(A \otimes B)'$, $A' \otimes B'$, tr $(A \otimes B)$, tr A tr B.

(ii) Find vec ABC and show that this vector is equal to $(C' \otimes A)$ vec B.

(iii) Find tr AB and show it is equal to $(\text{vec } A')'\text{vec } B$.

(iv) Find tr ABC and show it is equal to $(\text{vec } A')'(C' \otimes I)\text{vec } B$, for a suitable identity matrix I.

2. Let a and b be any column vectors. Show that $ab' = b' \otimes a = a \otimes b'$ and that vec $ab' = \text{vec } (b' \otimes a) = b \otimes a$.

Chapter 2

Simultaneous Linear Equations

2.1 Definitions

Most economic analysis is done in terms of linear economic models. A linear economic model consists of a system of linear equations, so we need to know how to handle such a system mathematically.

Definition
A **linear equation** in n variables $x_1, x_2, \ldots, x_n$ is

$$a_1 x_1 + a_1 x_2 + \cdots + a_n x_n = b$$

where $a_1, a_2, \ldots, a_n$ and b are constants (given real numbers).

Example

$$3x_1 + 4x_2 - 7x_3 = 10.$$

Note
  (i) In a linear equation all the variables have power of one.
      Thus $3x_1^2 + 4x_2 - 7x_3 = 10$ is not a linear equation.
      Also $3 \log x_1 + 4x_2 - 7x_3 = 10$ is not a linear function in x_1.
 (ii) We shall be concerned with m such linear equations in n variables. Thus
      m = number of equations
      n = number of variables.

Our analysis will be perfectly general, saying nothing about whether $m \geq$ or $\leq n$.

Write such a system as

$$a_{11}x_1 + a_{12}x_2 + \cdots + a_{1n}x_n = b_1$$
$$a_{21}x_1 + a_{22}x_2 + \cdots + a_{2n}x_n = b_2$$
$$\vdots \qquad\qquad \vdots \qquad \vdots$$
$$a_{m1}x_1 + a_{m2}x_2 + \cdots + a_{mn}x_n = b_m$$

where the a_{ij}s and the b_is are constants and the x_js are the variables.

Example

$$6x_1 + 5x_2 - 7x_3 = 10$$
$$-3x_1 + 2x_2 + 5x_3 = 11$$
$$4x_1 + 5x_2 \qquad\quad = 12$$
$$x_1 + 6x_2 + 7x_3 = 6.$$

Here $m = 4, n = 3$.
   In matrix notation we can represent our system as

$$\underset{m \times n}{A} \underset{n \times 1}{\mathbf{x}} = \underset{m \times 1}{\mathbf{b}}$$

where

$$\underset{m \times n}{A} = \begin{pmatrix} a_{11} & \cdots & a_{1n} \\ a_{21} & \cdots & a_{2n} \\ \vdots & \cdots & \vdots \\ a_{m1} & \cdots & a_{mn} \end{pmatrix}, \quad \underset{n \times 1}{\mathbf{x}} = \begin{pmatrix} x_1 \\ \vdots \\ x_n \end{pmatrix}, \quad \underset{m \times 1}{\mathbf{b}} = \begin{pmatrix} b_1 \\ \vdots \\ b_m \end{pmatrix}.$$

Example
Above example

$$\begin{pmatrix} 6 & 5 & -7 \\ -3 & 2 & 5 \\ 4 & 5 & 0 \\ 1 & 6 & 7 \end{pmatrix} \begin{pmatrix} x_1 \\ x_2 \\ x_3 \end{pmatrix} = \begin{pmatrix} 10 \\ 11 \\ 12 \\ 6 \end{pmatrix}$$
$$\qquad A \qquad\qquad \mathbf{x} \qquad\quad \mathbf{b}$$

We shall be concerned with solving these equations, that is, finding the most general $\mathbf{x}^*$ such that

$$A\mathbf{x}^* = \mathbf{b}.$$

Note

The following operations will not affect the solution:

 (i) Interchanging any pair of equations.
   $\Leftrightarrow$ Elementary row operation of interchanging 2 rows of $(A\ \mathbf{b})$.
 (ii) Multiplying both sides of an equation by a nonzero scalar.
   $\Leftrightarrow$ Elementary row operation of multiplying a row of $(A\ \mathbf{b})$ by a nonzero scalar.
 (iii) Adding a multiple of one equation to another.
   $\Leftrightarrow$ Elementary row operation of adding a multiple of one row of $(A\ \mathbf{b})$ to another.

Performing any elementary row operation on $(A\ \mathbf{b})$ leaves the solution unaltered!

Why don't we then perform elementary row operations on $(A\ \mathbf{b})$ in such a way that we end up with a system of equations that is easier to solve?

Note

The echelon form of $(A\ \mathbf{b})$ has steps with zero below the steps. If $(B\ \mathbf{k})$ is the echelon form of $(A\ \mathbf{b})$ then

$$B\mathbf{x} = \mathbf{k}$$

is a far simpler system of equations to solve, and has the same solution, if it exists, as $A\mathbf{x} = \mathbf{b}$!

2.2   Homogeneous Case $A\mathbf{x} = 0$

From the outset we can note the following:

 (i) It is clear that such a system always has a solution. Let $\mathbf{x} = \underset{n \times 1}{\mathbf{0}}$ then $\underset{m \times n}{A}\underset{n \times 1}{\mathbf{0}} = \underset{m \times 1}{\mathbf{0}}$. This is called the **trivial** solution.
 (ii) It is clear too that if a nontrivial solution exists an infinite number of solutions exist. Suppose $\mathbf{x}^*$ is a solution. That is

$$A\mathbf{x}^* = \mathbf{0}.$$

Therefore

$$\lambda A\mathbf{x}^* = \mathbf{0}$$

and

$$A(\lambda \mathbf{x}^*) = \mathbf{0} \text{ for any } \lambda \neq 0.$$

That is $\lambda \mathbf{x}^*$ is also a solution.

Whether a nontrivial solution exists or not depends on the $r(A)$.
Recall that $r(A) \leq \min(m, n)$, so

$$r(A) \leq n.$$

Also $r(A) =$ number of non-null rows of its echelon form B.

Case 1: $r(A) = r < n$
B has r non-null rows, so $B\mathbf{x} = \mathbf{0}$ represents r equations in n variables with $n > r$. Hence we can set $n - r$ variables to any values we like. Here we have an infinite number of solutions.

Example
Solve

$$
\begin{aligned}
x_1 + x_2 + x_3 + 3x_4 &= 0 \\
2x_1 - 2x_2 + 2x_3 + x_4 &= 0 \\
-2x_1 + 2x_2 - 2x_3 + 2x_4 &= 0 \\
x_1 + x_2 + x_3 + x_4 &= 0.
\end{aligned}
$$

In this system $m = 4, n = 4$.
In matrix notation we have

$$
\underbrace{\begin{pmatrix} 1 & -1 & 1 & 3 \\ 2 & -2 & 2 & 1 \\ -2 & 2 & -2 & 2 \\ 1 & 1 & 1 & 1 \end{pmatrix}}_{A} \underbrace{\begin{pmatrix} x_1 \\ x_2 \\ x_3 \\ x_4 \end{pmatrix}}_{\mathbf{x}} = \underbrace{\begin{pmatrix} 0 \\ 0 \\ 0 \\ 0 \end{pmatrix}}_{\mathbf{b}}.
$$

Our method is to perform elementary row operations on A to reduce A to its echelon form.

$$
\begin{array}{c}
A \cong \\
r_2' = r_2 - 2r_1 \\
r_3' = r_3 + 2r_1 \\
r_4' = r_4 - r_1
\end{array}
\begin{pmatrix}
1 & -1 & 1 & 3 \\
0 & 0 & 0 & -5 \\
0 & 0 & 0 & 8 \\
0 & 2 & 0 & -2
\end{pmatrix}
$$

$$
\begin{array}{c}
\cong \\
r_2 \leftrightarrow r_4
\end{array}
\begin{pmatrix}
1 & -1 & 1 & 3 \\
0 & 2 & 0 & -2 \\
0 & 0 & 0 & 8 \\
0 & 0 & 0 & -5
\end{pmatrix}
$$

$$
\begin{array}{c}
\cong \\
r_4' = r_4 + \dfrac{5}{8}r_3
\end{array}
\begin{pmatrix}
1 & -1 & 1 & 3 \\
0 & 2 & 0 & -2 \\
0 & 0 & 0 & 8 \\
0 & 0 & 0 & 0
\end{pmatrix}.
$$

This is the echelon form of A so we know

$$
r(A) = 3 < n = 4,
$$

and

$$
\begin{aligned}
x_1 - x_2 + x_3 + 3x_4 &= 0 \\
2x_2 \quad\quad - 2x_4 &= 0 \\
8x_4 &= 0,
\end{aligned}
$$

has the same solution as the original system.

Hence

$$
\begin{aligned}
x_4 &= 0 \\
x_2 &= 0 \\
x_1 &= -x_3.
\end{aligned}
$$

Let $x_3 = \lambda$, any scalar.

Then

$$\mathbf{x}^* = \begin{pmatrix} -\lambda \\ 0 \\ \lambda \\ 0 \end{pmatrix}$$

is the solution, which represents an infinite number of solutions.

Case 2: $r(A) = n$
B has n non-null rows.
   That is, B can be written as

$$n \left\{ B = \begin{pmatrix} * & & & & \\ 0 & * & & & \\ 0 & & \ddots & & \\ \vdots & & & * & \\ 0 & \cdots & \cdots & 0 \\ \vdots & \cdots & \cdots & \vdots \\ \vdots & \cdots & \cdots & \vdots \\ \vdots & \cdots & \cdots & \vdots \\ \vdots & & & \vdots \\ 0 & \cdots & \cdots & 0 \end{pmatrix} \right. ,$$

where the *s represent the entries above the steps.
   Then

$$B\mathbf{x} = \mathbf{0}$$

$$\Rightarrow x_n = 0$$

$$\Rightarrow x_{n-1} = 0$$

$$\vdots \qquad \vdots$$

$$\Rightarrow x_1 = 0.$$

i.e. Only the trivial solution exists.

Example
Solve

$$2x + y + 3z = 0$$
$$2x - y + z = 0$$
$$-4x + 4y + 2z = 0.$$

Let

$$A = \begin{pmatrix} 2 & 1 & 3 \\ 2 & -1 & 1 \\ -4 & 4 & 2 \end{pmatrix} \overset{\cong}{\underset{r_3' = r_3 + 2r_1}{r_2' = r_2 - r_1}} \begin{pmatrix} 2 & 1 & 3 \\ 0 & -2 & -2 \\ 0 & 6 & 8 \end{pmatrix}$$

$$\overset{\cong}{\underset{r_3' = r_3 + 3r_2}{}} \begin{pmatrix} 2 & 1 & 3 \\ 0 & -2 & -2 \\ 0 & 0 & 2 \end{pmatrix}.$$

Therefore $r(A) = 3 = n$ and

$$2x + y + 3z = 0$$
$$-2y - 2z = 0$$
$$2z = 0$$

has the same solutions as the original system. Clearly we have

$$z = 0$$
$$y = 0$$
$$x = 0.$$

Summary
Let A be $m \times n$. Then the system of linear equations $A\mathbf{x} = \mathbf{0}$ has a nontrivial solution if $r(A) < n$ where n is the number of variables. In this case there exists an infinite number of solutions.

Note
If $m < n$, the number of equations is less than the number of variables; then $r(A) < n$ and an infinite number of solutions always exist.

Exercises for 2.2

1. Consider the system of equations

$$x_1 \qquad + 2x_3 = 0$$
$$x_1 + 2x_2 + \ x_3 = 0$$
$$\alpha x_1 + \ x_2 + \ x_3 = 0.$$

    (i) For what values of α will the system only have the trivial solution?
    (ii) For what values of α will the system have an infinite number of solutions? Obtain the general solution for this case.

2. The system of equations

$$x_1 + 2x_2 + 2x_3 - \ 3x_4 = 0$$
$$x_1 \qquad - 2x_3 + 13x_4 = 0$$
$$3x_1 + 5x_2 + 4x_3 \qquad = 0$$

has an infinite number of solutions if a nontrivial solution exists. Why? Show that this is the case and obtain the general solution.

3. For what value of k do the following equations possess a nontrivial solution?

$$2x + 3y - 4z = 0$$
$$x + ky + 3z = 0$$
$$3x + ky - 2z = 0.$$

Find the solution.

2.3 Nonhomogeneous Case $Ax = b, \ b \neq 0$

It is now possible that no solution exists.

Definition
If no solution exists we say the equations are **inconsistent**.

Example
The equations

$$x + y = 4$$
$$x + y = 6,$$

have no solution.

We proceed as before and use elementary row operations to get the echelon form of $(A \; \mathbf{b})$. Suppose this is $(B \; \mathbf{k})$. Then

$$B\mathbf{x} = \mathbf{k}$$

has the same solution as $A\mathbf{x} = \mathbf{b}$, if it exists.

Test for consistency

Suppose $r(A \; \mathbf{b}) \neq r(A)$.

Let

$$r(A) = r \Rightarrow B \text{ has } r \text{ non-null rows.}$$

$$r(A \; \mathbf{b}) = r + 1 \Rightarrow (B \; \mathbf{k}) \text{ has } r + 1 \text{ non-null rows.}$$

What does $B\mathbf{x} = \mathbf{k}$ look like?

In general it looks like the following system

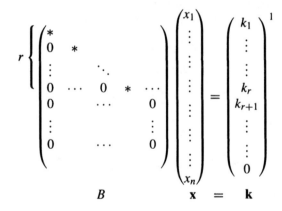

with $k_{r+1} \neq 0$.

Take the $(r + 1)$ equation in this system. We get $0x_1 + \cdots + 0x_n = k_{r+1}$, that is, $0 = k_{r+1} \neq 0$.

Clearly no solution exists. We have then the following theorem.

Theorem

If $r(A \; \mathbf{b}) \neq r(A)$ the equations are inconsistent.

---

[1] If the steps in the echelon form are not uniform, then without loss of generality variables can be renumbered to give this configuration.

Example

Test the following equations for consistency.

$$x_1 - 2x_2 + x_3 = 9$$

$$2x_1 + x_2 + x_3 = 10$$

$$-x_1 + 2x_2 - x_3 = -8$$

$$(A \ \mathbf{b}) = \begin{pmatrix} 1 & -2 & 1 & 9 \\ 2 & 1 & 1 & 10 \\ -1 & 2 & -1 & -8 \end{pmatrix}$$

$$\cong \begin{pmatrix} 1 & -2 & 1 & 9 \\ 0 & 5 & -1 & -8 \\ 0 & 0 & 0 & 1 \end{pmatrix},$$

so

$$r(A) = 2, \quad r(A \ \mathbf{b}) = 3.$$

$r(A) \neq r(A \ \mathbf{b})$, so the equations are inconsistent.

Case where the equations are consistent

Theorem

Suppose $A\mathbf{x} = \mathbf{b}$ has a particular solution $\mathbf{x} = \mathbf{p}$ and suppose $A\mathbf{x} = \mathbf{0}$ has a general solution $\mathbf{x} = \mathbf{z}$. Then all the solutions to $A\mathbf{x} = \mathbf{b}$ are given by

$$\mathbf{x} = \mathbf{p} + \mathbf{z}.$$

Proof

(i) Let $\mathbf{y}$ be an arbitrary solution to $A\mathbf{x} = \mathbf{b}$.

Then we wish to prove $\mathbf{y}$ can be written as the sum of a particular solution to $A\mathbf{x} = \mathbf{b}$ and the general solution to $A\mathbf{x} = \mathbf{0}$.

Let $\mathbf{p}$ be a particular solution to $A\mathbf{x} = \mathbf{b}$ and write

$$\mathbf{y} = \mathbf{p} + (\mathbf{y} - \mathbf{p}) = \mathbf{p} + \mathbf{z} \text{ say.}$$

Then

$$Az = Ay - Ap = 0.$$

Hence **z** is the general solution to $Ax = 0$.

(ii) Suppose **z** is any solution to $Ax = 0$. Now we wish to prove $y = p + z$ is the general solution to $Ax = b$. Clearly $Ay = Ap + Az = b + 0 = b$.

Note

If $r(A) = n$ then we have seen that the general solution to $Ax = 0$ is the trivial solution $x = 0$. For this case the nonhomogeneous equations have a general solution equal to a particular solution. That is it has a unique solution!

Summary: Rules of Rank for $Ax = b$

  (i) If $r(A \; b) \neq r(A)$, equations are inconsistent. No solution exists.
 (ii) If $r(A \; b) = r(A) = n$, an unique solution exists.
(iii) If $r(A \; b) = r(A) < n$, an infinite number of solutions exists.

Example

Test the following equations for consistency and find the solution if it exists:

$$x_1 + 3x_2 - 2x_3 = 11$$
$$2x_1 - 5x_2 + 7x_3 = -11$$
$$-x_1 + 2x_2 - 3x_3 = 4$$
$$x_1 + 2x_2 - x_3 = 8.$$

In this system $m = 4$, $n = 3$, and

$$(A \; b) = \begin{pmatrix} 1 & 3 & -2 & 11 \\ 2 & -5 & 7 & -11 \\ -1 & 2 & -3 & 4 \\ 1 & 2 & -1 & 8 \end{pmatrix}$$

$$\begin{matrix} \cong \\ r_2' = r_2 - 2r_1 \\ r_3' = r_3 + r_1 \\ r_4' = r_4 - r_1 \end{matrix} \begin{pmatrix} 1 & 3 & -2 & 11 \\ 0 & -11 & 11 & -33 \\ 0 & 5 & -5 & 15 \\ 0 & -1 & 1 & -3 \end{pmatrix}$$

$$\underset{\substack{r'_2 = \frac{1}{11}r_2 \\ r'_3 = \frac{1}{5}r_3}}{\cong} \begin{pmatrix} 1 & 3 & -2 & 11 \\ 0 & -1 & 1 & -3 \\ 0 & 1 & -1 & 3 \\ 0 & -1 & 1 & -3 \end{pmatrix}$$

$$\underset{\substack{r'_3 = r_3 + r_2 \\ r'_4 = r_4 - r_2}}{\cong} \begin{pmatrix} 1 & 3 & -2 & 11 \\ 0 & -1 & 1 & -3 \\ 0 & 0 & 0 & 0 \\ 0 & 0 & 0 & 0 \end{pmatrix}.$$

Hence $r(A \; \mathbf{b}) = r(A) = 2$ and the equations are consistent. Moreover

$$x_1 + 3x_2 - 2x_3 = 11$$

$$-x_2 + \; x_3 = -3$$

has the same solutions as the original system. A particular solution to the nonhomogeneous equations would be

$$x_3 = 0, \; x_2 = 3, \; x_1 = 2.$$

That is,

$$\mathbf{x} = \begin{pmatrix} 2 \\ 3 \\ 0 \end{pmatrix}.$$

Now the solution to $A\mathbf{x} = \mathbf{0}$ is given by

$$x_1 + 3x_2 - 2x_3 = 0$$

$$-x_2 + \; x_3 = 0.$$

Take $x_3 = \lambda$. Then $x_2 = \lambda$, $x_1 = -\lambda$.

Thus the general solution to the homogeneous equations is

$$\begin{pmatrix} -\lambda \\ \lambda \\ \lambda \end{pmatrix}, \quad \lambda \text{ being any real number,}$$

and to the nonhomogeneous equations is

$$\mathbf{x} = \begin{pmatrix} 2 - \lambda \\ 3 + \lambda \\ \lambda \end{pmatrix}.$$

Exercises for 2.3

1. For what value of c is the following system of equations consistent? Find the general solution when c takes this value:

$$x_1 + x_2 + x_3 = 2$$
$$2x_1 + x_2 + 2x_3 = 5$$
$$4x_1 + 3x_2 + 4x_3 = c.$$

2. Show that the equations

$$x + 3y - 2z = 9$$
$$3x - 17y + 8z = 49$$
$$3x - 4y + z = c$$

do not have a unique solution. For what values of c will they have (a) no solution, (b) an infinite number of solutions. For (b) obtain the general solution.

3. Consider the system of equations

$$x_1 + 4x_2 + 17x_3 + 4x_4 = 38$$
$$2x_1 + 12x_2 + 46x_3 + 10x_4 = 98$$
$$3x_1 + 18x_2 + 69x_3 + 17x_4 = 153.$$

   (i) Clearly if this system is consistent it has an infinite number of solutions. Why?
   (ii) Show that it is consistent and find the general solution.

2.4   Special Case $m = n$

Here the number of equations equals the number of variables. This is the case that most interests us as linear economic models are formulated in such a way that we essentially have n equations in n variables:

$$\underset{n \times n}{A\mathbf{x}} = \mathbf{b}.$$

Consider the case where $r(A) = n$. But $r(A) = n \Leftrightarrow |A| \neq 0 \Leftrightarrow A^{-1}$ exists. Premultiplying both sides by A^{-1} we have

$$A^{-1}A\mathbf{x} = A^{-1}\mathbf{b}.$$

That is, $\mathbf{x} = A^{-1}\mathbf{b}$ is the unique solution.

Note
We know that $A^{-1} = \mathrm{Adj}\,A/|A|$, so we can write the unique solution as

$$\mathbf{x} = \frac{\mathrm{Adj}\,A\mathbf{b}}{|A|}.$$

Example 1
Solve

$$3x_1 + 2x_2 = 7$$

$$4x_1 + \; x_2 = 1.$$

Here

$$A = \begin{pmatrix} 3 & 2 \\ 4 & 1 \end{pmatrix}, \quad \mathbf{b} = \begin{pmatrix} 7 \\ 1 \end{pmatrix}.$$

Now $|A| = 3 - 8 = -5 \neq 0$ so A^{-1} exists and we have an unique solution given by

$$\mathbf{x} = A^{-1}\mathbf{b} = \frac{\mathrm{Adj}\,A\mathbf{b}}{|A|}.$$

But

$$\mathrm{Adj}\,A = \begin{pmatrix} 1 & -4 \\ -2 & 3 \end{pmatrix}' = \begin{pmatrix} 1 & -2 \\ -4 & 3 \end{pmatrix},$$

so the unique solution is

$$\mathbf{x} = -\frac{1}{5}\begin{pmatrix} 1 & -2 \\ -4 & 3 \end{pmatrix}\begin{pmatrix} 7 \\ 1 \end{pmatrix} = -\frac{1}{5}\begin{pmatrix} 5 \\ -25 \end{pmatrix} = \begin{pmatrix} -1 \\ 5 \end{pmatrix}.$$

Example 2

Solve

$$x_1 + 2x_2 + 3x_3 = 3$$
$$x_1 + 3x_2 + 5x_3 = 0$$
$$x_1 + 5x_2 + 12x_3 = 6.$$

In matrix notation we have

$$\begin{pmatrix} 1 & 2 & 3 \\ 1 & 3 & 5 \\ 1 & 5 & 12 \end{pmatrix} \begin{pmatrix} x_1 \\ x_2 \\ x_3 \end{pmatrix} = \begin{pmatrix} 3 \\ 0 \\ 6 \end{pmatrix}.$$
$$A \qquad \mathbf{x} \quad = \quad \mathbf{b}$$

Now

$$\begin{matrix} |A| = \\ r_2' = r_2 - r_1 \\ r_3' = r_3 - r_1 \end{matrix} \begin{vmatrix} 1 & 2 & 3 \\ 0 & 1 & 2 \\ 0 & 3 & 9 \end{vmatrix} = 1(-1)^{1+1} \begin{vmatrix} 1 & 2 \\ 3 & 9 \end{vmatrix} = 9 - 6 = 3.$$

$$\begin{aligned}
\text{Adj}\, A &= \begin{pmatrix} (-1)^{1+1}\begin{vmatrix} 3 & 5 \\ 5 & 12 \end{vmatrix} & (-1)^{2+1}\begin{vmatrix} 1 & 5 \\ 1 & 12 \end{vmatrix} & (-1)^{1+3}\begin{vmatrix} 1 & 3 \\ 1 & 5 \end{vmatrix} \\ (-1)^{2+1}\begin{vmatrix} 2 & 3 \\ 5 & 12 \end{vmatrix} & (-1)^{2+2}\begin{vmatrix} 1 & 3 \\ 1 & 12 \end{vmatrix} & (-1)^{2+3}\begin{vmatrix} 1 & 2 \\ 1 & 5 \end{vmatrix} \\ (-1)^{3+1}\begin{vmatrix} 2 & 3 \\ 3 & 5 \end{vmatrix} & (-1)^{3+2}\begin{vmatrix} 1 & 3 \\ 1 & 5 \end{vmatrix} & (-1)^{3+3}\begin{vmatrix} 1 & 2 \\ 1 & 3 \end{vmatrix} \end{pmatrix}' \\
&= \begin{pmatrix} 11 & -7 & 2 \\ -9 & 9 & -3 \\ 1 & -2 & 1 \end{pmatrix}' \\
&= \begin{pmatrix} 11 & -9 & 1 \\ -7 & 9 & -2 \\ 2 & -3 & 1 \end{pmatrix}.
\end{aligned}$$

Hence

$$A^{-1} = \frac{1}{3} \begin{pmatrix} 11 & -9 & 1 \\ -7 & 9 & -2 \\ 2 & -3 & 1 \end{pmatrix},$$

and the unique solution is

$$\mathbf{x} = \frac{1}{3} \begin{pmatrix} 11 & -9 & 1 \\ -7 & 9 & -2 \\ 2 & -3 & 1 \end{pmatrix} \begin{pmatrix} 3 \\ 0 \\ 6 \end{pmatrix} = \frac{1}{3} \begin{pmatrix} 39 \\ -33 \\ 12 \end{pmatrix} = \begin{pmatrix} 13 \\ -11 \\ 4 \end{pmatrix}.$$

That is, $x_1 = 13$, $x_2 = -11$, $x_3 = 4$.

At this point it is convenient to introduce the following notation.

Notation

Let

$$A_{i\bullet} = i\text{th row of } A$$

and

$$A_{\bullet j} = j\text{th column of } A.$$

Using this notation we can write the ith element of the unique solution as

$$x_i = \frac{(\text{Adj}A)_{i\bullet}\mathbf{b}}{|A|}$$

An American mathematician noted a very useful way of writing this expression:

Cramer's Rule

The ith element of the solution can be written as

$$x_i = \begin{vmatrix} a_{11} & \cdots & b_1 & \cdots & a_{1n} \\ & \vdots & & & \vdots \\ a_{n1} & \cdots & b_n & \cdots & a_{nn} \end{vmatrix} \Big/ |A|. \tag{2.1}$$

In (2.1) the numerator is found by replacing the ith column of A by the vector $\mathbf{b}$ and taking the determinant.

Proof

Let c_{ij} be the cofactor of a_{ij} and recall that $\text{Adj}A = \{c_{ji}\}$. Expanding the determinant in the numerator of equation (2.1) using the ith column gives

$$\begin{vmatrix} a_{11} & \cdots & b_1 & \cdots & a_{1n} \\ & \vdots & & & \\ a_{n1} & \cdots & b_n & \cdots & a_{nn} \end{vmatrix} = \sum_j b_j c_{ji} = (\text{Adj } A)_{i\bullet}\mathbf{b}.$$

Example
Solve the equations

$$3x_1 + 2x_2 = 7$$
$$4x_1 + x_2 = 1.$$

Clearly in our notation

$$A = \begin{pmatrix} 3 & 2 \\ 4 & 1 \end{pmatrix} \quad \text{and} \quad \mathbf{b} = \begin{pmatrix} 7 \\ 1 \end{pmatrix}.$$

Now

$$|A| = 3 - 8 = -5 \neq 0.$$

Hence an unique solution exists, given by $\mathbf{x} = A^{-1}\mathbf{b}$.
Using Cramer's rule

$$x_1 = \frac{\begin{vmatrix} 7 & 2 \\ 1 & 1 \end{vmatrix}}{|A|} = \frac{7 - 2}{-5} = -1$$

$$x_2 = \frac{\begin{vmatrix} 3 & 7 \\ 4 & 1 \end{vmatrix}}{|A|} = \frac{3 - 28}{-5} = 5.$$

Exercises for 2.4

1. Using determinants decide whether the following systems of equations have an unique solution. If so use matrix inversion to obtain the solution. If no unique solution exists has the system an infinite number of solutions? If so find the general solution.
   (i)

$$x_1 + 2x_2 - 2x_3 = 1$$
$$2x_2 + x_3 = 4$$
$$x_1 \qquad + x_3 = 8.$$

(ii)

$$x_1 - x_2 - x_3 = 2$$
$$x_1 + 2x_2 + 3x_3 = 4$$
$$2x_1 - 2x_2 - 2x_3 = 5.$$

(iii)

$$x + y - 2z = 3$$
$$2x + 2y - 4z = 6$$
$$3x + 3y - 6z = 9.$$

2. State Cramer's rule. Use it to check your answers for question 1.

Chapter 3

Linear Economic Models

3.1 Introduction and Definitions

We come now to our first economic application of the mathematics we have learnt to date. Most economic analysis is done in terms of linear economic models, which involve a system of simultaneous linear equations. In some cases such a model may be a reasonable workable approximation to the real world economic phenomenon we are studying, but the real reason such models are used by economists is mathematical expediency. As we have seen, the mathematics of simultaneous linear equations is fully understood and such systems are relatively easy to solve. Moreover economists can call on the large body of knowledge about matrix algebra which backs up such systems.

Definitions
A **linear economic model** is then a system of simultaneous linear equations. These equations are of two sorts. First, are **definitional equations**, which represent relationships between variables which are true by definition. For example in a simple Keynesian model of a closed economy we would have the definitional equation

$$Y = C + I + G.$$

This gives us one way of defining gross national product. It is the sum of consumption, investment, and government expenditures. If we like, we could write the equation as

$$Y \equiv C + I + G,$$

where the $\equiv$ signifies that the relationship is true by definition.
The second sort of equation is called a **behavioral equation**. Such an equation purports to tell us something about the behavior of some "economic entity."

For example in a simple Keynesian model we may have the behavioural equation

$$C = \alpha + \beta Y, \quad \alpha \text{ and } \beta \text{ being constants,}$$

which tells us how consumers as a whole form their consumption expenditure. As another example, suppose that the demand equation in the microeconomic model of an individual market is given by

$$Q = a + bP + cY, \quad a, b, \text{ and } c, \text{ being constants.} \tag{3.1}$$

Again this equation tells us how buyers in this market determine the quantities they will purchase.

The equations themselves involve two sorts of variables: endogenous variables and exogenous variables. **Endogenous variables** form the focus of the model. The whole purpose of building the model in the first place is to get some insight into what determines the values of these variables and how these values change when given circumstances change. **Exogenous variables**, on the other hand, are variables whose values we take as given for the purposes of our economic analysis. They are usually one of three sorts. First, they can be noneconomic variables. For example, suppose that the supply function in a model for an agriculture good is

$$Q = e + fP + gR, \quad \text{with } e, f, g, \text{ constants.}$$

Here, R is a measure of rainfall and would be regarded as an exogenous variable. Second, they can be economic variables determined by noneconomic forces. For example in our Keynesian model, government expenditure G may be taken as an exogenous variable. It is certainly an economic variable but it is determined largely by political forces. Keynes himself regarded investment expenditure I as an exogenous variable being determined by "animal spirits." By this he meant that investment is largely determined by business men's expectations and Keynes thought these were largely psychological. Finally, exogenous variables can be economic variables determined by economic forces other than those at work in the model. For example in the above demand equation given by equation (3.1), national income Y may be regarded as an exogenous variable. Our model considers the market for a single good whereas Y is determined by the interaction of the thousands of markets that make up the economy. Our model concerns itself with microeconomic forces whereas Y is a macroeconomic variable.

The model itself comes in two forms, the structural form and the reduced form. The **structural form** is the original form of the model, as specified by economists. The **reduced form** is the solution to the model, when we solve for endogenous variables in terms of what we are given, namely exogenous variables. A model is said to be **complete** if

(i) the number of equations in the structural form is equal to the number of endogenous variables,
(ii) a unique solution exists.

The first condition, (i), ensures an economy of theorizing. We need no more equations than what is needed to do the job.

The solutions or values of the endogenous variables we obtain in the reduced form are called the **equilibrium values** of the endogenous variables. These are specified in terms of the given values of the exogenous variables.

Comparative static analysis concerns itself with how the equilibrium values of the endogenous variables change when we change the given values of the exogenous variables.

It is now time to give a mathematical presentation of our concepts. If we isolated the exogenous variables on the right hand side of our equations, we can always write the structural form of a complete model as

$$Ax = b,$$

where A is an $n \times n$ matrix of parameters of our model, x is an $n \times 1$ vector of the endogenous variables of the model, and b is an $n \times 1$ vector of the exogenous variables, or perhaps linear combinations of the exogenous variables. Completeness requires that $|A| \neq 0$ so the inverse of A exists and the reduced form is given by

$$x = A^{-1}b.$$

These are the equilibrium values of our endogenous variables. Sometimes we write

$$x^* = A^{-1}b \tag{3.2}$$

to remind ourselves that it is the equilibrium values we are dealing with in the reduced form.

The interesting thing about linear economic models is that the inverse A^{-1} embodies all the comparative static results of the model. Suppose we allow the values of some of our exogenous variables to change and these changes cause the vector b to change by Δb, then from equation (3.2) the resultant change in the equilibrium values of the endogenous variables is given by

$$\Delta x^* = A^{-1} \Delta b.$$

In summary we have the following:

Structural form:

$$Ax = b$$

Reduced form:

$$x^* = A^{-1} b$$

Comparative static analysis:

$$\Delta x^* = A^{-1} \Delta b.$$

Sometimes it requires considerable effort to obtain the entire reduced form of a linear economic model. After all, the models used by government agencies in the western world involve several hundred equations and it requires substantial computer technology along with complicated numerical techniques to invert the matrices involved. Moreover, often in our comparative static analysis we are only interested in how the changes in the values of the exogenous variables affect the values of certain key endogenous variables, perhaps only one key endogenous variable. In such a case we can use Cramer's rule to solve for the endogenous variable in question and conduct our comparative static analysis using that solution alone.

3.2 Examples of Linear Economic Models

Example 1

A simple supply and demand model

Structural form:

Demand equation: $Q = \alpha + \beta P \qquad \beta < 0$

Supply equation: $Q = a + b(P + S) \quad b > 0.$

In this model we have two behavioral equations, two endogenous variables quantity Q and price P, and one exogenous variable subsidy S.

Isolating the endogenous variables on the left hand side we have

$$Q - \beta P = \alpha$$

$$Q - bP = a + bS$$

or in matrix notation

$$\underset{A}{\begin{pmatrix} 1 - \beta \\ 1 - b \end{pmatrix}} \underset{x}{\begin{pmatrix} Q \\ P \end{pmatrix}} = \underset{b}{\begin{pmatrix} \alpha \\ a + bS \end{pmatrix}}.$$

Notice that the model is complete as the number of equations equals the number of endogenous variables and

$$|A| = \begin{vmatrix} 1 - \beta \\ 1 - b \end{vmatrix} = \beta - b \neq 0.$$

Reduced form:
Solving for our endogenous variables in terms of our exogenous variables we have

$$\begin{pmatrix} Q^* \\ P^* \end{pmatrix} = \frac{\text{Adj } Ab}{|A|} = \begin{pmatrix} -b & -1 \\ \beta & 1 \end{pmatrix}' \begin{pmatrix} \alpha \\ a + bS \end{pmatrix} \bigg/ (\beta - b).$$

$$= \begin{pmatrix} -b & \beta \\ -1 & 1 \end{pmatrix} \begin{pmatrix} \alpha \\ a + bS \end{pmatrix} \bigg/ (\beta - b).$$

That is,

$$Q^* = \frac{1}{\beta - b}(-b\alpha + \beta(a + bS))$$

$$P^* = \frac{1}{\beta - b}(-\alpha + a + bS).$$

These are the equilibrium values thrown up in the supply and demand diagram of elementary courses in economics:

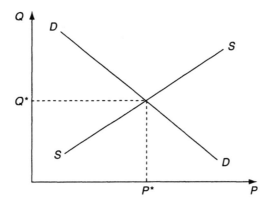

Comparative static analysis:
Suppose now the government decides to increase the subsidy by ΔS. As economists we are asked about the effect this will have on equilibrium price and quantity. Here

$$\Delta b = \begin{pmatrix} 0 \\ b\Delta S \end{pmatrix},$$

so

$$\begin{pmatrix} \Delta Q^* \\ \Delta P^* \end{pmatrix} = \frac{1}{\beta - b} \begin{pmatrix} -b & \beta \\ -1 & 1 \end{pmatrix} \begin{pmatrix} 0 \\ b\Delta S \end{pmatrix}$$

$$\Delta Q^* = \beta b \Delta S/(\beta - b)$$

$$\Delta P^* = b \Delta S/(\beta - b).$$

We can if we like put signs to these changes, as we are given that $\beta < 0, b > 0$, and $\Delta S > 0$. So

$$\Delta Q^* = (-\text{ve})(+\text{ve})(+\text{ve})/((-\text{ve}) - (+\text{ve})) = \frac{-\text{ve}}{-\text{ve}} = +\text{ve}$$

$$\Delta P^* = \frac{(+\text{ve})(+\text{ve})}{-\text{ve}} = -\text{ve}.$$

In our elementary economics course we would have solved this comparative static problem diagrammatically as follows:

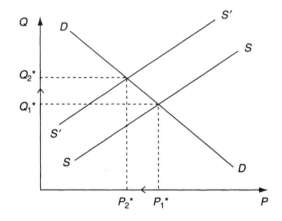

The increased subsidy causes the supply curve to move upwards and to the left thus increasing Q^* and decreasing P^*.

Notice that in the diagrammatic analysis all we get are the sign changes. In our mathematical analysis we get much more. We obtain the actual changes in Q^* and P^*. Using econometricians we could then estimate the crucial parameters β and b and so provide an estimate of the actual changes. This is the bread and butter stuff of economists!

Cramer's rule
Suppose now that in analyzing this model we are only interested in finding out how the increased subsidy affects the quantity of the good coming out of this market. If this is the case, we do not need the entire reduced form as we only want to solve for Q. We could if we liked use Cramer's rule to do this.

$$Q^* = \begin{vmatrix} \alpha & -\beta \\ a + bS & -b \end{vmatrix} \Big/ |A| = \frac{-b\alpha + \beta(a + bS)}{\beta - b}$$

so

$$\Delta Q^* = \frac{\beta b \Delta S}{\beta - b}$$

as before.

Example 2

A Keynesian macroeconomic model

Structural form:
This is given by

$$Y = C + I + G + X - M$$
$$C = \alpha + \beta Y \quad 0 < \beta < 1$$
$$M = a + bY \quad b > 0.$$

In this model we have one definitional equation and two behavioral equations. The endogenous variables are income Y, consumption C, and imports M. The exogenous variables are investment I, (following Keynes), government expenditure G, and exports X.

In elementary courses in economics we would probably solve this model recursively. First we would substitute the behavioral equations into the definitional equation and then solve for Y^*. Then we would substitute Y^* into the behavioral equations to obtain C^* and M^*. Certainly there is nothing wrong with this procedure but what we want to do is to use our newly acquired mathematical tools to find the reduced form in one fell swoop. Isolating the exogenous variables on the right hand side we have

$$
\begin{aligned}
Y - C + M &= I + G + X &&= E \\
-\beta Y + C & &&= \alpha \\
-bY + M & &&= a,
\end{aligned}
$$

where E stands for exogenous expenditure.

In matrix notation

$$
\begin{pmatrix} 1 & -1 & 1 \\ -\beta & 1 & 0 \\ -b & 0 & 1 \end{pmatrix} \begin{pmatrix} Y \\ C \\ M \end{pmatrix} = \begin{pmatrix} E \\ \alpha \\ a \end{pmatrix}
$$
$$A \qquad\qquad x \quad = \quad b \quad .$$

Again the model is complete as it has three equations and three endogenous variables and

$$
|A| = \begin{vmatrix} 1 & -1 & 1 \\ -\beta & 1 & 0 \\ -b & 0 & 1 \end{vmatrix} = \begin{vmatrix} 1 & -1 & 1 \\ 1-\beta & 0 & 1 \\ -b & 0 & 1 \end{vmatrix}
$$

$$
= (-1)(-1)^{1+2} \begin{vmatrix} 1-\beta & 1 \\ -b & 1 \end{vmatrix} = 1 - \beta + b \neq 0.
$$

Reduced form:

The reduced form is given by

$$\begin{pmatrix} Y^* \\ C^* \\ M^* \end{pmatrix} = A^{-1}b = \text{Adj } Ab/|A|.$$

Now

$$\text{Adj } A = \begin{pmatrix} 1 & \beta & b \\ 1 & 1+b & b \\ -1 & -\beta & 1-\beta \end{pmatrix}' = \begin{pmatrix} 1 & 1 & -1 \\ \beta & 1+b & -\beta \\ b & b & 1-\beta \end{pmatrix},$$

so

$$\begin{pmatrix} Y^* \\ C^* \\ M^* \end{pmatrix} = \frac{1}{1-\beta+b} \begin{pmatrix} 1 & 1 & -1 \\ \beta & 1+b & -\beta \\ b & b & 1-\beta \end{pmatrix} \begin{pmatrix} E \\ \alpha \\ a \end{pmatrix}.$$

Comparative static analysis:

Suppose now exports increase by ΔX and we want to know the effect of this on equilibrium income, consumption, and imports.

Here

$$\Delta b = \begin{pmatrix} \Delta X \\ 0 \\ 0 \end{pmatrix}$$

so

$$\begin{pmatrix} \Delta Y^* \\ \Delta C^* \\ \Delta M^* \end{pmatrix} = \frac{1}{1-\beta+b} \begin{pmatrix} 1 & 1 & -1 \\ \beta & 1+b & -\beta \\ b & b & 1-\beta \end{pmatrix} \begin{pmatrix} \Delta X \\ 0 \\ 0 \end{pmatrix}$$

$$= \frac{1}{1-\beta+b} \begin{pmatrix} \Delta X \\ \beta \Delta X \\ b \Delta X \end{pmatrix}.$$

Cramer's rule

Suppose in analyzing our model we want to determine the effect of an increase in government expenditure on equilibrium imports alone. Instead of solving for the entire reduced form, we could use Cramer's rule to solve for equilibrium M only.

Thus

$$M^* = \begin{vmatrix} 1 & -1 & E \\ -\beta & 1 & \alpha \\ -b & 0 & a \end{vmatrix} \Bigg/ |A|$$

$$= \begin{vmatrix} 1 & -1 & E \\ 1-\beta & 0 & E+\alpha \\ -b & 0 & a \end{vmatrix} \Bigg/ |A|$$

$$= (-1)(-1)^{1+2} \begin{vmatrix} 1-\beta & E+\alpha \\ -b & a \end{vmatrix} \Bigg/ (1-\beta+b)$$

$$= \frac{a(1-\beta) + b(E+\alpha)}{1-\beta+b}.$$

If G is increased by ΔG then E increases by ΔG so

$$\Delta M^* = \frac{b\Delta G}{1-\beta+b}.$$

Exercises for 3.2

1. (i) With reference to linear economic models define the following terms: endogenous variables, exogenous variables, definitional equations, behavioral equations, the structural form, the reduced form, equilibrium values of the endogenous variables, and a complete model.

   (ii) Again, referring to a linear model explain what is meant by comparative static analysis, and explain why Cramer's rule is often useful in deriving comparative static results.

2. Consider the simple Keynesian model (in structural form):

$$Y = C + I + G$$
$$C = a + bY$$
$$I = c + dY,$$

where G is exogenous government expenditure and b and d are the marginal propensities to consume and invest respectively.

   (i) Find the reduced form of the model.

   (ii) What are the effects on the equilibrium values of the endogenous variables caused by an unit change in the exogenous variable?

   (iii) Suppose we now change the consumption function to $C = a+b(Y-T)$, where taxation T is a new exogenous variable. How does this alter your

answer to (i)? How does your answer to (ii) change if we now let both
exogenous variables increase by unit amounts?

3. Suppose the market for Kiwi fruit can be modeled by

$$\text{Demand:} \quad Q = \alpha + \beta(P + T)$$
$$\text{Supply:} \quad Q = a + bP + cR.$$

In those equations the excise tax T and the level of rainfall R are exogenous variables, and we have the following a priori information about the
parameters of the model:

$$\alpha > 0, a > 0, \beta < 0, b > 0, c > 0.$$

Conduct a comparative static analysis to show the effects of
 (i) the government increasing the excise tax by ΔT,
 (ii) rainfall decreasing by ΔR.

4. Consider the following linear Keynesian macroeconomic model:

$$Y = C + I + G$$
$$C = \alpha + \beta Y \quad (\alpha > 0, \quad 0 < \beta < 1)$$
$$I = \gamma + \delta r \quad (\gamma > 0, \quad \delta < 0)$$
$$M = \tau Y + \lambda r \quad (\tau > 0, \quad \lambda < 0).$$

In the model, the money supply M and the government expenditure G are
regarded as exogenous variables. Using Cramer's rule find the reduced form
equations for national income Y and the interest rate r. Suppose that the
government wishes to increase its expenditure. How should it manipulate
the money supply M in order to prevent (equilibrium) interest rates from
rising?

3.3   The Use of Matrix Algebra in Statistics and Econometrics

We have seen in the previous section that often our comparative static results
in economics depend on a few crucial parameters from an underlying linear
economic model. It would be advantageous then if we could estimate these
parameters. Economists could then test hypotheses they may have about the
values of these parameters and use statistical techniques to forecast the values of
economic variables. This is the stuff in trade of an econometrician, a statistician
working in the field of economics.

In this section we have no intention of giving a survey of econometric techniques – that would take a text book larger than this one. What we want to do instead, is to illustrate how matrix algebra is used in statistics and econometrics. In particular, we seek to demonstrate how idempotent matrices and simultaneous linear equations arise naturally in their fields. We assume the reader has exposure to basic statistical concepts.

Suppose we have n random variables $X_1, X_2, \ldots, X_n$ which we place in an $n \times 1$ vector x say. Naturally enough x is called a **random vector**. Consider the matrices $A = i\,i'/n$ and $B = I - A$ where i is an $n \times 1$ vector whose elements are all one, and I is the $n \times n$ identity matrix. We saw in the exercises for 1.1 that these matrices are symmetric idempotent, i.e. $A' = A$ and $AA = A$ with similar results for B. Consider

$$Ax = i\,i'x/n.$$

Now

$$i'x/n = (11 \ldots 1) \begin{pmatrix} X_1 \\ X_2 \\ \vdots \\ X_n \end{pmatrix} \Big/ n = \sum_{i=1}^{n} X_i/n = \bar{X},$$

so

$$Ax = \bar{X}i = \begin{pmatrix} \bar{X} \\ \vdots \\ \bar{X} \end{pmatrix}, \tag{3.3}$$

a vector whose elements are the sample mean $\bar{X}$. It follows that

$$Bx = x - Ax = \begin{pmatrix} X_1 - \bar{X} \\ \vdots \\ X_n - \bar{X} \end{pmatrix}$$

is the vector of deviations from the sample mean.

A well-known statistic is the sample variance s^2 defined by

$$s^2 = \sum_{i=1}^{n} (X_i - \bar{X})^2/(n - 1).$$

But

$$(Bx)'\,(Bx) = (X_1 - \bar{X} \ldots X_n - \bar{X}) \begin{pmatrix} X_1 - \bar{X} \\ \vdots \\ X_n - \bar{X} \end{pmatrix} = \sum_{i=1}^{n} (X_i - \bar{X})^2,$$

and as B is symmetric and idempotent we have $(Bx)'(Bx) = x'B'Bx = x'BBx = x'Bx$. So we can then write our statistic as

$$s^2 = x'Bx/(n-1). \tag{3.4}$$

Further results concerning s^2 can be obtained using the fact that as $i'i = n$,

$$Ai = ii'i/n = i, \quad Bi = i - Ai = 0. \tag{3.5}$$

Suppose that μ is the population mean and consider

$$(x - \mu i)' B(x - \mu i).^1$$

Using our rules of matrix algebra we can write this expression as

$$x'Bx - 2\mu x'Bi + \mu^2 i'Bi = x'Bx$$

from equations (3.5). It follows that we can write

$$s^2 = x'Bx/(n-1) = (x - \mu i)'B(x - \mu i)/(n-1).$$

Consider now

$$(x - \mu i)'A(x - \mu i) = x'Ax - 2\mu i'Ax + \mu^2 i'Ai$$
$$= (Ax)'(Ax) - 2\mu i'Ax + \mu^2 (Ai)'(Ai)$$

where we have used the fact that A is symmetric idempotent. But using equations (3.3) and (3.5) we can now write

$$(x - \mu i)'A(x - \mu i) = n(\bar{X}^2 - 2\mu\bar{X} + \mu^2) = n(\bar{X} - \mu)^2. \tag{3.6}$$

The results given by equations (3.4) and (3.6) have important consequences for the distributions of common test statistics, such as the t test statistic.

Idempotent matrices also abound in linear regression analysis, which makes use of linear simultaneous equations. Econometrics grew out of regression analysis and the linear regression model still is the starting point of most text on econometrics. This model was designed by statisticians to capture the essence of 'near controlled experiments'. To illustrate what I mean by this, consider the classic example where agricultural economists believe that the yield from a

---

[1] This expression and $x'Bx$ are examples of quadratic forms studied in detail in the next chapter.

certain crop depends on crucial factors, such as the amounts of water, sunlight, fertilizer, and so on applied to the plots of land growing the crop. Our economists seek to study the effect of these crucial factors on yield, when considered in isolation. That is they hold all other factors that affect yield constant and only allow the crucial factors to vary. In *n* identical plots they plant identical seedlings, apply the same amounts of humidity, wind, and so on and allow the amounts of water, sunlight, fertilizer, and so on to vary across the plots. After a certain period of time the yields from the *n* plots are measured.

At first glance it looks as if our scientists have conducted a controlled experiment: they have held certain factors constant while allowing others to change. However, a little reflection reveals that this cannot be the case. For one thing there is no such thing as identical seedlings. Each seedling has its own genetic code that means the yield will vary slightly across the so-called "identical seedlings" even though the same amounts of water, sunlight, fertilizer, and so on have been applied. Moreover our agriculture economists cannot control for this variation.[2]

To allow for this inherent variation statisticians introduce a random variable into the equation.

Let

$$Y_i \; = \; \text{yield from plot } i,$$

$$X_{i1} = \text{amount of water applied to plot } i,$$

$$X_{i2} = \text{amount of sunlight applied to plot } i,$$

$$X_{i3} = \text{amount of fertilizer applied to plot } i,$$

$$\vdots \qquad\qquad \vdots$$

$$u_i \; = \; \text{a random variable.}$$

Suppose now there are *K* crucial factors and we believe the yield is linearly related to these factors. We could then write

$$Y_i = \alpha + \beta_1 X_{ii} + \beta_2 X_{i2} + \cdots + \beta_K X_{iK} + u_i, \quad i = 1, \ldots, n,$$

where u_i, is a random variable added to the end of the equation to capture the inherent variability associated with our experiment. This is called the **disturbance term**.

Statisticians then placed simplifying assumptions on the disturbance terms that allowed them to come up with interesting statistical results. These need not

---

[2]Recent research in genetics may soon make this statement incorrect.

concern us here, as our task is to illustrate how matrix algebra is used in their statistical model.

Writing our n yield equations out in full we have

$$Y_1 = \alpha + \beta_1 X_{11} + \beta_2 X_{12} + \cdots + \beta_k X_{1k} + u_1$$
$$Y_2 = \alpha + \beta_1 X_{21} + \beta_2 X_{22} + \cdots + \beta_k X_{2k} + u_2$$
$$\vdots \qquad \vdots \qquad \vdots \qquad \vdots \qquad \qquad \vdots \qquad \vdots$$
$$Y_n = \alpha + \beta_1 X_{n1} + \beta_2 X_{n2} + \cdots + \beta_k X_{nk} + u_n.$$

From our work in linear simultaneous equations we know that we can write such a system in matrix notation as

$$y = X\beta + u$$

where

$$\underset{n\times(k+1)}{X} = \begin{pmatrix} 1 & X_{11} & \cdots & X_{1k} \\ \vdots & \vdots & & \vdots \\ 1 & X_{n1} & \cdots & X_{nk} \end{pmatrix} \quad \underset{(k+1)\times 1}{\beta} = \begin{pmatrix} \alpha \\ \beta_1 \\ \vdots \\ \beta_k \end{pmatrix}, \; \underset{n\times 1}{y} = \begin{pmatrix} Y_1 \\ \vdots \\ Y_n \end{pmatrix}, \; \underset{n\times 1}{u} = \begin{pmatrix} u_1 \\ \vdots \\ u_n \end{pmatrix}.$$

Statisticians sought to make statistical inference about the parameters in β. The estimator they came up with is called the **ordinary least squares estimator**

$$\tilde{\beta} = (X'X)^{-1}X'y.^{[3]}$$

Using this estimator we can predict the yields that will result from a specified X by

$$\tilde{y} = X\tilde{\beta} = X(X'X)^{-1}X'y$$

Now consider the matrix

$$N = X(X'X)^{-1}X'.$$

Clearly

$$N' = \left(X(X'X)^{-1}X'\right)' = (X')'\left((X'X)'\right)^{-1}X' = X(X'X)^{-1}X' = N,$$

---

[3] We assume that $(X'X)^{-1}$ exists. It can be shown that this is the case if X has full column rank.

so N is a symmetric matrix. Moreover

$$NX = X(X'X)^{-1}X'X = X$$

so

$$NN = NX(X'X)^{-1}X' = N.$$

That is, N is idempotent. If we used $\tilde{y}$ as our predictor, we make **errors** given by the vector

$$e = y - \tilde{y} = y - Ny = My,$$

where $M = I - N$ and I is the $n \times n$ identity matrix. Now

$$MX = (I - N)X = X - NX = 0$$

so we can write the error vector as

$$e = M(X\beta + u) = Mu.$$

Moreover

$$M' = (I - N)' = I - N' = M$$

and

$$MM = (I - N)(I - N) = I - 2N + N^2 = I - N = M$$

so M too is a symmetric idempotent matrix.

The sum of the squared errors can be represented as

$$e'e = u'M'Mu = u'Mu.$$

These examples suffice to demonstrate that symmetric idempotent matrices abound in statistics and econometrics. In the next chapter we study expressions like $u'Mu$. These are called quadratic forms.

Chapter 4

Quadratic Forms and Positive Definite Matrices

4.1 Introduction

In this chapter we look at a branch of linear algebra which, although of considerable interest in itself, introduces concepts which are very important for us in later chapters, particularly those on optimization. A quadratic form in n variables is a generalization of a quadratic in a single variable. When written out in full, a **quadratic form** can be represented as

$$\sum_{i=1}^{n}\sum_{j=1}^{n} x_i a_{ij} x_j = a_{11}x_1^2 + a_{12}x_1x_2 + \cdots + a_{1n}x_1x_n$$

$$+ a_{21}x_2x_1 + a_{22}x_2^2 + \cdots + a_{2n}x_2x_n \qquad (4.1)$$

$$\vdots \qquad\qquad \vdots \qquad\qquad \vdots$$

$$+ a_{n1}x_nx_1 + a_{n2}x_nx_2 + \cdots + a_{nn}x_n^2,$$

where $x_1, x_2, \ldots, x_n$ represent the variables and the a_{ij}s are constants.

Example

$$8x_1^2 + 3x_1x_2 - 6x_1x_3 + 4x_2^2 - 5x_2x_3 + 2x_3^2. \qquad (4.2)$$

A quadratic form can always be written in matrix notation as $x'Ax$, where x is the $n \times 1$ vector $(x_1 \ldots x_n)'$ and A is the $n \times n$ matrix where the (i,j)th element is a_{ij}. Moreover, without loss of generality we can insist that the matrix A in the quadratic form is symmetric. For example the quadratic form given by (4.2) can be written as

$$(x_1 \quad x_2 \quad x_3) \begin{pmatrix} 8 & 1.5 & -3 \\ 1.5 & 4 & -2.5 \\ -3 & -2.5 & 2 \end{pmatrix} \begin{pmatrix} x_1 \\ x_2 \\ x_3 \end{pmatrix}.$$

The quadratic form, written out in full as in equation (4.1) is a rather ungainly beast. But it may be the case that regardless of the real values we feed in for the x s, the quadratic form always takes on a positive value (say). Of course if this happens it must result from a peculiar property of the constants of the quadratic form, the $a_{ij}s$. Moreover, given the ungainly nature of the expression, we may seek to simplify the quadratic form by some clever transformation of the variables. Hence in this chapter we seek to answer the following questions:

Question 1
Can we simplify the quadratic form by a clever transformation of variables?

Question 2
Is it the case that regardless of the real values we feed in for the variables $x_i s$ the quadratic form always takes on a certain sign?

Answering these questions involves talking about the eigenvalues and vectors of a given matrix. Again, in this Chapter if the readers want proofs for theorems presented here without them, they are referred to Hadley. G. (1964) "Linear Algebra," Chapter 7.

Definitions
With respect to question two, we have the following definitions:

(i) A matrix A is **positive definite** if $x'Ax > 0$ for all real x other than the null vector.

(ii) A matrix A is **positive semidefinite** if $x'Ax \geq 0$ for all real vectors x.

(iii) A matrix A is **negative definite** if $x'Ax < 0$ for all real x other than the null vector.

(iv) A matrix A is **negative semidefinite** if $x'Ax \leq 0$ for all real vectors x.

(v) A matrix A is **indefinite** if $x'Ax$ is positive for some vectors x and negative for others.

Instead of concentrating on the matrix A we often say that the quadratic form itself is positive definite if $x'Ax > 0$ for all x other than the null vector etc.

Exercises for 4.1
Express the following quadratic forms as $x'Ax$ where A is a symmetric matrix.

(i) $x_1^2 + x_1 x_2$

(ii) $13x^2 + 17y^2 + 32xy$

(iii) $3x_1^2 + x_2^2 + 3x_3^2 - 2x_1 x_2 + 3x_1 x_3 - 4x_2 x_3$

(iv) $-3x_1^2 - x_2^2 - 8x_3^2 + 2x_1 x_2 + 4x_2 x_3$

(v) $42x_1^2 + 3x_1 x_2 + 6x_2 x_3 + 8x_1 x_3 + 2x_2^2 - 7x_3^2$.

4.2   Eigenvalues of a Symmetric Matrix

Definition

Let A be an $n \times n$ matrix. An **eigenvalue** of A is a number λ, for which there exists a vector x, not equal to the null vector, such that

$$Ax = \lambda x.$$

The vector x is called an **eigenvector** of A.[1]

We can write the equation defining eigenvalues and eigenvectors of A as

$$(A - \lambda I)x = \mathbf{0},$$

which clearly is a system of homogeneous linear equations. Suppose that the matrix in this system $A - \lambda I$ is nonsingular. Then the only solution to this system would be the trivial solution, namely $x = \mathbf{0}$. To ensure that a nontrivial solution exists, we must insist that $|A - \lambda I| = 0$, that is, the $r(A - \lambda I) < n$. In this case we know from the rules of rank that an infinite number of solutions exist for the eigenvectors.

Consider now the expression that arises from $|A - \lambda I| = 0$.

In the case where A is a 2×2 matrix,

$$|A - \lambda I| = \begin{vmatrix} a_{11} - \lambda & a_{12} \\ a_{21} & a_{22} - \lambda \end{vmatrix}.$$

So when we set this determinant equal to zero we get

$$(a_{11} - \lambda)(a_{22} - \lambda) - a_{12}a_{21} = 0,$$

i.e.

$$\lambda^2 - (a_{11} + a_{22})\lambda + (a_{11}a_{22} - a_{12}a_{21}) = 0,$$

which is a quadratic equation in λ. More generally,

$$|A - \lambda I| = 0$$

represents a **polynomial equation of degree n** in λ, something of the form

$$b_0 + b_1\lambda + b_2\lambda^2 + \cdots + b_n\lambda^n = 0.$$

[1] Characteristic roots and characteristic vectors are an alternative terminology.

The **fundamental theorem of algebra** tells us that such an equation has exactly n roots, though these roots may be repeated and some of them may be complex numbers. A complex number is any number that involves $\sqrt{-1}$. When thinking of $\sqrt{-1}$ we are after a number which multiplied by itself gives -1. Clearly this number is not a positive number as two positive numbers when multiplied together give a positive number. Nor is it a negative number as two negative numbers when multiplied together also give a positive number. In fact, we cannot think of a number that is $\sqrt{-1}$. What we do is that we let $i = \sqrt{-1}$ and we treat i as any other number except that when we see i^2 we write -1. More formally, a **complex number** or **imaginary number** is $a + bi$ where a and b are real numbers and $i = \sqrt{-1}$.

Fortunately for us imaginary numbers need not concern us at this stage as we have the following theorem.

Theorem

If A is a symmetric matrix then all the eigenvalues of A are real numbers.

This theorem tells us that if A is symmetric, it has n eigenvalues which are real numbers and the roots of the polynomial equation

$$|A - \lambda I| = 0.$$

Example 1

Find the eigenvalues of

$$A = \begin{pmatrix} 2 & \sqrt{2} \\ \sqrt{2} & 1 \end{pmatrix}.$$

$$|A - \lambda I| = \begin{vmatrix} 2 - \lambda & \sqrt{2} \\ \sqrt{2} & 1 - \lambda \end{vmatrix} = (2 - \lambda)(1 - \lambda) - 2 = \lambda^2 - 3\lambda.$$

So $|A - \lambda I| = 0$ is the quadratic equation

$$\lambda^2 - 3\lambda = 0$$

i.e.

$$\lambda(\lambda - 3) = 0.$$

The two eigenvalues of A are then $\lambda_1 = 0$ and $\lambda_2 = 3$.

Example 2
Find the eigenvalues of

$$A = \begin{pmatrix} -3 & 2 & 0 \\ 2 & -3 & 0 \\ 0 & 0 & -5 \end{pmatrix}.$$

$$\begin{aligned}
|A - \lambda I| &= \begin{vmatrix} -3 - \lambda & 2 & 0 \\ 2 & -3 - \lambda & 0 \\ 0 & 0 & -5 - \lambda \end{vmatrix} \\
&= -(5 + \lambda)(-1)^{3+3} \begin{vmatrix} -3 - \lambda & 2 \\ 2 & -3 - \lambda \end{vmatrix} \\
&= -(5 + \lambda)\left[(3 + \lambda)^2 - 4\right] \\
&= -(5 + \lambda)(\lambda^2 + 6\lambda + 5) \\
&= -(5 + \lambda)(\lambda + 5)(\lambda + 1).
\end{aligned}$$

Setting $|A - \lambda I|$ equal to zero gives the eigenvalues $\lambda_1 = -5$, $\lambda_2 = -5$, $\lambda_3 = -1$. Notice in this example we have repeated eigenvalues.

Exercises for 4.2

1. Find the eigenvalues for the following symmetric matrices:

(i) $\begin{pmatrix} 1 & -1 \\ -1 & 1 \end{pmatrix}$ (ii) $\begin{pmatrix} 5 & 2 & 1 \\ 2 & 1 & 0 \\ 1 & 0 & 1 \end{pmatrix}$

(iii) $\begin{pmatrix} 2 & 1 & 1 \\ 1 & 1 & 0 \\ 1 & 0 & 1 \end{pmatrix}$ (iv) $\begin{pmatrix} -3 & 2 & 0 \\ 2 & -3 & 0 \\ 0 & 0 & -5 \end{pmatrix}.$

2. Show that it is impossible for any 2×2 symmetric matrix of the form

$$A = \begin{pmatrix} a_1 & b \\ b & a_2 \end{pmatrix}$$

with $b \neq 0$, to have identical eigenvalues.

4.3 Eigenvalues of Special Matrices

Similar matrices

Definition
Let A and B be $n \times n$ matrices. Then A is similar to B if there exists a nonsingular matrix C such that

$$B = C^{-1}AC.$$

Example
Let

$$A = \begin{pmatrix} 2 & 1 \\ 2 & 0 \end{pmatrix} \quad \text{and} \quad B = \begin{pmatrix} 0 & 1 \\ 2 & 2 \end{pmatrix}.$$

Consider $C = \begin{pmatrix} 1 & 1 \\ 0 & 1 \end{pmatrix}$. Clearly C is nonsingular with $C^{-1} = \begin{pmatrix} 1 & -1 \\ 0 & 1 \end{pmatrix}$. Moreover

$$B = C^{-1}AC,$$

so A and B are similar.

Theorem
If A and B are similar matrices, they have the same eigenvalues.

Proof
Let A and B be similar and consider

$$|B - \lambda I| = |C^{-1}AC - \lambda C^{-1}C|$$

$$= |C^{-1}(A - \lambda I)C|$$

$$= \frac{1}{|C|}|A - \lambda I||C|$$

$$= |A - \lambda I|.$$

Hence $|B - \lambda I| = 0$ is the same equation as $|A - \lambda I| = 0$.

Idempotent matrices

Recall A is idempotent if $A^2 = A$.

Theorem
The eigenvalues of an idempotent matrix are either one or zero.

Proof
Let A be idempotent and consider

$$Ax = \lambda x. \tag{4.3}$$

Premultiplying both sides by A we have

$$A^2 x = \lambda A x = \lambda^2 x,$$

that is,

$$Ax = \lambda^2 x. \tag{4.4}$$

Subtracting equation (4.3) from equation (4.4) gives

$$0 = \lambda(\lambda - 1)x$$

so

$$\lambda = 0 \text{ or } \lambda = 1 \text{ as } x \neq 0.$$

4.4   The Eigenvectors of a Symmetric Matrix

It turns out that the eigenvectors of a symmetric matrix can have special properties as well. To see this we need a few more definitions under our belt.

Definition
A set of vectors $x_1, x_2, \ldots, x_K$ are (pairwise) **orthogonal** if $x'_i x_j = 0$ for $i \neq j$.

Exercise
Show that the vectors

$$\begin{pmatrix} 1 \\ 2 \\ 1 \end{pmatrix}, \quad \begin{pmatrix} 1 \\ 0 \\ -1 \end{pmatrix}, \quad \begin{pmatrix} -1 \\ 1 \\ -1 \end{pmatrix}$$

are orthogonal.

Definition

A vector x is **normalized** if

$$x'x = 1.$$

Exercise

Show that $\frac{1}{\sqrt{6}}\begin{pmatrix} 1 \\ 2 \\ 1 \end{pmatrix}$ is normalized.

Definition

A set of vectors $x_1, x_2, \ldots, x_K$ are **orthonormal** if

$$x'_i x_j = \delta_{ij} \begin{cases} = 0 & i \neq j \\ = 1 & i = j \end{cases}.$$

That is, these vectors are orthogonal and normalized.

Exercise

Show that

$$\frac{1}{\sqrt{6}}\begin{pmatrix} 1 \\ 2 \\ 1 \end{pmatrix}, \quad \frac{1}{\sqrt{2}}\begin{pmatrix} 1 \\ 0 \\ -1 \end{pmatrix}, \quad \frac{1}{\sqrt{3}}\begin{pmatrix} -1 \\ 1 \\ -1 \end{pmatrix}$$

form an orthonormal set of vectors.

We now seek to show that if A is symmetric, then there exists for A a set of orthonormal eigenvectors.

First we have seen that an infinite number of eigenvectors correspond to a given eigenvalue. If

$$Ax = \lambda x$$

then clearly

$$A(\mu x) = \lambda(\mu x)$$

for any scalar μ. So why don't we pick the eigenvector x that corresponds to λ as the one that is normalized?

Next we have the following theorem.

Theorem

If A is a symmetric matrix, then eigenvectors corresponding to different eigenvalues are orthogonal.

Proof

Let λ_i and λ_j be two distinct eigenvalues of A with corresponding eigenvectors x_i and x_j respectively. Thus we have

$$Ax_i = \lambda_i x_i \tag{4.5}$$

and

$$Ax_j = \lambda_j x_j. \tag{4.6}$$

Premultiplying both sides of equation (4.5) by x'_j and both sides of equation (4.6) by x'_i gives

$$x'_j A x_i = \lambda_i x'_j x_i \tag{4.7}$$

$$x'_i A x_j = \lambda_j x'_i x_j. \tag{4.8}$$

Now as $x'_j x_i$ is a scalar, $(x'_j x_i)' = x'_i x_j$ is the same scalar. Likewise $(x'_j A x_i)' = x'_i A' x_j = x'_j A x_i$. But as A is symmetric we have $x'_i A' x_j = x'_i A x_j$. Subtracting equation (4.8) from equation (4.7) gives

$$0 = (\lambda_i - \lambda_j)x'_i x_j.$$

But $\lambda_i \neq \lambda_j$ so $x'_i x_j = 0$.

The above theorem caters for eigenvectors corresponding to different eigenvalues. The next theorem, given without proof, caters for eigenvectors corresponding to repeated eigenvalues.

Theorem

If λ_i is an eigenvalue repeated K times, there exist K eigenvectors corresponding to λ_i which together with the other eigenvectors form an orthogonal set.

Finding the eigenvectors

The eigenvector(s) corresponding to the eigenvalue λ_i is found by solving the equations

$$(A - \lambda_i I)x = 0.$$

As we want our eigenvectors to form an orthonormal set we solve these equations together with the normalization condition

$$x'x = 1.$$

Example 1

Find an orthonormal set of eigenvectors for $A = \begin{pmatrix} 2 & \sqrt{2} \\ \sqrt{2} & 1 \end{pmatrix}$.

We have already seen that the two eigenvalues of A are $\lambda_1 = 0$ and $\lambda_2 = 3$.

$\underline{\lambda_1 = 0}$

$$(A - \lambda_1 I)x = 0 \text{ gives } Ax = 0$$

that is,

$$\begin{pmatrix} 2 & \sqrt{2} \\ \sqrt{2} & 1 \end{pmatrix} \begin{pmatrix} x_1 \\ x_2 \end{pmatrix} = 0,$$

or

$$2x_1 + \sqrt{2}x_2 = 0$$

$$\sqrt{2}x_1 + x_2 = 0.$$

Both equations give $x_2 = -\sqrt{2}x_1$. Hence $x_1^2 + x_2^2 = 1 \Rightarrow 3x_1^2 = 1 \Rightarrow x_1 = \frac{1}{\sqrt{3}}$.

For our eigenvector we take

$$x_1 = \frac{1}{\sqrt{3}} \begin{pmatrix} 1 \\ -\sqrt{2} \end{pmatrix}.$$

$\underline{\lambda_2 = 3}$

$$(A - \lambda_2 I)x = 0 \text{ gives } \begin{pmatrix} -1 & \sqrt{2} \\ \sqrt{2} & -2 \end{pmatrix} \begin{pmatrix} x_1 \\ x_2 \end{pmatrix} = \begin{pmatrix} 0 \\ 0 \end{pmatrix}.$$

that is, $x_1 = \sqrt{2}x_2$.

Our normalization condition $x_1^2 + x_2^2 = 1$ requires

$$3x_2^2 = 1.$$

that is, $x_2 = \frac{1}{\sqrt{3}}$.

Therefore we take $x_2 = \frac{1}{\sqrt{3}} \begin{pmatrix} \sqrt{2} \\ 1 \end{pmatrix}$ as our second eigenvector.

Example 2

Find an orthonormal set of eigenvectors for

$$A = \begin{pmatrix} -3 & 2 & 0 \\ 2 & -3 & 0 \\ 0 & 0 & -5 \end{pmatrix}.$$

We know the eigenvalues of A are $\lambda_1 = \lambda_2 = -5$ and $\lambda_3 = -1$.

$\underline{\lambda_3 = -1}$

$$(A - \lambda_3 I)x = 0 \text{ is } \begin{pmatrix} -2 & 2 & 0 \\ 2 & -2 & 0 \\ 0 & 0 & -4 \end{pmatrix} \begin{pmatrix} x_1 \\ x_2 \\ x_3 \end{pmatrix} = \begin{pmatrix} 0 \\ 0 \\ 0 \end{pmatrix}.$$

that is,

$$x_1 = x_2$$
$$x_3 = 0.$$

Then $x_1^2 + x_2^2 + x_3^2 = 1 \Rightarrow 2x_1^2 = 1 \Rightarrow x_1 = \frac{1}{\sqrt{2}}$, so we have $x_3 = \frac{1}{\sqrt{2}} \begin{pmatrix} 1 \\ 1 \\ 0 \end{pmatrix}$ as our eigenvector.

$\underline{\lambda_1 = \lambda_2 = -5}$

$$(A - \lambda_1 I)x = 0 \Rightarrow \begin{pmatrix} 2 & 2 & 0 \\ 2 & 2 & 0 \\ 0 & 0 & 0 \end{pmatrix} \begin{pmatrix} x_1 \\ x_2 \\ x_3 \end{pmatrix} = \begin{pmatrix} 0 \\ 0 \\ 0 \end{pmatrix}.$$

that is, $x_1 = -x_2, x_3$ any value.

Take $x_3 = 0$
Then our normalization condition requires

$$2x_1^2 = 1$$

so

$$x_1 = \frac{1}{\sqrt{2}}.$$

our eigenvector would then be

$$x_1 = \frac{1}{\sqrt{2}} \begin{pmatrix} 1 \\ -1 \\ 0 \end{pmatrix}.$$

Take $x_3 = 1$
Then $x_1^2 + x_2^2 + x_3^2 = 1$ requires

$$2x_1^2 + 1 = 1.$$

that is, $x_1 = 0$.

Take as our eigenvector $x_2 = \begin{pmatrix} 0 \\ 0 \\ 1 \end{pmatrix}$.

Notice, as these examples illustrate, that the orthonormal set of eigenvectors associated with a symmetric matrix A is not unique.

Exercises for 4.4

1. (i) What is meant by orthogonal vectors and orthonormal vectors?

 (ii) Find three vectors that are orthogonal to $x = \begin{pmatrix} 1 \\ -1 \\ 3 \end{pmatrix}$.

 (iii) Consider $x_1 = \frac{1}{\sqrt{3}} \begin{pmatrix} 1 \\ 1 \\ 1 \end{pmatrix}$. Find two other vectors x_2 and x_3 such that the three vectors x_1, x_2, x_3 form an orthonormal set.

2. Find an orthonormal set of eigenvectors for the following matrices:

 (i) $\begin{pmatrix} 2 & 4 \\ 4 & 2 \end{pmatrix}$ (ii) $\begin{pmatrix} 4 & 2 \\ 2 & 1 \end{pmatrix}$ (iii) $\begin{pmatrix} 2 & 1 & 1 \\ 1 & 1 & 0 \\ 1 & 0 & 1 \end{pmatrix}$.

4.5 The Matrix Whose Columns are the Eigenvectors of a Symmetric Matrix

Suppose A is a symmetric matrix with eigenvalues $\lambda_1, \lambda_2, \ldots, \lambda_n$ and an orthonormal set of eigenvectors $x_1, x_2, \ldots, x_n$. In this section we consider the properties of the matrix Q say, whose columns are these eigenvectors. That is, $Q = (x_1, x_2, \ldots, x_n)$.

Properties of Q

Definition

A matrix B is **orthogonal** if

$$B^{-1} = B'.$$

Theorem

Q is an orthogonal matrix.

Proof

Clearly

$$Q' = \begin{pmatrix} x'_1 \\ x'_2 \\ \vdots \\ x'_n \end{pmatrix},$$

So $Q'Q = \{x'_i x_j\} = \{\delta_{ij}\} = I.$

Hence $Q' = Q^{-1}$ as only the inverse has this property.

Theorem

The matrix $Q'AQ$ is a diagonal matrix whose main diagonal elements are the eigenvalues of A.

Proof

$$(Q'AQ)_{ij} = (Q'A)_{i\bullet} Q_{\bullet j}$$
$$= x'_i A x_j$$
$$= \lambda_j x'_i x_j$$
$$= \lambda_j \delta_{ij}.$$

Exercises for 4.5

1. Show that the following matrices are orthogonal

(i) $\dfrac{1}{\sqrt{2}} \begin{pmatrix} 1 & -1 \\ 1 & 1 \end{pmatrix}$ (ii) $\dfrac{1}{\sqrt{6}} \begin{pmatrix} 0 & \sqrt{2} & 2 \\ \sqrt{3} & -\sqrt{2} & 1 \\ -\sqrt{3} & -\sqrt{2} & 1 \end{pmatrix}$

(iii) $\dfrac{1}{\sqrt{30}} \begin{pmatrix} 0 & \sqrt{5} & 5 \\ \sqrt{6} & -2\sqrt{5} & 2 \\ -2\sqrt{6} & -\sqrt{5} & 1 \end{pmatrix}.$

2. Consider $A = \begin{pmatrix} 2 & \sqrt{2} \\ \sqrt{2} & 1 \end{pmatrix}$. We have seen that an orthonormal set of eigenvectors for A is

$$x_1 = \frac{1}{\sqrt{3}} \begin{pmatrix} 1 \\ -\sqrt{2} \end{pmatrix}, \quad x_2 = \frac{1}{\sqrt{3}} \begin{pmatrix} \sqrt{2} \\ 1 \end{pmatrix},$$

and these correspond to the eigenvalues $\lambda_1 = 0$ and $\lambda_2 = 3$. Consider

$$Q = \frac{1}{\sqrt{3}} \begin{pmatrix} 1 & \sqrt{2} \\ -\sqrt{2} & 1 \end{pmatrix}.$$

Show that $Q'Q = I$ and $Q'AQ = \begin{pmatrix} 0 & 0 \\ 0 & 3 \end{pmatrix}$.

3. For the matrix

$$A = \begin{pmatrix} -3 & 2 & 0 \\ 2 & -3 & 0 \\ 0 & 0 & -5 \end{pmatrix},$$

find an orthogonal matrix Q such that $Q'AQ$ is diagonal. What are the main diagonal elements of this matrix?

4. (i) For each of the following matrices find an orthogonal matrix Q such that $Q'AQ$ is a diagonal matrix. What are the main diagonal elements of this matrix?

(a) $A = \begin{pmatrix} 1 & -1 \\ -1 & 1 \end{pmatrix}$ (b) $A = \begin{pmatrix} 5 & 2 & 1 \\ 2 & 1 & 0 \\ 1 & 0 & 1 \end{pmatrix}$ (c) $A = \begin{pmatrix} 2 & 1 & 1 \\ 1 & 1 & 0 \\ 1 & 0 & 1 \end{pmatrix}$.

(ii) For each of the matrices in part (i) can we say anything about the definiteness of A and the sign of the quadratic form $x'Ax$ for all vectors x?

4.6 Diagonalization of Quadratic Forms

We are now in a position to answer the two questions posed in the introduction of this chapter. Recall that we want to know if it is possible to simplify the quadratic form

$$x'Ax = \sum_{i=1}^{n} \sum_{j=1}^{n} x_i a_{ij} x_j,$$

with A symmetric and whether we can put a sign to it.

The first question is easily answered. Let Q be the matrix whose columns are an orthonormal set of eigenvectors for A. Consider the nonsingular transformation of variables.

$$x = Qy \text{ or } y = Q'x.$$

Then

$$x'Ax = y'Q'AQy = y'Dy$$

where D is the diagonal matrix $\{\lambda_j\delta_{ij}\}$.
Thus $x'Ax = \lambda_1 y_1^2 + \lambda_2 y_2^2 + \ldots + \lambda_n y_n^2$, a far simpler expression than the one we started with.

To answer the second question requires a little more work. If we allow x to vary over all of E^n the set of values taken by $x'Ax$ is called the **range** of the quadratic form. As for any x there is a unique y, and vice versa such that $x'Ax = y'Dy$, the quadratic forms $x'Ax$, $y'Dy$ must have the same range.

Suppose now that A is positive or negative definite; so $x'Ax = 0$ only if $x = 0$. We wish to show that the only value for y which gives $y'Dy = 0$ is $y = 0$. But this must be the case as $y = Q'x$ so $y = 0$ is the only value of y for which $x = 0$.

What we have proved in the last two paragraphs, is that the definiteness of a quadratic form remains the same when we make a nonsingular transformation of variables. So $x'Ax$ has the same definiteness as $y'Dy = \lambda_1 y_1^2 + \lambda_2 y_2^2 + \ldots + \lambda_n y_n^2$.

If each eigenvalue of A is positive (negative), then this expression is positive (negative) for all y other than the null vector and vice versa. If one of the eigenvalues say λ_1 is zero, then we can set $y_2 = y_3 = \cdots = y_n = 0$ and our expression is zero for any y_1; hence $y'Dy = 0$ for $y \neq 0$.

If some of the λs are positive while others are negative clearly we cannot put a sign to $y'Dy$. These results lead to the following theorem:

Theorem

(i) The quadratic form $x'Ax$ is positive (negative) definite if and only if every eigenvalue of A is positive (negative).

(ii) The quadratic form $x'Ax$ is positive (negative) semidefinite if and only if all eigenvalues of A are nonnegative (nonpositive) and at least one is zero.

(iii) The quadratic form $x'Ax$ is indefinite if and only if A has both positive and negative eigenvalues.

Example 1

As the eigenvalues of $A = \begin{pmatrix} 2 & \sqrt{2} \\ \sqrt{2} & 1 \end{pmatrix}$ are 0 and 3, A is positive semidefinite so $2x_1^2 + x_2^2 + 2\sqrt{2}x_1x_2 \geq 0$ for all x_1 and x_2.

Example 2

As the eigenvalues of

$$A = \begin{pmatrix} -3 & 2 & 0 \\ 2 & -3 & 0 \\ 0 & 0 & -5 \end{pmatrix}$$

are -5 and -1, A is negative definite so $-3x_1^2 - 3x_2^2 - 5x_3^2 + 4x_1x_2 < 0$ for all x_1, x_2, x_3 other than the point $x_1 = x_2 = x_3 = 0$.

Exercises for 4.6

1. For the matrices

   (i) $A = \begin{pmatrix} 2 & \sqrt{2} \\ \sqrt{2} & 1 \end{pmatrix}$,   (ii) $A - \begin{pmatrix} -3 & 2 & 0 \\ 2 & 3 & 0 \\ 0 & 0 & -5 \end{pmatrix}$,

   find the transformation of variables that diagonalizes the quadratic form $x'Ax$.
2. Find a symmetric matrix for the quadratic form $x^2 + 4xy + y^2$. Find a matrix transformation which takes $\begin{pmatrix} x \\ y \end{pmatrix}$ to the vector $\begin{pmatrix} v_1 \\ v_2 \end{pmatrix}$ such that

   $$x^2 + 4xy + y^2 = 3v_1^2 - v_2^2.$$

   Can we say anything about the definiteness of the quadratic form?
3. Suppose that A is a positive definite symmetric matrix. Prove that there exists a nonsingular matrix P such that $A = P'P$.

4.7   Eigenvalues and $|A|$, $r(A)$, and tr A

In the above discussion, we used the eigenvalues of a matrix to determine its definiteness. However those values are intimately linked with the determinant of A, the rank of A, and the trace of A.

Recall that

$$Q'AQ = \begin{pmatrix} \lambda_1 & & 0 \\ & \ddots & \\ 0 & & \lambda_n \end{pmatrix}.$$

Now the determinant of a diagonal matrix is just the product of the main diagonal elements.

So

$$|Q'AQ| = \lambda_1 \lambda_2 \ldots \lambda_n.$$

But

$$|Q'AQ| = |Q'||A||Q| = \frac{1}{|Q|}|A||Q| = |A|$$

as

$$|Q'| = |Q^{-1}| = 1/|Q|.$$

This gives the following result.

Theorem
For a symmetric matrix A, $|A| = \lambda_1 \ldots \lambda_n$.

Consider next

$$r(Q'AQ) = r \begin{pmatrix} \lambda_1 & & 0 \\ & \ddots & \\ 0 & & \lambda_n \end{pmatrix} = \text{number of nonzero eigenvalues of } A.$$

But the rank of a matrix is unaltered when a matrix is premultiplied or postmultiplied by a nonsingular matrix. Thus,

Theorem
For a symmetric matrix A, $r(A)$ is equal to the number of nonzero eigenvalues of A.

Finally,

$$\text{tr } Q'AQ = \lambda_1 + \lambda_2 + \cdots + \lambda_n.$$

But

$$\text{tr } Q'AQ = \text{tr } AQQ' = \text{tr } A,$$

giving the following:

Theorem
For a symmetric matrix A, $\operatorname{tr} A = \lambda_1 + \lambda_2 + \cdots + \lambda_n$.

For a symmetric idempotent matrix, other than the identity matrix, we know the eigenvalues are zero or one so for this matrix the determinant is zero, that is, it is singular and its rank must equal its trace.

Exercises for 4.7

1. Let i be an $n \times 1$ vector whose elements are all ones and let I be the $n \times n$ identity matrix. Show that $A = i'i/n$ and $B = I - A$ are symmetric idempotent matrices and that $AB = 0$. What are the ranks of A and B? What are their eigenvalues? What are their definiteness and their determinants?
2. Let $N = X(X'X)^{-1}X'$ and $M = I - N$, where X is an $n \times K$ matrix with rank K, and I is the $n \times n$ identity matrix. Show that M and N are symmetric idempotent matrices and that $MN = 0$. What are their ranks? What are their eigenvalues and determinants?
3. For each of the following matrices, show that the trace is the sum of the eigenvalues and the determinant is the product of the eigenvalues. What is the rank of the matrix?

$$
\text{(i)} \begin{pmatrix} 2 & 1 & 1 \\ 1 & 1 & 0 \\ 1 & 0 & 1 \end{pmatrix} \qquad \text{(ii)} \begin{pmatrix} 5 & 2 & 1 \\ 2 & 1 & 0 \\ 1 & 0 & 1 \end{pmatrix} \qquad \text{(iii)} \begin{pmatrix} 2 & 1 & 1 \\ 1 & 1 & 1 \\ 1 & 1 & 1 \end{pmatrix}.
$$

4.8 An Alternative Approach Using Determinants

We have studied matrix algebra long enough by now to realize that there is always more than one way of doing things and one of the ways, more often than not involves the use of determinants. This is also the case in evaluating the definiteness of matrix.

We want to determine the definiteness of

$$
A_{n\times n} = \begin{pmatrix} a_{11} & \cdots & a_{1n} \\ \vdots & & \vdots \\ a_{n1} & \cdots & a_{nn} \end{pmatrix},
$$

where again we restrict ourselves to the case where A is symmetric. The criteria we use involve the use of certain minors we can form from A.

Definition

The **leading principal minors** of A are

$$a_{11}, \begin{vmatrix} a_{11} & a_{12} \\ a_{21} & a_{22} \end{vmatrix}, \begin{vmatrix} a_{11} & a_{12} & a_{13} \\ a_{21} & a_{22} & a_{23} \\ a_{31} & a_{32} & a_{33} \end{vmatrix}, \ldots, |A|.$$

Example

Consider

$$A = \begin{pmatrix} 1 & -1 & 0 \\ -1 & 6 & -2 \\ 0 & -2 & 3 \end{pmatrix}.$$

The leading principal minors are

$$1, \begin{vmatrix} 1 & -1 \\ -1 & 6 \end{vmatrix} = 5, |A| = \begin{vmatrix} 1 & -1 & 0 \\ 0 & 5 & -2 \\ 0 & -2 & 3 \end{vmatrix} = 1(-1)^{1+1} \begin{vmatrix} 5 & -2 \\ -2 & 3 \end{vmatrix} = 11.$$

Theorem

Let A be an $n \times n$ symmetric matrix. Then,

(i) A is positive definite if and only if all the n leading principal minors of A are positive.

(ii) A is negative definite if and only if the leading principal minors alternate in sign: the first being negative, the next positive etc.

Example 1

Consider the above matrix A whose leading principal minors are 1, 5, and 11. So A is positive definite, that is,

$$x'Ax = x_1^2 + 6x_2^2 + 3x_3^2 - 2x_1x_2 - 4x_2x_3 > 0$$

for all x s other than $x_1 = x_2 = x_3 = 0$.

Example 2

Consider

$$A = \begin{pmatrix} -1 & 2 & 0 \\ 2 & -6 & 1 \\ 0 & 1 & -1 \end{pmatrix}.$$

The leading principal minors are

$$-1, \quad \begin{vmatrix} -1 & 2 \\ 2 & -6 \end{vmatrix} = 2,$$

$$|A| = \begin{vmatrix} -1 & 2 & 0 \\ 2 & -5 & 0 \\ 0 & 1 & -1 \end{vmatrix} = -1|-1|^{3+3} \begin{vmatrix} -1 & 2 \\ 2 & -5 \end{vmatrix} = -1(5-4) = -1.$$

The leading principal minors alternate in sign, the first being negative, so A is negative definite. That is,

$$x'Ax = -x_1^2 - 6x_2^2 - x_3^2 + 4x_1x_2 + 2x_1x_3 < 0$$

for all x s other than $x_1 = x_2 = x_3 = 0$.

Definition
A **principal minor** of $A_{n \times n}$ is the determinant of a square submatrix of A obtained by deleting certain columns of A and the same numbered rows of A.

Example

$$A = \begin{pmatrix} a_{11} & a_{12} & a_{13} \\ a_{21} & a_{22} & a_{23} \\ a_{31} & a_{32} & a_{33} \end{pmatrix}.$$

The principal minors of A are

a_{11} formed by deleting c.2, c.3 and r.2, r3,

a_{22} formed by deleting c.1, c.3 and r.1, r.3,

a_{33} formed by deleting c.1, c.2 and r.1, r.2.

$\begin{vmatrix} a_{11} & a_{12} \\ a_{21} & a_{22} \end{vmatrix}$ formed by deleting c.3 and r.3

$\begin{vmatrix} a_{11} & a_{13} \\ a_{31} & a_{33} \end{vmatrix}$ formed by deleting c.2 and r.2

$\begin{vmatrix} a_{22} & a_{23} \\ a_{32} & a_{33} \end{vmatrix}$ formed by deleting c.1 and r.1.

$|A|$ formed by deleting no columns nor rows.

Example
Consider

$$A = \begin{pmatrix} 1 & 2 & 0 \\ 2 & 4 & 5 \\ 0 & 5 & 6 \end{pmatrix}.$$

The principal minors of A are

$$1, 4, 6$$

$$\begin{vmatrix} 1 & 2 \\ 2 & 4 \end{vmatrix} = 0, \quad \begin{vmatrix} 1 & 0 \\ 0 & 6 \end{vmatrix} = 6, \quad \begin{vmatrix} 4 & 5 \\ 5 & 6 \end{vmatrix} = -1$$

$$|A| = \begin{vmatrix} 1 & 2 & 0 \\ 0 & 0 & 5 \\ 0 & 5 & 6 \end{vmatrix} = 1(-1)^{1+1} \begin{vmatrix} 0 & 5 \\ 5 & 6 \end{vmatrix} = -25.$$

Theorem

Let A be a symmetric matrix. Then,

(i) A is positive semidefinite if and only if every principal minor of A is ≥ 0.

(ii) A is negative semidefinite if and only if every principal minor of odd order is ≤ 0 and every principal minor of even order is ≥ 0.

Example 1

$$A = \begin{pmatrix} 1 & -1 & -1 \\ -1 & 1 & 1 \\ -1 & 1 & 3 \end{pmatrix}.$$

Principal minors are

$$1, 1, 3 \text{ all} \geq 0$$

$$\begin{vmatrix} 1 & -1 \\ -1 & 1 \end{vmatrix} = 0, \quad \begin{vmatrix} 1 & -1 \\ -1 & 3 \end{vmatrix} = 2, \quad \begin{vmatrix} 1 & 1 \\ 1 & 3 \end{vmatrix} = 2 \text{ all} \geq 0$$

$$|A| = \begin{vmatrix} 0 & 0 & 0 \\ -1 & 1 & 1 \\ -1 & 1 & 3 \end{vmatrix} = 0 \geq 0.$$

Hence A is positive semidefinite and

$$x'Ax = x_1^2 + x_2^2 + 3x_3^2 - 2x_1x_2 - 2x_1x_3 + 2x_2x_3 \geq 0$$

for all x.

Examples

$$A = \begin{pmatrix} -1 & 1 & 0 \\ 1 & -1 & 0 \\ 0 & 0 & -2 \end{pmatrix}.$$

Principal minors are

$$-1, -1, -2 \le 0$$

$$\begin{vmatrix} -1 & 1 \\ 1 & -1 \end{vmatrix} = 0, \quad \begin{vmatrix} -1 & 0 \\ 0 & -2 \end{vmatrix} = 2, \quad \begin{vmatrix} -1 & 0 \\ 0 & -2 \end{vmatrix} = 2 \text{ all } \ge 0$$

$$|A| = \begin{vmatrix} 0 & 0 & 0 \\ 1 & -1 & 0 \\ 0 & 0 & -2 \end{vmatrix} = 0 \le 0.$$

Hence A is negative semidefinite, so

$$x'Ax = -x_1^2 - x_2^2 - 2x_3^2 + 2x_1 x_2 \le 0 \text{ for all } x.$$

Theorem
If A is an $n \times n$ symmetric matrix and the principal minors of A fit none of the above categories, then A is indefinite.

Above example

$$A = \begin{pmatrix} 1 & 2 & 0 \\ 2 & 4 & 5 \\ 0 & 5 & 6 \end{pmatrix}$$

$$x'Ax = x_1^2 + 4x_2^2 + 6x_3^2 + 4x_1 x_2 + 10x_2 x_3 < 0 \quad \text{for some } x \text{ and}$$
$$> 0 \quad \text{for some } x$$

Exercise for 4.8

1. By considering the leading principal minors of the following matrices show that they are both negative definite.

$$\text{(i)} \quad \begin{pmatrix} -3 & 2 & 0 \\ 2 & -3 & 0 \\ 0 & 0 & -5 \end{pmatrix} \qquad \text{(ii)} \quad \begin{pmatrix} -3 & 1 & 0 \\ 1 & -1 & 2 \\ 0 & 2 & -8 \end{pmatrix}.$$

2. By considering the principal minors of

$$\begin{pmatrix} 2 & 1 & 1 \\ 1 & 1 & 0 \\ 1 & 0 & 1 \end{pmatrix}$$

   show that this matrix is positive semidefinite.

3. Show that

$$A = \begin{pmatrix} 1 & 2 & 0 \\ 2 & 3 & 6 \\ 0 & 6 & 8 \end{pmatrix}$$

   is an indefinite matrix.

Part II

Functions of Many Variables
and Optimization

Chapter 5

Functions of Many Variables

5.1 Functions in General

A **function** f is a rule that takes us from elements of one set S to elements of another set T such that each element of S goes to one and only one element of T.

Diagrammatically we can represent a function as follows:

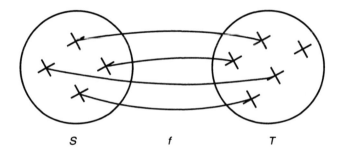

For the rule to be a function it must accommodate each element in S. The following rule is not a function:

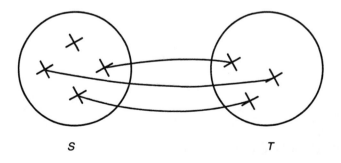

Moreover, each element in S must go to one and only one element in T. The following rule then is not a function:

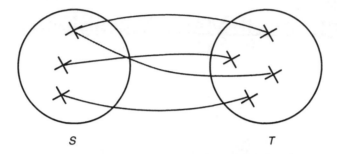

An unspecified element x in S is called the **independent variable(s)**. If x goes to y in T we write $y = f(x)$ and y is called the **image** of x or the **dependent variable**. The set S is called the **domain** of the function while the set T is called the **target space** of the function. The set of images is called the **range** of the function.

Diagrammatically,

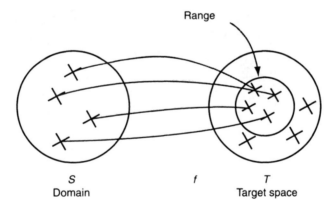

Notation

We write

$$f : S \to T$$

or

$$y = f(x)$$

which tells us how to get the image of x.

If the domain is R^n or a subset of R^n and the target space is R, the set of real numbers, we have a (real) **function of many variables**. Our notation for such a function is

$$y = f(\pmb{x}) = f(x_1, \ldots, x_n).$$

The $n \times 1$ vector $\pmb{x}$ is often called a **point**. In our work we will often talk of the distance between two points, using Euclidean distance, so the domain will usually be E^n, or some subset of E^n, rather than R^n.

Economic examples of functions of two variables which we will come across a lot are as follows:

Cobb-Douglas function

$$y = Ax_1^\alpha x_2^\beta, \quad A, \alpha, \beta \text{ constants.}$$

Constant elasticity of substitution (CES) production function

$$y = (ax_1^{-\beta} + bx_2^{-\beta})^{-1/\beta} \quad a, b > 0.$$

The domain of these functions is the **nonnegative orthant** of R^2 (or E^2) which is the set

$$\left\{ \begin{pmatrix} x_1 \\ x_2 \end{pmatrix} \Big/ x_1 \geq 0, x_2 \geq 0 \right\}.$$

5.2   Partial Differentiation

Recall for a moment the definition of a derivative for a function of a single variable $y = f(x)$. The **derivative** of y with respect to x is defined as

$$\frac{dy}{dx} = \lim_{\Delta x \to 0} \frac{\Delta y}{\Delta x} = \lim_{\Delta x \to 0} \frac{f(x + \Delta x) - f(x)}{\Delta x}. \tag{5.1}$$

This derivative is an approximation for the rate of change $\Delta y / \Delta x$ where the change in x, Δx, is small.

Now let $y = f(\pmb{x})$ be a function of many variables. Then the **partial derivative** of y with respect to x_i, $\partial y / \partial x_i$ is defined as

$$\frac{\partial y}{\partial x_i} = \lim_{\Delta x_i \to 0} \frac{f(x_1, \ldots, x_i + \Delta x_i, \ldots, x_n) - f(x_1, \ldots, x_i, \ldots, x_n)}{\Delta x_i} \tag{5.2}$$

Comparing equation (5.1) with equation (5.2) we see that the definitions are essentially the same, provided in equation (5.2) we are prepared to treat all the other variables $x_1, x_2, \ldots, x_{i-1}, x_{i+1}, \ldots x_n$ as constants. This gives the following procedure for partial differentiation:

Procedure

When partially differentiating $y = f(x_1, \ldots, x_n)$ with respect to x_i we treat x_i as the only variable, the other variables being treated as constants.

Notations

Various notations are used for the partial derivative of $y = f(x_1, \ldots, x_n)$ with respect to x_i. They are

$$\frac{\partial y}{\partial x_i}, \frac{\partial f}{\partial x_i}, f_{x_i}, f_i.$$

When we partially differentiate, the usual rules of differentiation apply. To emphasize this point, in the following table (Table 5.1), on the left hand side we have examples of the rules applied to derivatives of a function of a single variable, whereas on the right hand side we have examples of the corresponding rules applied to partial derivatives of a function of many variables.

Generalizations of the chain rule

There are a few generalizations of the chain rule we need to know. These are introduced by way of examples.

Example 1

Suppose $C = C(Y^D(Y(G, T)))$.

Our notation says that C is a function of Y^D, Y^D is a function of Y, which in its turn is a function of G and T. Then

$$\frac{\partial C}{\partial T} = \frac{dC}{dY^D} \cdot \frac{dY^D}{dY} \cdot \frac{\partial Y}{\partial T}.$$

Example 2

Consider $L = L(r(G, T), Y(G, T))$.

That is, L is a function of r and Y but these variables are functions of G and T. Then

$$\frac{\partial L}{\partial G} = \frac{\partial L}{\partial r} \cdot \frac{\partial r}{\partial G} + \frac{\partial L}{\partial Y} \cdot \frac{\partial Y}{\partial G}.$$

Table 5.1   Rules of differentiation.

Function of a single variable	Function of many variables
Power rule	
$y = 8x^{-7} + 3x^2$	$y = 3x_1^2 x_2 + 8x_2^{-5} x_1^3$
$\dfrac{dy}{dx} = -56x^{-8} + 6x$	$\dfrac{\partial y}{\partial x_1} = 6x_1 x_2 + 24x_2^{-5} x_1^2$
	$\dfrac{\partial y}{\partial x_2} = 3x_1^2 - 40x_2^{-6} x_1^3$
Chain rule	
(i) $y = e^{x^2}$	$y = e^{x_1^3 + 2x_2^{-7}}$
$\dfrac{dy}{dx} = e^{x^2} 2x$	$\dfrac{\partial y}{\partial x_1} = e^{x_1^3 + 2x_2^{-7}} 3x_1^2$
	$\dfrac{\partial y}{\partial x_2} = e^{x_1^3 + 2x_2^{-7}}\left(-14x_2^{-8}\right)$
(ii) $y = (6 + 7x^3)^8$	$y = (6x_1^2 + 6x_1 x_2 + 9x_2)^{-3}$
$\dfrac{dy}{dx} = 8(6 + 7x^3)^7 21x^2$	$\dfrac{\partial y}{\partial x_1} = -3(6x_1^2 + 6x_1 x_2 + 9x_2)^{-4}$
	$\times (12x_1 + 6x_2)$
	$\dfrac{\partial y}{\partial x_2} = -3(6x_1^2 + 6x_1 x_2 + 9x_2)^{-4}(6x_1 + 9)$
(iii) $y = \log(7x^{-3} + 6x^2)$	$y = \log(3x_1^3 + 7x_1 x_2 + x_2^4)$
$\dfrac{dy}{dx} = \dfrac{1}{7x^{-3} + 6x^2}$	$\dfrac{\partial y}{\partial x_1} = \dfrac{1}{3x_1^3 + 7x_1 x_2 + x_2^4}(9x_1^2 + 7x_2)$
$\times (-21x^{-4} + 12x)$	$\dfrac{\partial y}{\partial x_2} = \dfrac{1}{3x_1^3 + 7x_1 x_2 + x_2^4}(7x_1 + 4x_2^3)$
Product rule	
$y = x^3 e^{-7x}$	$y = x_1^2 x_2^{-7} e^{x_1 x_2}$
$\dfrac{dy}{dx} = 3x^2 e^{-7x} - 7x^3 e^{-7x}$	$\dfrac{\partial y}{\partial x_1} = 2x_1 x_2^{-7} e^{x_1 x_2} + x_1^2 x_2^{-7} e^{x_1 x_2} x_2$
	$\dfrac{\partial y}{\partial x_2} = -7x_1^2 x_2^{-8} e^{x_1 x_2} + x_1^2 x_2^{-7} e^{x_1 x_2} x_1$

Meaning of a partial derivative

(i) The partial derivative, $\partial y/\partial x_i$ gives an approximation to the rate of change in y when there is a small change in x_i, all other variables remaining constant.

Example

Let $y = 3x_1^2 x_2 + 8x_2^{-5}x_1^3$.

Suppose at point $x_1 = 2$, $x_2 = 1$, x_1 changes by a small amount. Find an approximation to the resultant rate of change in y.

We have $\partial y/\partial x_1 = 6x_1 x_2 + 24x_2^{-5}x_1^2$, which we evaluate at the point to obtain

$$\frac{\partial y}{\partial x_1}(2, 1) = 6.2.1 + 24.1.4 = 108.$$

This is our approximation.

(ii) If $\partial y/\partial x_i$ is positive this means that an increase in x_i leads to an increase in y; a decrease in x_i to a decrease in y. If negative, the two variables move in opposite directions.

(iii) Marginal analysis in economics essentially involves looking at rates of change in the dependent variable when there is a small change in one of the independent variables. That is, marginal analysis in economics involves partial derivatives. Consider for example the Cobb-Douglas function $Q = Ax_1^\alpha x_2^\beta$ and suppose that this is a production function. Then the **marginal product** of input 1 is

$$\frac{\partial Q}{\partial x_1} = \alpha Ax_1^{\alpha-1}x_2^\beta.$$

Suppose $U(x_1, x_2) = \log x_1 + \log x_2$ is a consumer's utility function then the **marginal utility** of good 2 is

$$\frac{\partial U}{\partial x_2} = \frac{1}{x_2}.$$

Neoclassical economists with their marginal analysis were actually reinventing differentiation!

Second-order partial derivatives

From the above table it is clear that the partial derivatives themselves are functions of the x s. We can think of taking the partial derivatives of the partial derivatives to give us **second order partial derivatives**:

$$\frac{\partial^2 f(x)}{\partial x_1^2} = \frac{\partial}{\partial x_1}\left(\frac{\partial f(x)}{\partial x_1}\right) = f_{11}$$

$$\frac{\partial^2 f(x)}{\partial x_2 \partial x_1} = \frac{\partial}{\partial x_2}\left(\frac{\partial f(x)}{\partial x_1}\right) = f_{12}$$

$$\frac{\partial^2 f(x)}{\partial x_1 \partial x_2} = \frac{\partial}{\partial x_1}\left(\frac{\partial f(x)}{\partial x_2}\right) = f_{21}, \text{ etc.}$$

Example

Consider the Cobb-Douglas function

$$Q = 4K^{3/4}L^{1/4}.$$

Then

$$\frac{\partial Q}{\partial K} = 3K^{-1/4}L^{1/4} = Q_K, \qquad \frac{\partial Q}{\partial L} = K^{3/4}L^{-3/4} = Q_L.$$

Now

$$\frac{\partial^2 Q}{\partial K^2} = \frac{\partial}{\partial K}\left(\frac{\partial Q}{\partial K}\right) = -\frac{3}{4}K^{-5/4}L^{1/4} = Q_{KK}$$

$$\frac{\partial^2 Q}{\partial L \partial K} = \frac{\partial}{\partial L}\left(\frac{\partial Q}{\partial K}\right) = \frac{3}{4}K^{-1/4}L^{-3/4} = Q_{KL}$$

$$\frac{\partial^2 Q}{\partial K \partial L} = \frac{\partial}{\partial K}\left(\frac{\partial Q}{\partial L}\right) = \frac{3}{4}K^{-1/4}L^{-3/4} = Q_{LK}$$

$$\frac{\partial^2 Q}{\partial L^2} = \frac{\partial}{\partial L}\left(\frac{\partial Q}{\partial L}\right) = -\frac{3}{4}K^{3/4}L^{-7/4} = Q_{LL}$$

Note

In this example $Q_{KL} = Q_{LK}$. This result is an example of the following theorem.

Young's theorem

Let $y = f(x) = f(x_1, \ldots, x_n)$. Then

$$\frac{\partial^2 f(x)}{\partial x_i \partial x_j} = \frac{\partial^2 f(x)}{\partial x_j \partial x_i},$$

provided that the derivatives are continuous.[1]

Young's theorem says that it does not matter in what order you carry out the differentiation!

[1] Continuous functions are defined in the next section.

The gradient vector and the Hessian matrix

Associated with any function, $y = f(x) = f(x_1, \ldots, x_n)$ are an important vector and an important matrix, called the gradient vector and the Hessian matrix.

Definition
The **gradient vector** of $f(x)$ denoted by $\nabla f(x)$ is the $n \times 1$ vector of first order partial derivatives, that is,

$$\nabla f(x) = \begin{pmatrix} f_1(x) \\ \vdots \\ f_n(x) \end{pmatrix} \quad \text{where } f_i(x) = \frac{\partial f(x)}{\partial x_i}.$$

Definition
The **Hessian matrix** of $f(x)$ denoted by $H(x)$ is the matrix of all second order partial derivatives:

$$H(x) = \begin{bmatrix} f_{11}(x) & \cdots & f_{1n}(x) \\ f_{21}(x) & \cdots & f_{2n}(x) \\ \vdots & & \vdots \\ f_{n1}(x) & \cdots & f_{nn}(x) \end{bmatrix}.$$

Note
By Young's theorem $f_{ij} = f_{ji}$, so $H(x)$ is symmetric.

Example

$$f(x_1, x_2) = 3x_1^2 + x_2^3 - 3x_1 x_2$$
$$f_1 = 6x_1 - 3x_2, \quad f_2 = 3x_2^2 - 3x_1.$$

Hence

$$\nabla f(x) = \begin{pmatrix} 6x_1 - 3x_2 \\ 3x_2^2 - 3x_1 \end{pmatrix}$$

Now

$$f_{11} = 6, \, f_{12} = -3 = f_{21}, \, f_{22} = 6x_2$$

so

$$H(x) = \begin{pmatrix} 6 & -3 \\ -3 & 6x_2 \end{pmatrix}.$$

Exercises for 5.2

1. Define the gradient vector and Hessian matrix of a function of many variables. Compute the gradient vector and Hessian matrix for the following functions:
   (i) $y = x_1^3 x_2^2$
   (ii) $y = x_1^5 - 3x_1^2 x_2 + x_2^2$
   (iii) $y = x_1/x_2$
   (iv) $y = x_1 - x_2/x_1 + x_2$
   (v) $y = (x_1^2 - 2x_2^2)^5$
   (vi) $y = \log(x_1^{-2} + x_2^{-3})$
   (vii) $y = e^{2x_1 + 3x_2}$
   (viii) $y = 3x_1^2 x_2 - 7x_1 \sqrt{x_2}$.
2. Let $y = \frac{1}{2} \log(x_1^2 + x_2^2)$. Show that

$$\frac{\partial^2 y}{\partial x_1^2} + \frac{\partial^2 y}{\partial x_2^2} = 0.$$

5.3 Special Sorts of Functions

Continuous functions

Let $y = f(x)$ be a function of many variables. This function is **continuous at point** x_0 if whenever a sequence of points $\{x_n\}, n = 1, 2, \ldots$ converge to x_0, the images of these points converge to the image of x_0:
That is,

$$x_n \to x_0 \Rightarrow f(x_n) \to f(x_0).$$

The function is said to be **continuous** if it is continuous at every point in its domain.

Essentially a function of a single variable is continuous if its graph can be drawn without taking one's pen off the paper. Figures 5.1 and 5.2 illustrates this.

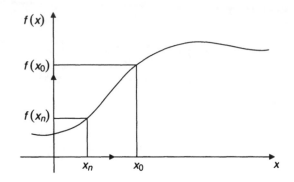

Figure 5.1   A continuous function of a single variable.

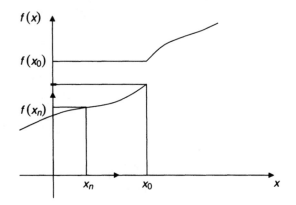

Figure 5.2   A function discontinuous at x_0.

As far as functions of a single variable are concerned, all polynomials are continuous and all rational functions are continuous for all points where the denominator is not zero. The function $y = f(x)$ is **a polynomial of degree n** if

$$f(x) = a_0 x^n + a_1 x^{n-1} + \cdots + a_{n-1} x + a_n$$

for $-\infty < x < \infty$ and is a **rational function** if

$$f(x) = \frac{F(x)}{G(x)},$$

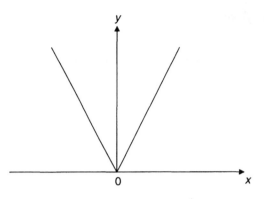

Figure 5.3   Graph of $y = |x|$.

where $F(x)$ and $G(x)$ are polynomials. The sum of continuous functions is continuous, as is the product of continuous functions. Suppose now we have two functions $f : R^m \to R^n, g : R^n \to R^p$. Then the **composite function** of f and g, denoted by $g \circ f : R^m \to R^p$ is defined by $g \circ f(x) = g(f(x))$ for all $x \in R^m$. If f is continuous and g is continuous, then $g \circ f$ is continuous.

The derivative of a function does not exist at a point of discontinuity. This is easily seen for a function of a single variable, when one remembers that a derivative of such a function at a point gives the slope of the tangent at that point. Clearly no tangent exists at a point of discontinuity. Most continuous functions are differentiable. One exception is the **absolute value function**

$$y = |x|,$$

where $|x| = x$ if x is positive, $|x| = -x$ if x is negative, and $|x| = 0$ if $x = 0$. The graph of this function presented in Figure 5.3 clearly shows it is continuous.

The derivative of this function, however, does not exist at $x = 0$, as no obvious tangent exists at this point.

Continuous functions require the existence of a convergent sequence of points for the independent variables. That is, these variables must not be discrete. If the independent variables can only take on discrete values, then the function will be discontinuous and nondifferentiable. If such a function is relevant to economies, then neoclassical analysis is not applicable. Other mathematical tools such as integer programing must be appealed to, but unfortunately for economics, integer programing is still in its infancy.

Homogeneous functions

Definition
$y = f(x) = f(x_1, \ldots, x_n)$ is a **homogeneous** function of degree r if

$$f(\lambda x_1, \ldots, \lambda x_n) = \lambda^r f(x_1, \ldots, x_n) \text{ for all } \lambda > 0.$$

Example 1
Consider $f(x_1, x_2) = x_1^2 x_2 - x_1 x_2^2$.
Then

$$f(\lambda x_1, \lambda x_2) = (\lambda x_1)^2 (\lambda x_2) - (\lambda x_1)(\lambda x_2)^2$$
$$= \lambda^3 x_1^2 x_2 - \lambda^3 x_1 x_2^2$$
$$= \lambda^3 f(x_1, x_2),$$

so the function is homogeneous of degree 3.

Example 2
Cobb-Douglas Function $Q = A K^\alpha L^\beta$.
Then

$$Q(\lambda K, \lambda L) = A(\lambda K)^\alpha (\lambda L)^\beta = \lambda^{\alpha + \beta} A K^\alpha L^\beta$$
$$= \lambda^{\alpha + \beta} Q(K, L),$$

so the function is homogeneous of degree $\alpha + \beta$.

Two important theorems concerning homogeneous functions are the following:

Theorem
If $y = f(x)$ is homogeneous of degree r then the first order partial derivatives $\partial y / \partial x_i$ are homogeneous of degree $r - 1$.

Proof
Suppose $y = f(x_1, \ldots, x_n)$ is homogeneous of degree r so

$$f(\lambda x_1 \ldots \lambda x_n) = \lambda^r f(x_1, \ldots, x_n).$$

Differentiating both sides of this equation with respect to x_i we obtain

$$f_i(\lambda x_1 \ldots \lambda x_n)\lambda = \lambda^r f_i(x_1 \ldots x_n).$$

That is $\partial f / \partial x_i$ is homogeneous of degree $r - 1$.

Euler's theorem

If $y = f(x)$ is homogeneous of degree r and differentiable then

$$x_1 \frac{\partial f(x)}{\partial x_1} + x_2 \frac{\partial f(x)}{\partial x_2} + \cdots + x_n \frac{\partial f(x)}{\partial x_n} = rf(x).$$

Proof

Suppose $y = f(x)$ is homogenous of degree r so

$$f(\lambda x_1 \ldots \lambda x_n) = \lambda^r f(x_1, \ldots, x_n).$$

Differentiating both sides of this equation with respect to λ renders

$$x_1 f_1(\lambda x_1 \ldots \lambda x_n) + \cdots + x_n f_n(\lambda x_1 \ldots \lambda x_n) = r\lambda^{r-1} f(x_1, \ldots, x_n).$$

Letting $\lambda = 1$ gives the result.

Example

Above example $f(x_1, x_2) = x_1^2 x_2 - x_1 x_2^2$.

The partial derivatives are

$$f_1 = 2x_1 x_2 - x_2^2, \quad f_2 = x_1^2 - 2x_1 x_2.$$

Now

$$
\begin{aligned}
f_1(\lambda x_1, \lambda x_2) &= 2(\lambda x_1)(\lambda x_2) - (\lambda x_2)^2 \\
&= 2\lambda^2 x_1 x_2 - \lambda^2 x_2^2 \\
&= \lambda^2 (2x_1 x_2 - x_2^2) \\
&= \lambda^2 f_1(x_1, x_2),
\end{aligned}
$$

so $f_1(x_1, x_2)$ is homogeneous of degree 2.

Also

$$
\begin{aligned}
x_1 f_1 + x_2 f_2 &= x_1(2x_1 x_2 - x_2^2) + x_2(x_1^2 - 2x_1 x_2) \\
&= 2x_1^2 x_2 - x_1 x_2^2 + x_1^2 x_2 - 2x_1 x_2^2 \\
&= 3(x_1^2 x_2 - x_1 x_2^2) \\
&= 3f(x_1, x_2),
\end{aligned}
$$

as we would expect from Euler's Theorem.

Convex and concave function

Convex and concave functions have nice mathematical properties and we study these functions in this section. Convex functions are often confused with another concept, that of convex sets. We define the latter first.

Convex sets
Line segments

Let u, v be points belonging to R^n. The **line segments** joining u and v is the set

$$L(u, v) = \{x/x = \lambda u + (1 - \lambda)v, 0 \leq \lambda \leq 1\}.$$

Example

In E^2, a line segment can be represented as the following set of points:

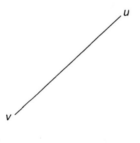

Note

A point on the line segment joining u and v can be written as $x = \lambda u + (1 - \lambda)v$ for a given λ between 0 and 1.

Example

$x = \frac{1}{4}u + \frac{3}{4}v$ is a point lying on the line segment joining u and v.

Consider now a set X contained in E^n, that is, a set of $n \times 1$ vectors.

Definition

X is a **convex set** if whenever u, v belong to X, the line segment joining u and v is contained in X. That is, $u, v \in X \Rightarrow \lambda u + (1 - \lambda)v \in X$ for all $0 \leq \lambda \leq 1$.

Convex sets have nice mathematical properties, and confining ourselves to them rules out "nasty" looking sets in E^2.

Example
Consider the following sets in E^2:

Clearly these are not convex. On the other hand, convex sets have nice geometric features:

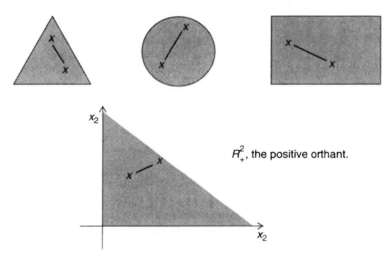

R^2_+, the positive orthant.

Example
In E^1, the **interval** $\{x \in E^1 / a < x < b\}$ is convex. Diagrammatically,

Convex functions

Definition
Let $y = f(x)$ be a function of many variables. Then $f(x)$ is a **convex function** on a convex set X contained in R^n if $\lambda f(u) + (1 - \lambda)f(v) \geq f(\lambda u + (1 - \lambda)v)$, $0 \leq \lambda \leq 1$, for all u, v belonging to X.

The function $f(x)$ is **strictly convex** on a convex set X contained in R^n if

$$\lambda f(u) + (1 - \lambda)f(v) > f(\lambda u + (1 - \lambda)v), 0 < \lambda < 1,$$

and for all u, v belonging to X.

If the function $f(x)$ is convex on its domain we simply say it is convex.

Example 1

The graph of a strictly convex function of a single variable looks like the following:

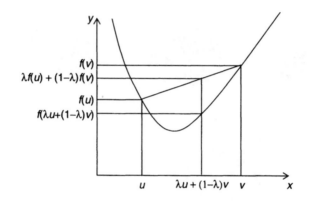

Notice that we have the following inequality:
Height of the line segment > Height of the arc.

Example 2

The graph of a convex function of a single variable may look like Figure 5.4.

The graphs of the corresponding functions of two variables look as in Figures 5.5 and 5.6.

Definition

The function $y = f(x)$ is **concave** on a set X contained in R^n if

$$\lambda f(u) + (1 - \lambda)f(v) \leq f(\lambda u + (1 - \lambda)v), \ 0 \leq \lambda \leq 1,$$

for all u, v belonging to X, and **strictly** concave if the inequality is a strict inequality for

$$0 < \lambda < 1.$$

If the function $f(x)$ is concave on its domain we simply say it is concave.

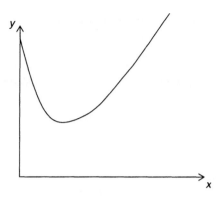

Figure 5.4   A convex function of a single variable.

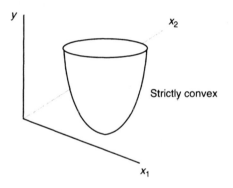

Figure 5.5   A strictly convex function of two variables.

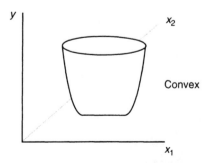

Figure 5.6   A convex function of two variables.

Examples of graphs of concave functions would be as shown in Figure 5.7–5.10.

Note
If $f(x)$ is convex then $-f(x)$ is concave and vice versa. When we are concerned with the convexity or concavity of a function, we say we are concerned with the **curvature** of the function. The following theorem allows us to determine strict concavity:

Theorem
The function $f(x)$ is strictly convex (concave) on a convex set $X \subset R^n$ if the Hessian matrix $H(x)$ is positive (negative) definite for all x belonging to X.

Recall
The matrix H is positive definite if all the leading principal minors of H are > 0 and H is negative definite if all the leading principal minors of H alternate in sign the first being negative.

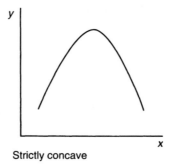

Strictly concave

Figure 5.7   A strictly concave function of a single variable.

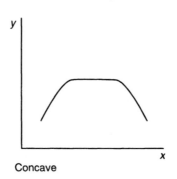

Concave

Figure 5.8   A concave function of a single variable.

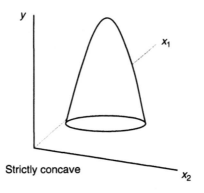

Figure 5.9 A strictly concave function of two variables.

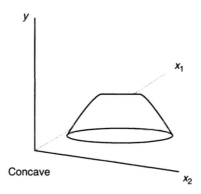

Figure 5.10 A concave function of two variables.

Example

Show that $f(x_1, x_2) = x_1^{1/4} x_2^{1/2}$ is strictly concave on the **positive orthant**,

$$R_+^2 = \left\{ x = \begin{pmatrix} x_1 \\ x_2 \end{pmatrix} \Big/ x_1 > 0, x_2 > 0 \right\}$$

Now

$$f_1 = \frac{1}{4} x_1^{-3/4} x_2^{1/2}, \quad f_2 = \frac{1}{2} x_1^{1/4} x_2^{-1/2}$$

$$f_{12} = \frac{1}{8} x_1^{-3/4} x_2^{-1/2}, \quad f_{11} = -\frac{3}{16} x_1^{-7/4} x_2^{1/2}, \quad f_{22} = -\frac{1}{4} x_1^{1/4} x_2^{-3/2},$$

so the Hessian matrix is

$$H(x) = \frac{1}{16} \begin{pmatrix} -3x_1^{-7/4}x_2^{1/2} & 2x_1^{-3/4}x_2^{-1/2} \\ 2x_1^{-3/4}x_2^{-1/2} & -4x_1^{1/4}x_2^{-3/2} \end{pmatrix}.$$

The first leading principal minor is

$$-\frac{3}{16}x_1^{-7/4}x_2^{1/2} < 0 \quad \text{for } x_1 > 0, \quad x_2 > 0.$$

The second leading principal minor is

$$|H| = \frac{1}{256}\left(12x_1^{-6/4}x_2^{-1} - 4x_1^{-6/4}x_2^{-1}\right)$$

$$= \frac{1}{32}x_1^{-3/2}x_2^{-1} > 0 \quad \text{for } x_1 > 0, \quad x_2 > 0.$$

Thus $f(x_1, x_2)$ is strictly concave on R_+^2.
For convexity and concavity we have the following theorem:

Theorem
The function $f(x)$ is convex (concave) on a convex set $X \subset R^n$ if and only if $H(x)$ is positive (negative) semidefinite for all x belonging to X.

Recall
H is positive semidefinite if and only if all the principal minors of H are ≥ 0.
H is negative semidefinite if and only if odd order principal minors are ≤ 0 and even order principal minors are ≥ 0.

Example 1
Show $f(x_1, x_2) = x_1 - x_2 - x_1^2$ is concave.
Now

$$f_1 = 1 - 2x_1, \quad f_2 = -1, \quad f_{12} = 0, \quad f_{11} = -2, \quad f_{22} = 0.$$

Thus

$$H(x) = \begin{pmatrix} -2 & 0 \\ 0 & 0 \end{pmatrix}.$$

The first principal minors are $-2, 0 \leq 0$ and the second principal minor is $|H| = 0 \geq 0$.

Hence the function is concave.

Example 2

What can we say about the convexity and concavity of $f(x_1, x_2) = x_1 x_2$?

The required derivatives are

$$f_1 = x_2, \quad f_2 = x_1, \quad f_{11} = 0, \quad f_{22} = 0, \quad f_{12} = 1.$$

Hence the Hessian matrix is

$$H = \begin{pmatrix} 0 & 1 \\ 1 & 0 \end{pmatrix}.$$

The first principal minors are $0, 0$ and the second principal minor is $|H| = -1$.

This establishes that H is indefinite. As the above theorems concerning convexity and concavity are "if and only if" theorems, $f(x_1, x_2)$ is neither convex nor concave.

Exercises for 5.3

1. (i) Let A and B be the following sets. Graph their intersection $A \cap B$ and their union $A \cup B$ indicating which of these sets are convex.
   (a) $A = \{x \in E^2 / x_1 > 2\}, B = \{x \in E^2 / x_1 < 3\}$
   (b) $A = \{x \in E^2 / x_1^2 + x_2^2 \leq 4\}, B = \{x \in E^2 / (x_1 - 1)^2 + x_2^2 \leq 4\}$
   (c) $A = \{x \in E^2 / x_1 \geq 0, x_2 \geq 0, x_1 \leq 1, x_2 \leq 1\}$
       $B = \{x \in E^2 / (x_1 - 1)^2 + x_2^2 \leq 1\}$.
   (ii) Prove that the following sets are convex
   (a) $X = \{x \in E^n / c'x = z\}$
   (b) $X = \{x \in E^n / Ax = b\}$
   (c) $X = \{x \in E^n / Ax \leq b\}$
   (d) $X = \{x \in E^n / x_i \geq 0\}$
2. Suppose that S is a convex set in E^n with a finite number of elements. How many elements can S have?
3. The Cartesian product of any two sets S and T in E^n is defined by

$$S \times T = \{(s, t) / s \in S, t \in T\}$$

   (i) Prove that if S and T are both convex sets in E^n then $S \times T$ is also convex.
   (ii) Let S and T be intervals of the real line. Graph $S \times T$.

4. Prove that if X_1 and X_2 are convex sets of E^n then their intersection $X_1 \cap X_2$ is a convex set. Is their union $X_1 \cup X_2$ convex? If not give a counter example.

5. Define a homogeneous function and state Euler's Theorem. Show that Euler's Theorem holds for the following functions:

   (i) $f(x, y) = x^{1/2}y^{1/2} + 3x^2y^{-1}$

   (ii) $f(x, y) = x^{3/4}y^{1/4} + 6x$

   (iii) $f(x, y) = (x^2 - y^2)/(x^2 + y^2) + 3$

   (iv) $f(x, y) = 3x^5y + 2x^2y^4 - 3x^3y^3$.

6. Two functions that are used a lot in economics are the Cobb-Douglas function given by $Q(K, L) = AK^\alpha L^\beta$ and the CES production function given by $Q(K, L) = A(a_1K^\rho + a_2L^\rho)^{1/\rho}$.

   (i) Show that these functions are homogeneous. Of what degrees are they?

   (ii) Show that Euler's Theorem holds for these functions.

   (iii) Are the marginal products Q_K and Q_L of the Cobb-Douglas and CES production functions homogeneous functions? If so, of what degree?

7. If $y = f(x_1, x_2)$ is a homogeneous function of degree r show that

$$x_1^2 f_{11} + 2x_1 x_2 f_{12} + x_2^2 f_{22} = r(r - 1)f.$$

8. Define a convex function and a convex set. A theorem, stated in the text, says that $y = f(x_1 \ldots x_n)$ is convex (concave) on a convex set X if and only if the Hessian matrix of the function is positive (negative) semidefinite at every point in X. Use this theorem to check the concavity or convexity of the follow functions on R^2:

   (i) $f(x_1 x_2) = x_1 x_2$

   (ii) $f(x, y) = x^4 + y^4 + 3x^2y^2$

   (iii) $f(x, y) = -3x^2 + 2xy - y^2 + 3x - 4y + 1$

   (iv) $f(x, y) = e^{x+y} + e^{x-y} - \frac{3}{2}x - \frac{1}{2}y$

   (v) $f(x, y) = 2x - y - x^2 - 2xy - y^2$

   (vi) $f(x, y) = x + y - e^x - e^{x+y}$.

9. Use the theorem quoted in question 8 to find the largest convex domain in E^2 on which the function

$$f(x, y) = x^2 - y^2 - xy - x^3$$

is concave.

10. Another theorem stated in the text says that $y = f(x_1 \ldots x_n)$ is strictly convex (concave) on a convex set X if the Hessian matrix of the function is positive (negative) definite for all points in X. Use this theorem to check out the strict convexity or strict concavity of the following functions:

   (i) $f(x, y) = -3x^2 + 2xy - y^2 + 3x - 4y + 1$ on R^2,

(ii) $f(x, y) = x^4 + x^2 y^2 + y^4 - 3x - 8y$ on R^2 excluding the null vector,

(iii) $f(x, y) = x^{1/4} y^{1/4}$ on the positive orthant R^2_+,

(iv) $f(x, y, z) = 3e^x + 5y^4 - \log z$ on the positive orthant.

11. Show that the Cobb-Douglas function

$$Q = AK^a L^b$$

is

(i) concave on the positive orthant if $A > 0, a \geq 0, b \geq 0$, and $a + b \leq 1$

(ii) strictly concave on the positive orthant if A, a, and b are all positive and $a + b < 1$.

12. Let $f(x)$ and $g(x)$ be convex functions defined on R^n. Let a and b be positive numbers. Prove that $af(x) + bg(x)$ is a convex function on R^n.

13. Prove that if $f(x)$ is a convex function then

$$S^{\leq} = \{x / f(x) \leq k\}$$

is a convex set for any constant k. What is the corresponding result for a concave function?

5.4   Comparative Statics and Nonlinear Economic Models

Introduction

In linear economic models comparative static analysis is a relatively simple matter. In mathematical terms we know we can write the structural form as

$$A x = b$$

where x is the vector of endogenous variables and b is the vector containing linear combinations of the exogenous variables.

The equilibrium values of the endogenous variables are given by

$$x^* = A^{-1} b \text{ or } x_j^* = \frac{\begin{vmatrix} a_{11} & \cdots & b_1 & \cdots & a_{n1} \\ \vdots & & \vdots & & \vdots \\ a_{n1} & \cdots & b_n & \cdots & a_{nn} \end{vmatrix}}{|A|}.$$

All our comparative static results are contained in the system of equations

$$\Delta x^* = A^{-1} \Delta b$$

or by using Cramer's rule to see how x_j^* changes when we change the values of the exogenous variables.

In this section we ask ourselves the question, how do we conduct comparative static analysis in an economic model where we insist that the equations are nonlinear?

In answering this question we need new mathematics.

Implicit function theorems

Suppose we have a nonlinear equation, say

$$F(y, x_1, x_2, \ldots, x_n) = 0.$$

We seek to determine when this equation can be solved to give y as a function of $x_1, \ldots, x_n$, say

$$y = f(x_1, \ldots, x_n).$$

Such a function if it exists is called the **implicit function** defined by the nonlinear equation.

Implicit function theorem 1

Suppose the nonlinear function F has continuous partial derivatives $F_y, F_1, F_2, \ldots, F_n$ and consider any point $y^0, x_1^0, \ldots, x_n^0$ that satisfies the equation $F(y, x_1, \ldots, x_n) = 0$. If the derivative F_y is nonzero when evaluated at this point then an implicit function exists at least in the neighborhood of this point. Moreover the partial derivatives $\partial f / \partial x_i$ exist and are continuous.

Note
If such an implicit function exists it makes sense to talk of the derivatives $\partial y / \partial x_1, \ldots, \partial y / \partial x_n$. Moreover these can be obtained by differentiating $F = 0$ with respect to x_i, say, remembering y is a function of $x_1, \ldots, x_n$.

Example
At what points does

$$y^3 x_1^2 + x_2^3 + y x_1 x_2 - 3 = 0, \tag{5.3}$$

have an implicit function for y in terms of x_1 and x_2? Find $\partial y / \partial x_1$ when this implicit function exists. Now

$$F(y, x_1, x_2) = y^3 x_1^2 + x_2^3 + y x_1 x_2 - 3$$

and clearly F_y, F_1, F_2 exist and are continuous. Moreover $F_y = 3y^2x_1^2 + x_1x_2$, so an implicit function exists at any point (y, x_1, x_2) satisfying $F = 0$ such that $F_y \neq 0$. Take, for example, the point $(1, 1, 1)$. For this point $F(1, 1, 1) = 1 + 1 + 1 - 3 = 0$, and

$$F_y(1, 1, 1) = 3 + 1 = 4 \neq 0.$$

Differentiating both sides of (5.3) with respect to x_1 we get

$$2x_1y^3 + x_1^2 3y^2 \frac{\partial y}{\partial x_1} + yx_2 + x_1x_2 \frac{\partial y}{\partial x_1} = 0.$$

Collecting terms we have

$$\frac{\partial y}{\partial x_1}(3y^2x_1^2 + x_1x_2) = -(y^3 2x_1 + yx_2)$$

giving

$$\frac{\partial y}{\partial x_1} = -\frac{y^3 2x_1 + yx_2}{3y^2x_1^2 + x_1x_2}.$$

Note
From this example, we have found $\partial y / \partial x_1$ even though we do not know what the implicit function is!

Economic application

Suppose in a nonlinear economic model, the equilibrium condition is given by the nonlinear equation

$$F(y, x_1, \ldots, x_n) = 0,$$

where y is an endogenous variable and $x_1, \ldots, x_n$ are the exogenous variables.

We want to know when an equilibrium solution exists, that is, when can we solve for the endogenous variable y as a function of the exogenous variables $x_1, \ldots, x_n$. We also want to conduct comparative static analysis by looking at $\partial y / \partial x_j$, say.

Example
Consider the simple Keynesian macroeconomic model for a closed economy:

$$Y = C + I + G$$
$$C = C(Y) \quad 0 < C' < 1$$
$$I = I(Y) \quad 0 < I' < 1.$$

Substituting the behavioral equations into the definition equation gives our equilibrium condition

$$Y = C(Y) + I(Y) + G$$

or

$$Y - C(Y) - I(Y) - G = 0. \tag{5.4}$$

Equation (5.4) is of the form $F(Y, G) = 0$. We want to conduct a comparative static exercise for this model, by looking at dY/dG, to give us an indication of the effect of a change in government expenditure on equilibrium income. But it only makes sense to talk of the derivative dY/dG if we are first persuaded that our equilibrium condition has a solution $Y = Y(G)$. The Implicit Function Theorem assures us it does for any points where

$$F_Y = 1 - C' - I' \neq 0.$$

Moreover, if this condition holds we can obtain the derivative we want by differentiating both sides of equation (5.4) with respect to G, remembering now that $Y = Y(G)$. We get

$$\frac{dY}{dG} - C'\frac{dY}{dG} - I'\frac{dY}{dG} - 1 = 0,$$

so

$$\frac{dY}{dG}(1 - C' - I') = 1$$

and

$$\frac{dY}{dG} = \frac{1}{1 - C' - I'}.$$

Generalization of the implicit function theorem

Suppose we have two nonlinear equations[2]

$$F^1(y_1, y_2, x_1, \ldots, x_n) = 0$$
$$F^2(y_1, y_2, x_1, \ldots, x_n) = 0.$$

When is it possible to solve these for y_1 and y_2 as functions of $x_1, \ldots, x_n$ whose partial derivatives exist? Before we give the appropriate implicit function theorem, we have the following definition:

Definition
The **Jacobian Determinant** is

$$|J| = \begin{vmatrix} \dfrac{\partial F^1}{\partial y_1} & \dfrac{\partial F^1}{\partial y_2} \\ \dfrac{\partial F^2}{\partial y_1} & \dfrac{\partial F^2}{\partial y_2} \end{vmatrix}.$$

Implicit function theorem 2

Suppose F^1 and F^2 have continuous partial derivatives with respect to $y_1, y_2, x_1, \ldots, x_n$. Then implicit functions $y_1 = y_1(x_1, \ldots, x_n)$ and $y_2 = y_2(x_1, \ldots, x_n)$ exist at any point satisfying the equations where the Jacobian determinant is nonzero. Moreover these implicit functions have continuous partial derivatives.

Example
Consider the following version of the IS-LM model where the product market is portrayed by the equations

$$Y = C + I + G$$
$$C = C(Y) \quad 0 < C' < 1$$
$$I = I(r) \quad I' < 0,$$

and the money market is portrayed by the equations

$$L^T = kY$$
$$L^S = L(r).$$

[2]This section is easily generalized to any number of nonlinear equations.

The equilibrium conditions for the two markets are

$$Y = C(Y) + I(r) + G$$
$$kY + L(r) = m.$$

In this model the exogenous variables are government expenditure G and the money supply m, whereas the endogenous variables are income Y and the interest rate r. The equilibrium conditions are equivalent to the nonlinear equations

$$F^1(Y, r, G, m) = Y - C(Y) - I(r) - G = 0 \qquad (5.5)$$

$$F^2(Y, r, G, m) = kY + L(r) - m = 0, \qquad (5.6)$$

and we ask ourselves when these equations have implicit solutions $Y = Y(m, G)$ and $r = r(m, G)$?

The Jacobian determinant is

$$|J| = \begin{vmatrix} 1 - C' & -I' \\ k & L' \end{vmatrix}$$
$$= L'(1 - C') + kI',$$

so solutions exist at points where

$$L'(1 - C') + kI' \neq 0.$$

If this condition holds then it makes sense to talk of the partial derivatives, such as $\partial Y / \partial m$ or $\partial r / \partial G$, and to use them as our approximations in comparative static analysis.

Suppose for example government expenditure changes and we want to know how this will affect equilibrium income and interest rate. We are interested in $\partial Y / \partial G$ and $\partial r / \partial G$. Differentiating the equilibrium conditions, given by equations (5.5) and (5.6), (remembering now that we can regard Y and r as functions of m and G), we get

$$\frac{\partial Y}{\partial G} - C' \frac{\partial Y}{\partial G} - I' \frac{\partial r}{\partial G} - 1 = 0$$

$$k \frac{\partial Y}{\partial G} + L' \frac{\partial r}{\partial G} = 0$$

or in matrix notation

$$\begin{pmatrix} 1 - C' & -I' \\ k & L' \end{pmatrix} \begin{pmatrix} \dfrac{\partial Y}{\partial G} \\ \dfrac{\partial r}{\partial G} \end{pmatrix} = \begin{pmatrix} 1 \\ 0 \end{pmatrix}.$$

Using Cramer's rule to solve for $\partial Y/\partial G$, for example, we get

$$\frac{\partial Y}{\partial G} = \frac{\begin{vmatrix} 1 & -I' \\ 0 & L' \end{vmatrix}}{\begin{vmatrix} 1 - C' & -I' \\ k & L' \end{vmatrix}}$$

$$= \frac{L'}{L'(1 - C') + kI'}.$$

Exercises for 5.4

1. In the content of a single nonlinear equation, what question does the Implicit Function Theorem address? Why is this theorem important for comparative static analysis in economics?
2. Given the nonlinear equation $F(x, y) = 0$ shown below, is an implicit function $y = f(x)$ defined in the neighborhood of the point $x = 1, y = 1$? If so find dy/dx in the neighborhood:
   (i) $x^3 + 4x^2y - 7xy^2 + 2 = 0$
   (ii) $x^2 + 8xy + y^4 - 10 = 0$.
3. Does the nonlinear equation

$$x_1 + 3x_1x_2 + 2x_2y + x_2^2 + y^2 - 5 = 0$$

define an implicit function $y = f(x_1, x_2)$ around the point $x_1 = 1, x_2 = 1, y = 0$?

   If so, find $\partial y/\partial x_1$, and $\partial y/\partial x_2$ and evaluate them at this point.
4. Consider the nonlinear macroeconomic model of an open economy

$$Y = C + I + G + X - M$$
$$C = C(Y), \quad 0 < C' < 1$$
$$I = I(Y), \quad I' > 0$$
$$M = M(Y), \quad M' > 0,$$

where exports X and government expenditure G are considered exogenous variables. Our equilibrium condition is

$$Y = C(Y) + I(Y) + G + X - M(Y).$$

What condition do we need to ensure that a solution $Y = Y(G, X)$ exists? Assuming this condition holds find $\partial Y / \partial G$.

5. Consider the nonlinear equations

$$y_1^5 + y_2 - x = 0$$
$$y_1^2 + y_2^3 - x^2 = 0.$$

Do these equations define implicit functions $y_1 = y_1(x)$ and $y_2 = y_2(x)$ around the point $y_1 = 1, y_2 = 0$, and $x = 1$? If so compute dy_1/dx and dy_2/dx and evaluate these derivatives at this point.

6. Consider the nonlinear macroeconomic (the IS-LM model) whose equilibrium equations are given by

$$Y = C(Y) + I(r) + G$$
$$L(r, Y) = M.$$

The exogenous variables are government expenditure G and the real money supply M while the endogenous variables are national income Y and the interest rate r. We have the following information on derivations:

$$0 < C' < 1, \quad I' < 0, \quad L_r < 0, \quad L_Y > 0.$$

(i) What condition do we need to ensure that equilibrium solutions $Y = Y(G, M)$ and $r = r(G, M)$ exists?

(ii) Monetary policy in this model is represented by changes in M. Analyze the comparative statics of the model when M increases by assigning signs to the derivatives $\partial Y / \partial M$ and $\partial r / \partial M$. (We assume the condition derived in (i) holds.)

5.5   Differentials and Taylor's Approximation

We finish this chapter with a section on an important approximation which is used extensively in the next chapter. We give this approximation first for a function of a single variable and then we generalize it for a function of many variables. The latter leads into a discussion on differentials and total derivatives.

Taylor's theorem for a function of a single variable

Theorem
Let $y = f(x)$ be a differentiable function of a single variable and let x_0 be a point in the domain of the function. Then

$$f(x) = f(x_0) + \frac{f'(x_0)}{1!}(x - x_0) + \frac{f''(x_0)}{2!}(x - x_0)^2 + \frac{f'''(x_0)}{3!}(x - x_0)^3 + \cdots$$

$$+ \frac{f^{(n)}(x_0)}{n!}(x - x_0)^n + R_n,$$

where R_n is a remainder term, $n!$ is the nth factorial defined by $n! = n(n - 1)(n - 2) \ldots 2.1$, and $f^{(n)}(x_0)$ signifies the nth derivative of $f(x)$ evaluated at x_0.

Mathematicians are interested in the form of the remainder term R_n, but our interest is to use this theorem to obtain an approximation. Suppose x and x_0 are points in the domain of the function which are close to each other. Then $dx = x - x_0$ represents a small change in x and the terms $(dx)^2, (dx)^3 \ldots$ will be getting smaller. Thus we can write

$$f(x) \approx f(x_0) + \frac{f'(x_0)}{1!} \; dx \; + \frac{f''(x_0)}{2!} \; (dx)^2 + \cdots + \frac{f^{(n)}(x_0)}{n!} \; (dx)^n.$$

This is called the nth order Taylor approximation. For example the first order Taylor approximation would be

$$f(x) \approx f(x_0) + f'(x_0)dx$$

whereas the second order approximation would be

$$f(x) \approx f(x_0) + f'(x_0)dx + \frac{f''(x_0)}{2}(dx)^2,$$

and so on.

Example
Compute the third order Taylor approximation for $f(x) = 1/(1 + x)$ at $x_0 = 1$ and use this approximation to estimate $f(1.1)$.

We evaluate $f(x)$ and the first three derivatives of $f(x)$, at the point $x_0 = 1$:

$$f(x) = (1+x)^{-1} \qquad f(1) = \frac{1}{2}$$

$$f'(x) = -(1+x)^{-2} \qquad f'(1) = -\frac{1}{2^2} = -\frac{1}{4}$$

$$f''(x) = 2(1+x)^{-3} \qquad f''(1) = \frac{2}{2^3} = \frac{1}{4}$$

$$f'''(x) = -6(1+x)^{-4} \qquad f'''(1) = -\frac{6}{2^4} = -\frac{3}{8}.$$

Our approximation then is $f(x) \approx \frac{1}{2} - \frac{1}{4}(x-1) + \frac{1}{8}(x-1)^2 - \frac{1}{16}(x-1)^3$.
Evaluating both sides at $x = 1.1$ we obtain

$$f(1.1) \approx \frac{1}{2} - \frac{1}{4}(0.1) + \frac{1}{8}(0.1)^2 - \frac{1}{16}(0.1)^3$$

$$= \frac{1}{2} - 0.025 + 0.00125 - 0.0000625 = 0.4761875.$$

Note that $f(1.1) = 1/2.1 = 0.4761905$, so our approximation is fairly accurate.
 Essentially the closer the point x is to x_0, the smaller $dx = x - x_0$ is, and the more accurate is the approximation obtained. The small change $dx = x - x_0$ is called the **differential** of x.

Taylor's approximation for a function of many variables

We now present the second order Taylor's approximation for a function of many variables.

 Let $f(x)$ be a function of many variables. Then for all points x and x^0 in the domain of the function

$$f(x) \approx f(x^0) + \sum_{j=1}^{n} \frac{\partial f(x^0)}{\partial x_j}(x_j - x_j^0) + \frac{1}{2}\sum_{i=1}^{n}\sum_{j=1}^{n} \frac{\partial^2 f(x^0)}{\partial x_i \partial x_j}(x_i - x_i^0)(x_j - x_j^0)$$

where $x = (x_1, x_2, \ldots, x_n)'$ and $x^0 = (x_1^0, x_2^0, \ldots, x_n^0)'$.

 As in the case of a function of a single variable, the closer x^0 is to x, the more accurate the approximation. When x^0 is close to $x, x_j - x_j^0$ represents a small change in x_j, which we denote by dx_j. Such a small change is called the **differential** in x_j.

Taylor's approximation can conveniently be put into matrix notation using the gradient vector and Hessian matrix of the function. Recall that the gradient vector $\nabla f(x)$ is the (column) vector of first order partial derivatives of $f(x)$ and the Hessian matrix $H(x)$ is the matrix of all second order partial derivatives of $f(x)$. Now let dx be the $n \times 1$ vector of the differentials of the n independent variables.

That is,

$$dx = \begin{pmatrix} x_1 - x_1^0 \\ x_2 - x_2^0 \\ \vdots \\ x_n - x_n^0 \end{pmatrix}.$$

Then we can write

$$f(x) \approx f(x^0) + dx' \nabla f(x^0) + \tfrac{1}{2} dx' H(x^0) dx$$

or

$$f(x) - f(x^0) \approx dx' \nabla f(x^0) + \tfrac{1}{2} dx' H(x^0) dx. \qquad (5.7)$$

The first term in the approximation is a linear function of the differentials, with the coefficients of this function being the elements of the gradient vector evaluated at x^0. The second term involves a quadratic form in the differentials, the matrix of the quadratic form being the Hessian matrix evaluated at x^0.

The differential of $y = f(x)$

We noted that small changes in the independent variables are called differentials of these variables. We now want to define what we mean by the differential of the dependent variable y. Suppose we make Taylor's approximation even cruder by considering only the first term in equation (5.7),

$$f(x) - f(x^0) \approx dx' \nabla f(x^0) = \sum_{j=1}^{n} \frac{\partial f(x^0)}{\partial x_j} dx_j. \qquad (5.8)$$

The left hand side gives the change in y and the right hand side gives an approximation for this change. This approximation is called the **differential** of y. More formally we have the following definition.

Definition

The differential of $y = f(x)$ is given by

$$dy = \frac{\partial f}{\partial x_1} dx_1 + \frac{\partial f}{\partial x_2} dx_2 + \cdots + \frac{\partial f}{\partial x_n} dx_n.$$

When we evaluate dy at the point x^0 we get the right hand side of equation (5.8).

The differential of y then gives an approximation to the change in y that results from small changes in $x_1, x_2, \ldots, x_n$. For a function of a single variable, the following diagram illustrates this approximation:

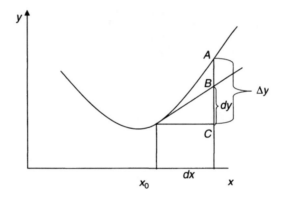

Suppose we are at x_0 and we let x change by dx. Then the corresponding change in y will be Δy given by AC. The differential of y, is

$$dy = f'(x_0)dx = BC.$$

Clearly the smaller dx becomes, the better dy is as an approximation to Δy.

Example

Suppose $y = x_1^2 x_2 + 3x_2^2 x_1$. Find an approximation for the change in y when, from the point $x^0 = (1, 1)'$, x_1 increases by 0.1 and x_2 decreases by 0.1.

Our approximation, using a different notation, is

$$dy = f_1 dx_1 + f_2 dx_2$$
$$= (2x_1 x_2 + 3x_2^2)dx_1 + (x_1^2 + 6x_2 x_1)dx_2.$$

Now

$$x_1 = 1, x_2 = 1, dx_1 = 0.1, dx_2 = -0.1,$$

so

$$dy = (2 + 3)(0.1) + (1 + 6)(-0.1) = -0.2.$$

The total derivative of $y = f(x)$

For a function of a single variable,

$$dy = f'(x)dx$$

so

$$\frac{dy}{dx} = f'(x).$$

That is the ratio of differentials is the derivative. Now consider a function of two variables $y = f(x_1, x_2)$. Then

$$dy = \frac{\partial f}{\partial x_1}dx_1 + \frac{\partial f}{\partial x_2}dx_2.$$

Dividing through both sides of this equation by dx_1 we have

$$\frac{dy}{dx_1} = \frac{\partial f}{\partial x_1} + \frac{\partial f}{\partial x_2}\frac{dx_2}{dx_1}.$$

Again the ratio of differentials dy/dx_1 is a derivative. It is called the **total derivative** of y with respect to x_1.

What then distinguishes this total derivative of y with respect to x_1, dy/dx_1, from the partial derivative $\partial y/\partial x_1$?

First, suppose that the variable x_2 is not a function of x_1. Then $dx_2/dx_1 = 0$ and

$$\frac{dy}{dx_1} = \frac{\partial y}{\partial x_1}.$$

The two derivatives differ then when x_2 is a function of x_1. The partial derivative $\partial y/\partial x_1$ gives an approximation to the rate of change in y when x_1 changes, if we insist that we treat x_2 as a constant. If x_2 is a function in x_1, clearly this would be unrealistic and the total derivative dy/dx_1 is the appropriate approximation for the rate of change, picking up both the direct effect of a change in x_1 on y (given by $\partial y/\partial x_1$) and the indirect effect through x_2 (given by $\partial y/\partial x_2 \cdot dx_2/dx_1$).

Example
Suppose $y = 3x_1 - x_2^2$ and $x_2 = 2x_1^2 + x_1 + 4$. Find the partial derivative $\partial y/\partial x_1$ and the total derivative dy/dx_1. Check your answer for dy/dx_1 using a different method.

Clearly

$$\frac{\partial y}{\partial x_1} = 3, \frac{\partial y}{\partial x_2} = -2x_2 \quad \text{and} \quad \frac{dx_2}{dx_1} = 4x_1 + 1.$$

Now

$$\frac{dy}{dx_1} = \frac{\partial y}{\partial x_1} + \frac{\partial y}{\partial x_2}\frac{dx_2}{dx_1}$$
$$= 3 - 2x_2(4x_1 + 1).$$

As a check, substitute for x_2 in y to give

$$y = 3x_1 - (2x_1^2 + x_1 + 4)^2.$$

Then

$$\frac{dy}{dx_1} = 3 - 2(2x_1^2 + x_1 + 4)(4x_1 + 1)$$
$$= 3 - 2x_2(4x_1 + 1).$$

Exercises for 5.5

1. (i) Compute Taylor's approximation of order three for $y = x^{1/2}$. Use this approximation to estimate $\sqrt{4.05}$.
   (ii) Compute Taylor's approximation of order three for
   (a) $y = (x + 1)^{1/2}$ about $x^0 = 0$,
   (b) $y = e^x$ about $x^0 = 0$, and
   (c) $y = \log x$ about $x^0 = 1$,
   in terms of small changes dx in x. Then compute the values of these approximations for $dx = 0.2$.
2. (i) For a function of two variables $y = f(x_1, x_2)$ write out Taylor's approximation of order two.
   (ii) For the Cobb-Douglas function

$$y = f(x_1, x_2) = x_1^{1/4} x_2^{3/4}$$

compute Taylor's approximation of order two, at the point $x_1^0 = 1$ and $x_2^0 = 1$ in terms of small changes dx_1 and dx_2 in x_1 and x_2 respectively. Use this approximation to estimate $f(x_1, x_2)$ at the point $x_1 = 1.1$ and $x_2 = 0.9$.

(iii) For the function given in (ii) compute the differential. Use it to approximate the changes in y when we move from point $x_1^0 = 1$, and $x_2^0 = 1$ to point $x_1 = 1.1$ and $x_2 = 0.9$.

3. For the function $y = f(x_1, x_2)$ distinguish between the partial derivative of y with respect to x_1 and the total derivative of y with respect to x_1. Suppose $y = x_1^3 + 7x_2^2$ and $x_2 = \log 5x_1$. Find the partial derivative $\partial y / \partial x_1$ and the total derivative dy/dx_1.

4. For a function of two variables $y = f(x) = f(x_1, x_2)$, as the differential dy is a function of x_1, x_2 as well, we can think of taking the differential of the differential. This is called the **second order differential** and is denoted by d^2y. So

$$d^2y = d(dy).$$

Show that $d^2y = dx'H(x)dx$ where $H(x)$ is the Hessian matrix of $f(x)$.

Chapter 6

Optimization

6.1 Unconstrained Optimization

Introduction

Many of the problems confronting economists are optimization problems. For example in microeconomics, the problem neoclassical economics gives to the consumer is one of maximizing utility subject to a budget constraint. Likewise to the firm, neoclassical economics assigns the problem of profit maximization.

It is often argued that economists, through their marginal analysis in dealing with problems like the above, reinvented calculus several 100 years after it had been invented by mathematicians. These days economists are only too happy to call on the body of knowledge built up by mathematicians on optimization problems.

Let $y = f(x)$ be a function of many variables. Then $f(x)$ has an optimum at point x^0 if $f(x)$ takes a maximum or minimum at x^0. The process of finding the optima associated with a function is called **optimization**. We start our discussion by distinguishing between local optima and global optima and between ordinary optima and strict optima.

Local versus global optima

Recall that the Euclidian distance between two points or vectors x, y belonging to E^n is

$$d(x, y) = \sqrt{(x_1 - y_1)^2 + \cdots + (x_n - y_n)^2}.$$

We have the following definition.

Definition

An ε **neighborhood** of point x^0 is the set of points:

$$\{x/d(x,x^0) < \varepsilon\}.$$

Usually we take ε as a small positive number and we use the ε neighborhood to signify points which are close to x^0.

Example

In E^1 the ε neighborhood is the interval:

In E^2, the ε neighborhood is the set of points contained in a circle centered at x^0:

In E^3 the ε neighborhood forms a sphere.

The concept of an ε neighborhood is used to distinguish between local and global optima.

Definition

The function $f(x)$ has a **local maximum at x^0** if $f(x^0) \geq f(x)$ for all points x in an ε neighborhood of x^0.

The function $f(x)$ has a **local minimum at x^0** if $f(x^0) \leq f(x)$ for all points x in an ε neighborhood of x^0.

The function $f(x)$ has a **global maximum** at x^0 if $f(x^0) \geq f(x)$ for all x in the domain of $f(x)$.

The function $f(x)$ has a **global minimum** at x^0 if $f(x^0) \leq f(x)$ for all x in the domain of $f(x)$.

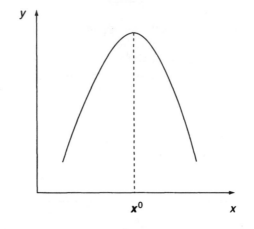

Figure 6.1   A strict local and global maximum.

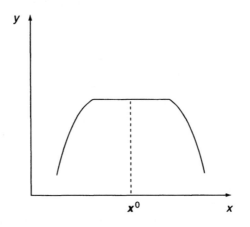

Figure 6.2   A local and global maximum.

Strict optima versus optima

To get the corresponding definitions for **strict optima,** we replace all the above inequality signs by strict inequality signs.

Examples

Consider the graphs of Figures 6.1–6.3 functions of a single variable.

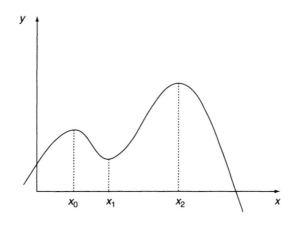

Figure 6.3 Strict local and global optima.

We know that calculus has to do with finding approximations for rates of changes and actual changes in y when there are small changes in the xs. Small changes in the independent variables mean that we stay close to the initial point x_0. So we suspect that calculus can help us find local optima. This is indeed the case and in what follows, we develop procedures based on calculus for finding strict local optima, though our discussion is easily generalized to local – though not necessarily strict – optima. In the classification of strict local optima we shall make use of our previous work with positive definite matrices and convex functions. We start our search for local optima by finding all the critical points of the function.

Definition
Let the $y = f(x)$ be a function of many variables. Then any point x^* that satisfies

$$f_1 = f_2 = \cdots = f_n = 0$$

is called a **critical point** of the function.

Critical points provide us with all the possible candidates for a local optima.

Theorem
If x^* is a local maximum or minimum of $y = f(x)$ then x^* is a critical point.

To illustrate the proof of this theorem consider the graphs of strict local optima for a function of two variables which also happen to be global optima.

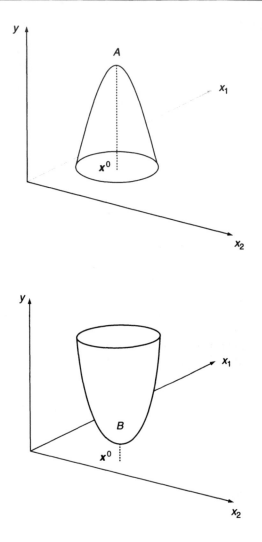

At A, we have a (strict) local maximum which is also a global maximum. Similarly at B, we have a (strict) local minimum which is also a global minimum. In either case y is no longer changing so $dy = 0$. But $dy = f_1 dx_1 + f_2 dx_2$ for small changes dx_1, dx_2 in x_1 and x_2 respectively. So $dy = 0 \Leftrightarrow f_1 = f_2 = 0$.

The proof is easily generalized.

All the local optima come from the pool of critical points. But not all critical points are local optima, as the following graph of a function in two variables illustrated in Figure 6.4.

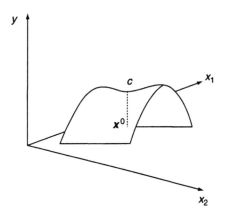

Figure 6.4   A saddle point.

At C we have $dy = 0$ or $f_1 = f_2 = 0$ so x_0 is a critical point. But it is neither a local maximum nor a local minimum. The point is called a **saddle point** for obvious reasons.

Question
What additional conditions do we require to ensure a critical point x^* is a strict local optimum?

We answer this question in three different ways using concepts that we are now familiar with.

1   Using Taylor's approximation
Recall Taylor's approximation

$$f(x) \approx f(x^0) + \nabla f(x^0)'dx + \tfrac{1}{2}dx'H(x^0)dx.$$

If x^0 is a critical point then $\nabla f(x^0) = \mathbf{0}$ so $f(x) \approx f(x^0) + \tfrac{1}{2}dx'H(x^0)dx$, at any critical point.

Suppose now that the Hessian matrix $H(x)$ is negative definite when evaluated at x^0. Then $dx'H(x^0)dx$ is less than zero for all dx implying

$$f(x) < f(x^0).$$

That is, $H(x)$ being negative definite when evaluated at x^0, is enough to ensure that we have a strict local maximum at x^0.

2   *Using differentials*

Consider a strict local maximum as illustrated at point A. When we leave such a point in any direction, y must decrease. So at the strict local maximum $dy = 0$, then $dy < 0$. That is $d^2y < 0$ at the strict local maximum. But $d^2y = dx'H(x)dx$, so $d^2y < 0$ at x^0 is equivalent to $H(x)$ being negative definite when evaluated at x^0.

3   *Using convexity or concavity*

For a critical point x^* to be a strict local optimum, we want the function to have the right curvature at x^*. Again consider the graph of functions of two variables which have strict local optima:

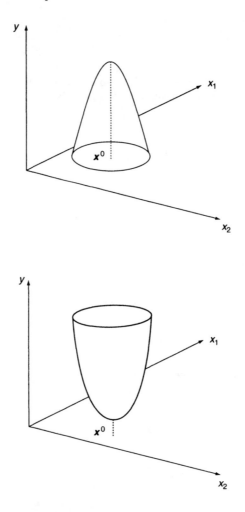

For our strict local maximum we want the function to be strictly concave at x^0. But we know that this is equivalent to $H(x)$ being negative definite when evaluated at x^0. Similarly a strict local minimum at x^0 requires the function to be strictly convex at x^0 which is equivalent to insisting that $H(x)$ is positive definite at x^0.

Regardless of the approach we choose we obtain the following theorem:

Theorem 1
Let x^* be a critical point of $f(x)$.

  (i) If the Hessian matrix $H(x)$ is negative definite when evaluated at x^*, then x^* is a strict local maximum of $f(x)$.
 (ii) If the Hessian matrix $H(x)$ is positive definite when evaluated at x^*, then x^* is a strict local minimum of $f(x)$.

Notice that this theorem gives us a two-step procedure for finding strict local optima.

Step 1
Find the critical points of the function by solving

$$f_1 = f_2 = \cdots f_n = 0.$$

These are often called the **first order conditions** of optimization as they involve first order derivatives.

Step 2
Evaluate the definiteness of $H(x)$ at the critical points.

The conditions involved in step 2 are called **second order conditions** as the Hessian matrix requires us to obtain second order derivatives.

The next theorem caters for saddle points.

Theorem 2
If x^* is a critical point of $f(x)$ and $H(x)$ is indefinite at x^*, then x^* is a saddle point.

Recall now that determining whether a matrix such as $H(x)$ is negative definite or positive definite requires us to look at the signs of the leading principal minors of $H(x)$, whereas establishing that $H(x)$ is indefinite requires us to look at the signs of all the principal minors.

Example 1
Find and evaluate the critical points of $f(x_1, x_2) = x_1^3 - x_2^3 + 9x_1x_2$.

Our first order conditions are

$$f_1 = 3x_1^2 + 9x_2 = 0 \text{ and}$$
$$f_2 = -3x_2^2 + 9x_1 = 0.$$

From the first equation,

$$x_2 = -\tfrac{1}{3}x_1^2.$$

Substituting into the second equation gives

$$-\tfrac{1}{3}x_1^4 + 9x_1 = 0$$

or

$$x_1(27 - x_1^3) = 0,$$

so $x_1 = 0$ or $x_1 = 3$ which leads to $x_2 = 0$ or $x_2 = -3$ respectively. We have then, two critical points

$$x_1^* = \begin{pmatrix} 0 \\ 0 \end{pmatrix}, \quad x_2^* = \begin{pmatrix} 3 \\ -3 \end{pmatrix}.$$

Now consider the second order derivatives

$$f_{11} = 6x_1, f_{12} = 9, \quad \text{and} \quad f_{22} = -6x_2.$$

So the Hessian matrix is

$$H(x) = \begin{pmatrix} 6x_1 & 9 \\ 9 & -6x_2 \end{pmatrix}.$$

Critical point x_1^*
The Hessian matrix when evaluated at x_1^* is

$$H(x_1^*) = \begin{pmatrix} 0 & 9 \\ 9 & 0 \end{pmatrix}$$

which has principal minors of 0, 0 and -81, so $H(x_1^*)$ is indefinite and x_1^* is a saddle point.

Critical point x_2^*

$$H(x_2^*) = \begin{pmatrix} 18 & 9 \\ 9 & 18 \end{pmatrix}$$

which has leading principal minors of 18 and 243, so $H(x_2^*)$ is positive definite and x_2^* is a strict local minimum.

Example 2

Let $y = -x_1^3 + 3x_1x_3 + 2x_2 - x_2^2 - 3x_3^2$.

  (i) Find the critical points of this function.

 (ii) Determine if any of these are local optima.

  (i) The first order conditions are

$$f_1 = -3x_1^2 + 3x_3 = 0$$

$$f_2 = 2 - 2x_2 = 0$$

$$f_3 = 3x_1 - 6x_3 = 0.$$

The second equation gives $x_2 = 1$ and from the third equation we have $x_1 = 2x_3$. Substituting in the first equation gives

$$-4x_3^2 + x_3 = 0$$

or

$$x_3(1 - 4x_3) = 0,$$

so

$$x_3 = 0 \quad \text{or} \quad x_3 = 1/4.$$

We have then two critical points

$$x_1^* = \begin{pmatrix} 0 \\ 1 \\ 0 \end{pmatrix} \quad \text{and} \quad x_2^* = \begin{pmatrix} \frac{1}{2} \\ 1 \\ \frac{1}{4} \end{pmatrix}.$$

(ii) The second order derivatives are

$$f_{11} = -6x_1, \quad f_{12} = 0, \quad f_{13} = 3 \quad \text{and}$$
$$f_{22} = -2, \quad f_{23} = 0, \quad f_{33} = -6,$$

so the Hessian matrix is

$$H(x) = \begin{pmatrix} -6x_1 & 0 & 3 \\ 0 & -2 & 0 \\ 3 & 0 & -6 \end{pmatrix}.$$

Critical point x_1^*

The Hessian matrix evaluated at this point is

$$H(x_1^*) = \begin{pmatrix} 0 & 0 & 3 \\ 0 & -2 & 0 \\ 3 & 0 & -6 \end{pmatrix}.$$

The first principal minors are 0, -2, and -6 which are all less than or equal to 0. The second order principal minors are

$$\begin{vmatrix} 0 & 0 \\ 0 & -2 \end{vmatrix} = 0 \quad \text{and} \quad \begin{vmatrix} 0 & 3 \\ 3 & -6 \end{vmatrix} = -9,$$

which is sufficient to establish that $H(x_1^*)$ is indefinite, so our critical point is a saddle point.

Critical point x_2^*

$$H(x_2^*) = \begin{pmatrix} -3 & 0 & 3 \\ 0 & -2 & 0 \\ 3 & 0 & -6 \end{pmatrix}.$$

The first leading principal minor is $-3 < 0$. The second leading principal minor is

$$\begin{vmatrix} -3 & 0 \\ 0 & -2 \end{vmatrix} = 6 > 0.$$

The last leading principal minor is

$$|H(x_2^*)| = \begin{vmatrix} 0 & 0 & -3 \\ 0 & -2 & 0 \\ 3 & 0 & -6 \end{vmatrix} = 3(-1)^{3+1} \begin{vmatrix} 0 & -3 \\ -2 & 0 \end{vmatrix} = -18 < 0.$$

These minors establish that $H(x_2^*)$ is negative definite so x_2^* is a strict local maximum.

Finally, on leaving the section, it is clear from our analysis that a critical point x^* is a local maximum, though not necessarily strict, if $H(x^*)$ is negative semidefinite, and this requires us to look at all the principal minors of the matrix. Similarly, a critical point x^* is a local minimum if $H(x^*)$ is a positive semidefinite.

Exercises for 6.1

1. For each of the following functions find the critical points and classify them:
   (i) $f(x_1, x_2) = x_1^3 - x_2^3 + 9x_1x_2$
   (ii) $f(x, y) = -x^3 + xy + y^2 + x$
   (iii) $f(x, y) = x^4 + x^2 - 6xy + 3y^2$
   (iv) $f(x_1, x_2, x_3) = x_1^2 + 3x_2^2 - 3x_1x_2 + 4x_2x_3 + 6x_3^2$
   (v) $f(x_1, x_2, x_3) = x_1x_3 + x_1^2 - x_2 + x_2x_3 + x_2^2 + 3x_3^2$
   (vi) $f(x, y, z) = x^2 + 6xy + y^2 - 3yz + 4z^2 + 6x + 17y - 2z$.
2. Show that the function $f(x, y) = xy^2 + x^3y - xy$ has six critical points. Find the ones that are strict local maxima or strict local minima.

6.2 Local Optima and Global Optima

The first and second order conditions give us a procedure for establishing local optima. But what we are usually after in solving optimization problems in economics, are the global optima. When then, is a local optimum a global optimum? The answer to this question again brings in the concept of the curvature of the function we are trying to optimize and is provided by the following theorem.

Theorem 3: globality theorem I
Let $f : D \to R$ and suppose D is a convex subset of R^n.

(i) If $f(x)$ is a concave function on D and x^* is a critical point then x^* is a global maximum.
(ii) If $f(x)$ is a convex function on D and x^* is a critical point then x^* is a global minimum.

To apply this theorem we need to recall that $f(x)$ is concave (convex) on D if and only if $H(x)$ is negative semidefinite (positive semidefinite) for all points x in the domain D of the function. Moreover negative semidefiniteness and positive semidefiniteness involves us in looking at the signs of the principal minors of $H(x)$.

Note the difference between Theorem 1 and Theorem 3. To establish a local maximum at x^0 we must show that the function is concave at x^0, that is that the Hessian matrix $H(x)$ is negative semidefinite when evaluated at x^0.

To establish a global maximum at x^0, not necessarily strict, we need to show that $f(x)$ is concave not only at x^0 but over the entire domain. Equivalently we need to show that the Hessian matrix $H(x)$ is negative semidefinite for all points in the domain of the function.

Example 3

Consider the function $f(x)$ from the set of real numbers to the set of nonnegative numbers given by

$$f(x) = x^4.$$

Now

$$f'(x) = 4x^3,$$

so $x = 0$ is a critical point. Moreover $f''(x) = 12x^2 \geq 0$ for all real x.

So $x = 0$ is a global minimum.

Example 4

Suppose a firm that produces one good under perfect competition has a production function given by

$$Q(L, K) = 4L^{1/4}K^{1/4}.$$

Suppose p is the price of output, w is the wage rate, and r is the unit cost of capital. Find the firm's demand functions for its inputs.

The total profit for the firm is

$$\pi = pQ - wL - rK$$
$$= 4pL^{1/4}K^{1/4} - wL - rK.$$

The first order conditions for the maximization of this function are

$$\pi_L = pL^{-3/4}K^{1/4} - w = 0$$
$$\pi_K = pL^{1/4}K^{-3/4} - r = 0.$$

The first condition gives $K^{1/4} = wL^{3/4}/p$ so from the second equation we have

$$pL^{1/4}\left(\frac{w}{p}\right)^{-3} L^{-9/4} - r = 0.$$

That is

$$L^{-2} = rw^3/p^4,$$

or

$$L^2 = p^4/rw^3,$$

so

$$L^* = p^2/\sqrt{rw^3}.$$

By symmetry

$$K^* = p^2/\sqrt{wr^3}.$$

So we have one critical point given by L^* and K^*.

The second order derivatives are

$$\pi_{LL} = -\tfrac{3}{4}pL^{-7/4}K^{1/4}$$
$$\pi_{LK} = p\tfrac{1}{4}L^{-3/4}K^{-3/4}$$
$$\pi_{KK} = -\tfrac{3}{4}pL^{1/4}K^{-7/4},$$

so the Hessian matrix is

$$H\begin{pmatrix} L \\ K \end{pmatrix} = \frac{1}{4}p\begin{pmatrix} -3L^{-7/4}K^{1/4} & L^{-3/4}K^{-3/4} \\ L^{-3/4}K^{-3/4} & -3L^{1/4}K^{-7/4} \end{pmatrix}.$$

Now the domain of the profit function we are seeking to maximize is the nonnegative orthant of R^2, namely

$$D = \left(\begin{pmatrix} K \\ L \end{pmatrix} \middle/ L \geq 0, K \geq 0 \right).$$

The first order principal minors of H are

$$-\tfrac{3}{4}pL^{-7/4}K^{1/4} \quad \text{and} \quad -\tfrac{3}{4}pL^{1/4}K^{-7/4}$$

which are both less than or equal to zero on this domain. The second order principal minor is

$$|H| = \tfrac{1}{2}p^2L^{-3/2}K^{-3/2}$$

which is greater than or equal to zero on D. It follows that the Hessian matrix is negative semidefinite and that $\pi(L, K)$ is concave on D. According to Globality Theorem I, the critical point L^*, K^* is a global maximum. The firm's demand functions for inputs then are

$$L^* = p^2/\sqrt{rw^3} \quad \text{and} \quad K^* = p^2/\sqrt{wr^3}.$$

As an exercise the reader might like to show that these functions are homogeneous of degree zero.

Exercises for 6.2

1. Suppose that a firm that produces one good under perfect competition has a production function given by

$$Q(L, K) = L^{1/2} + K^{1/2}.$$

Suppose p is the price of output, w is the wage rate, and r is the unit cost of capital.
   (i) Find an expression for total profit as a function of L and K.
   (ii) Find the critical point of this function.
   (iii) Show that this critical point is a global maximum, remembering that L and Q being quantities must be greater than or equal to zero.
   (iv) The critical point gives the firm's demand functions for labor L^* and capital K^*. Are these functions homogeneous?
   (v) How does the demand for labour and the demand for capital change with a small change in w and r respectively?
   (vi) The firm's profit function is defined as the maximum total profit regarded as a function of the parameters p, w, and r. How does this function change when there is a small change in each of these parameters?
2. Repeat Question 1 when the firm has a Cobb-Douglas production function given by

$$Q(L, K) = 4L^{1/4}K^{1/2}.$$

6.3   Constrained Optimization

Introduction

Unconstrained optimization problems abound in economics. But perhaps even more prevalent are constrained optimization problems, where we optimize a function subject to an equality constraint. One has only to think of the problem neoclassical economics assigns the consumer, namely that of maximizing utility subject to a budget constraint, or that assigned to the firm of cost minimization subject to production being set at a given level. Perhaps more relevant to the multinationals that confront us today in Western economies is the problem of maximizing sales or total revenue subject to the constraint that profits must be at an acceptable level to satisfy shareholders.

The optimization problem we study in this section then is the following

$$\text{Optimize} \quad y = f(x_1, \ldots, x_n)$$
$$\text{subject to} \quad g(x_1, \ldots, x_n) = c,$$

or more succinctly

$$\text{Optimize} \quad y = f(x)$$
$$\text{subject to} \quad g(x) = c.$$

The function $f(x)$ that we are trying to optimize is called the **objective function**. The function $g(x)$ in the equality constraint is called the **constraint function.**

The effect of imposing an equality constraint on the problem can be illustrated as in Figure 6.5.

A is the unconstrained maximum, when we are free to optimize over the entire domain of the function. The constraint function, $g(x_1, x_2)$ is linear, insisting that

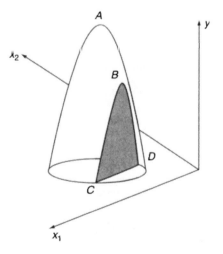

Figure 6.5   Unconstrained and constrained maxima.

we only consider the points on the line segment CD. Such points, satisfying the constraints, form the **set of feasible solutions.** The constrained maximum is then B.

The Lagrangian multiplier technique

Essentially, Lagrange's method for tackling the problem is to convert it into an unconstrained problem by the introduction of a new variable called the Lagrangian multiplier. He did this by referring to the following function:

Definition
The **Lagrangian function** is

$$Z(x, \lambda) = f(x) + \lambda(c - g(x))$$

where λ is the **Lagrangian multiplier.**

Suppose we can ensure that $g(x) = c$. Then the last term in the Lagrangian function is zero for all λ and Z becomes the objective function $f(x)$. We could then optimize Z freely instead of optimizing $f(x)$ subject to the equality constraint.

Ensuring that the constraint holds is easy, consider

$$\frac{\partial Z}{\partial \lambda} = c - g(x).$$

If we set this derivative as equal to zero, then $g(x) = c$.

This discussion leads to the following theorem.

Theorem
Suppose x^* is a solution to the problem:

$$\text{Optimize}\quad f(x)$$

$$\text{subject to } g(x) = c.$$

Then there is a number λ^* such that (x^*, λ^*) is a critical point of the Lagrangian function

$$Z(x, \lambda) = f(x) + \lambda(c - g(x)).^{[1]}$$

This theorem gives us the first order conditions for our problem, namely

$$\frac{\partial Z}{\partial x_1} = \frac{\partial Z}{\partial x_2} = \cdots = \frac{\partial Z}{\partial x_n} = \frac{Z}{\partial \lambda} = 0.$$

---

[1] Theoretically, x^* cannot also be a critical point of the constraint function $g(x)$.

The second order conditions

In the unconstrained problem the first order conditions are equivalent to $dy = 0$, whereas the first order conditions listed above are equivalent to $dy = 0$ subject to $g(x) = c$.

The second order conditions allow us to distinguish between maxima and minima. For the unconstrained problem we require the following

$$\text{Maximum}: d^2y < 0 \quad \text{for all small changes } dx_1, dx_2, \ldots, dx_n.$$

$$\text{Minimum}: d^2y > 0 \quad \text{for all small changes } dx_1, dx_2, \ldots, dx_n.$$

For a constrained maximum we also want $d^2y < 0$ but not for all small changes $dx_1, dx_2, \ldots, dx_n$, but rather only those that satisfy the constraint $g(x) = c$. Taking the differential of both sides of the constraint we have

$$g_1 dx_1 + g_2 dx_2 + \cdots + g_n dx_n = 0, \tag{6.1}$$

so the differentials $dx_1, dx_2, \ldots, dx_n$ that satisfy the constraint are those that satisfy equation (6.1).

Second order conditions can then be obtained by studying the problem

$$d^2y = dx'H(x)dx < 0$$

subject to $\nabla g(x)'dx = 0$.

That is, we have to look at when a quadratic form in dx is negative definite given that dx is subject to a linear constraint.

Consideration of such a problem is outside the scope of this book. Instead we list the conditions by way of a theorem. But first a definition.

Definition
Consider the Lagrangian function

$$Z(x, \lambda) = f(x) + \lambda(c - g(x)).$$

The **bordered** Hessian matrix associated with this function is

$$\bar{H}(x, \lambda) = \begin{pmatrix} 0 & g_1 & \cdots & g_n \\ g_1 & Z_{11} & \cdots & Z_{1n} \\ \vdots & & & \\ g_n & Z_{n1} & \cdots & Z_{nn} \end{pmatrix}$$

where $g_i = \partial g / \partial x_i$ and $Z_{ij} = \partial Z / \partial x_i \partial x_j$.

The border of this matrix consists of the first order partial derivatives of the constraint function, and a zero. The main body of the matrix is the Hessian matrix of the Lagrangian function, formed when we ignore the Lagrangian multiplier.

In the following theorem we consider the following leading principal minors of $\bar{H}$:

$$|\bar{H}_2| = \begin{vmatrix} 0 & g_1 & g_2 \\ g_1 & Z_{11} & Z_{12} \\ g_2 & Z_{21} & Z_{22} \end{vmatrix}$$

$$|\bar{H}_3| = \begin{vmatrix} 0 & g_1 & g_2 & g_3 \\ g_1 & Z_{11} & Z_{12} & Z_{13} \\ g_2 & Z_{21} & Z_{22} & Z_{23} \\ g_3 & Z_{31} & Z_{32} & Z_{33} \end{vmatrix}$$

$$\vdots$$

$$|\bar{H}|.$$

Theorem 4

Let (x^*, λ^*) be a critical point of the Lagrangian function. Then

(i) x^* is a local maximum of the constrained problem if when evaluated at this point

$$|\bar{H}_2| > 0, |\bar{H}_3| < 0, \ldots, (-1)^n |\bar{H}| > 0,$$

(ii) x^* is a local minimum of the constrained problem if when evaluated at this point

$$|\bar{H}_2| < 0, |\bar{H}_3| < 0, \ldots, |\bar{H}| < 0.$$

For a local maximum then the leading principal minors must alternate in sign the first being positive. For a local minimum they must all be negative.

Example 1

Find the (local) maximum of the following problem:

$$\text{Maximum}: \quad y = x_1^2 + 3x_1x_2 - 3x_2^2$$

$$\text{subject to} \quad x_1 + 3x_2 = 6.$$

The Lagrangian function for this problem is

$$Z = x_1^2 + 3x_1x_2 - 3x_2^2 + \lambda(6 - x_1 - 3x_2)$$

and the first order conditions are

$$Z_\lambda = 6 - x_1 - 3x_2 = 0,$$
$$Z_1 = 2x_1 + 3x_2 - \lambda = 0, \text{ and}$$
$$Z_2 = 3x_1 - 6x_2 - 3\lambda = 0.$$

Solving these linear equations gives the following critical point for the Lagrangian function:

$$x_1^* = 15, x_2^* = -3, \lambda^* = 21.$$

Now

$$g_1 = 1, g_2 = 3, Z_{11} = 2, Z_{12} = 3, Z_{22} = -6,$$

so the bordered Hessian matrix is

$$\bar{H} = \begin{pmatrix} 0 & 1 & 3 \\ 1 & 2 & 3 \\ 3 & 3 & -6 \end{pmatrix}.$$

Consider the leading principal minor

$$|\bar{H}_2| = |\bar{H}| = \begin{vmatrix} 0 & 1 & 3 \\ 1 & 2 & 3 \\ 0 & -3 & -15 \end{vmatrix}$$

$$= (-1)^{1+2} \begin{vmatrix} 1 & 3 \\ -3 & -15 \end{vmatrix}$$

$$= 6,$$

so $x_1^* = 15, x_2^* = -3$ is a constrained local maximum.

Exercises for 6.3

1. Find the local maximum of the following problem:

$$\text{Maximum} \quad y = (x_1 + 1)(x_2 + 2)$$
$$\text{subject to} \quad 2x_1 + 4x_2 = 12.$$

Show that the second order condition holds.

2. Suppose the consumer seeks to maximize his or her utility function $U(x_1, x_2) = x_1 x_2$ subject to a budget constraint $p_1 x_1 + p_2 x_2 = Y$, where x_1 and x_2 represent the quantities of goods consumed, p_1 and p_2 are the prices of the two goods and Y represents the consumer's income.

   (i) What is the Lagrangian function for the problem?

   (ii) Find the first order conditions for this problem.

   (iii) Show that the second order condition holds.

   (iv) Solving the first order conditions for x_1 and x_2 gives the consumer's demand functions $x_1^* = x_1^*(p_1, p_2, Y)$ and $x_2^* = x_2^*(p_1, p_2, Y)$.

   Find these functions and show that they are homogeneous at degree zero. Why would you expect this result?

   (v) The consumer's indirect utility function is defined as

   $$M(p_1, p_2, Y) = \max U(x_1, x_2) = U(x_1^*, x_2^*).$$

   Find this function. How does the consumer's optimal utility change when there is a small change in (a) p_1, and (b) Y?

   (vi) What is the value of the Lagrangian multiplier associated with the optimal point?

3. Suppose a firm uses inputs K and L of capital and labour respectively to produce a single output Q, according to a production function given by $Q(L, K) = 4K^{1/4}L^{1/4}$. Let w be the wage rate and r be the unit cost of capital. Suppose further that the firm wishes to minimize total cost subject to the constraint that output must equal Q_0.

   (i) What is the Lagrangian function for the problem?

   (ii) Find the first order conditions for this problem.

   (iii) Find the bordered Hessian matrix for this problem. What does the second order condition require? (You need not show that it does in fact hold).

   (iv) Solve the first order conditions for L and K in terms of w, r, and Q_0. (These are called the firm's conditional demand functions for inputs).

   (v) Substituting L^* and K^* into the objective function, find the minimum cost as a function of w, r, and Q_0. (This is called the cost function.)

   (vi) Differentiating the cost function, determine how the minimum cost changes when the wage rate changes by a small amount, and when Q_0 is increased by a small amount.

   (vii) What is the value of the Lagrangian multiplier associated with the optimal point?

4. Consider a consumer whose utility function is

   $$U = x_1^a x_2^b, \quad a, b > 0, \quad a + b = 1.$$

This consumer wishes to minimize the expenditure $p_1x_1 + p_2x_2$ needed to achieve a certain level of utility u_0.

(i) What are the first order conditions for this optimization problem?

   Hint: Do not treat $a + b = 1$ as a constraint as it is a condition on the parameters not the variables.

(ii) What is the bordered Hessian matrix for this problem?

(iii) What does the second order condition require? (You need not show that it does in fact hold.)

(iv) Find the optimal values for x_1 and x_2. (These are called the Hicksian demand function.)

(v) Using the fact that $a + b = 1$ show that the minimum value function is

$$M = a^{-a}b^{-b}p_1^a p_2^b u_0$$

(This function is called the expenditure function).

(vi) How does this minimum value function change when there is a small change in p_1?

6.4   Constrained Local Optima Versus Constrained Global Optima

Theorem 4 allows us to obtain all local optima of our constrained optimization problem. But when are these local optima also global optima? As is expected from our discussion in the unconstrained problem, our objective function must have the right curvature over the set of feasible solutions. But the set of feasible solutions must also have the appropriate mathematical properties. The Globality Theorem seeks to answer this question in the most general constrained optimization framework, where we seek to optimize an objective function subject to any number of constraints. The set of points satisfying these constraints is called the **set of feasible solutions**.

Theorem 4: Globality Theorem II

If the set of feasible solutions is a closed convex set and if the objective function is a continuous concave (convex) function over this set, then any local maximum (minimum) is also a global maximum (minimum). If the objective function is strictly concave (convex) over the feasible set, then the global maximum (minimum) is unique.

A **closed** set is one whose boundary points are included in the set.

Definition

A point a belonging to set X, is a **boundary point** of X, if every ε neighborhood of a includes points belonging to X and points not belonging to X.

An important example of a closed convex set is a hyperplane.

Definition
A **hyperplane** X is the following set of points:

$$X = \{x/a'x = b\}.$$

In other words, a hyperplane is the set of points that satisfies the **linear constraint**

$$a_1x_1 + a_2x_2 + \cdots + a_nx_n = b.$$

Exercise
Show that a hyperplane is a convex set.

A hyperplane is closed, as every point in the set that forms the hyperplane is a boundary point. With these concepts under our belt we can now tackle an application of the Globality Theorem II.

Example
Suppose a consumer's utility function is

$$U(x_1x_2) = x_1^{1/4}x_2^{1/2}$$

and the consumer seeks to maximize this function subject to the budget constraint

$$p_1x_1 + p_2x_2 = Y.$$

Find the values x_1^* and x_2^* that maximize the utility function subject to the budget constraint.

At the onset let us satisfy ourselves that the local maximum we achieve will be a global maximum. We do this by appealing to Globality Theorem II. As the budget constraint is linear, the set of feasible solutions is closed and convex. We have seen from the example in Section 5.3 of Chapter 5 that the objective function is strictly concave over its entire domain. Thus the Globality Theorem assures us that the local maximum will also be a global maximum.

The Lagrangian function is

$$Z = x_1^{1/4}x_2^{1/2} + \lambda(Y - p_1x_1 - p_2x_2),$$

the first order conditions are

$$Z_1 = \tfrac{1}{4}x_1^{-3/4}x_2^{1/2} - \lambda p_1 = 0,$$

$$Z_2 = \tfrac{1}{2}x_1^{1/4}x_2^{-1/2} - \lambda p_2 = 0, \text{ and}$$

$$Z_\lambda = Y - p_1 x_1 - p_2 x_2 = 0.$$

From the first two equations we have

$$\frac{1}{2}\frac{x_2}{x_1} = \frac{p_1}{p_2},$$

so

$$x_2 = 2p_1 x_1 / p_2.$$

Substituting into the third equation gives

$$x_1^* = Y/3p_1$$

and then

$$x_2^* = \frac{2Y}{3p_2}.$$

Finally we need to assure ourselves that x_1^* and x_2^* do in fact represent a local maximum. Now

$$g_1 = p_1, \quad g_2 = p_2, \quad Z_{11} = \tfrac{3}{16}x_1^{-7/4}x_2^{1/2},$$

$$Z_{12} = \tfrac{1}{8}x_1^{-3/4}x_2^{-1/2}, \quad Z_{22} = -\tfrac{1}{4}x_1^{1/4}x_2^{-3/2}.$$

So the bordered Hessian matrix is

$$\bar{H} = \begin{pmatrix} 0 & p_1 & p_2 \\ p_1 & -\tfrac{3}{16}x_1^{-7/4}x_2^{1/2} & \tfrac{1}{8}x_1^{-3/4}x_2^{-1/2} \\ p_2 & \tfrac{1}{8}x_1^{-3/4}x_2^{-1/2} & -\tfrac{1}{4}x_1^{1/4}x_2^{-3/2} \end{pmatrix}.$$

As an exercise, the reader can show that $|\bar{H}| > 0$ for all positive p_1, p_2, x_1, and x_2, thus x_1^* and x_2^* represent a local and global maximum. They are, of course, the demand functions of the consumer.

Exercise for 6.4

Suppose a consumer seeks to maximize the utility function $U = -1/x_1 - 1/x_2$ subject to the budget constraint $p_1 x_1 + p_2 x_2 = Y$. (Believe it or not, U qualifies as a utility function!). Show that the conditions of the Globality Theorem hold so any local maximum will be a global maximum. Then repeat question 2 of exercises for 6.3 with this new utility function.

*6.5   An Introduction to Matrix Calculus

The techniques of multivariate calculus discussed in this chapter usually suffice for the optimization problems we encounter in economics and we shall study some of these problems in detail in the next chapter. But optimization problems associated with classical statistical techniques in statistics and econometrics are another matter. Here the function we seek to optimize is often very complicated and it is no easy task obtaining the derivatives we need to form the graduate vector or the Hessian matrix of the function. Moreover, even when we have these derivatives in hand, it is often very difficult to recognize what we have got. Instead one is confronted with a hopeless mess.

Fortunately, the whole procedure can be streamlined if we are prepared to learn a few rules relating to **matrix calculus**, the calculus that evolves when we allow for the possibility of differentiating a vector with respect to another vector. Consider an $m \times n$ matrix Y whose elements y_{ij} are differentiable functions of the elements x_{kl} of a $p \times q$ matrix X. Then we have mnpq partial derivatives that we can consider:

$$\frac{\partial y_{ij}}{\partial x_{k\ell}} \quad \begin{aligned} i &= 1, \cdots, m \\ j &= 1, \cdots, n \\ k &= 1, \cdots, p \\ \ell &= 1, \cdots, q. \end{aligned}$$

The question is how to arrange these derivatives. Different arrangements give rise to different concepts of derivatives in matrix calculus. A useful approach is to consider the vectors $y = \text{vec } Y$ and $x = \text{vec } X$ and define a notation of a derivative of a vector y with respect to another vector x.

Definition

Let $y = (y_i)$ be an $m \times 1$ vector whose elements are differentiable functions of the elements of an $n \times 1$ vector $x = (x_i)$. We write $y = y(x)$ and say that y is a **vector function** of x.

The **derivative** of y with respect to x, denoted by $\partial y / \partial x$, is the $n \times m$ matrix given by

$$
\frac{\partial y}{\partial x} = \begin{bmatrix} \dfrac{\partial y_1}{\partial x_1} & \cdots & \dfrac{\partial y_m}{\partial x_1} \\ \vdots & & \vdots \\ \dfrac{\partial y_1}{\partial x_n} & \cdots & \dfrac{\partial y_m}{\partial x_n} \end{bmatrix}.
$$

Note that under this definition if y is a scalar, so $y(x)$ is a **scalar function** of x, the derivative $\partial y / \partial x$ is the $n \times 1$ vector given by

$$
\frac{\partial y}{\partial x} = \begin{bmatrix} \dfrac{\partial y}{\partial x_1} \\ \vdots \\ \dfrac{\partial y}{\partial x_n} \end{bmatrix}
$$

which is the usual gradient vector of the function. Similarly, if x is a scalar and y is an $m \times 1$ vector then the derivative $\partial y / \partial x$ is the $1 \times m$ vector

$$
\frac{\partial y}{\partial x} = \begin{bmatrix} \dfrac{\partial y_1}{\partial x} \cdots \dfrac{\partial y_m}{\partial x} \end{bmatrix}.
$$

For the general case covered in the definition, the jth column of the matrix $\partial y / \partial x$ is the derivative of a scalar function with respect to a vector, namely $\partial y_j / \partial x$, whereas the ith row of the matrix $\partial y / \partial x$ is the derivative of a vector with respect to a scalar, namely $\partial y / \partial x_i$. Row vectors are accommodated by the following definition:

Definition
By the symbol $\partial y / \partial x'$ we mean the $m \times n$ matrix defined by

$$
\frac{\partial y}{\partial x'} = \left(\frac{\partial y}{\partial x} \right)'
$$

and we define

$$
\frac{\partial y'}{\partial x} = \frac{\partial y}{\partial x}.
$$

Example
Let

$$y_1 = x_1^2 + x_2^2 - x_3^2$$
$$y_2 = x_3^3 - 3x_1x_2 - 2x_2x_3.$$

Then

$$\frac{\partial y}{\partial x} = \begin{pmatrix} 2x_1 & -3x_2 \\ 2x_2 & -3x_1 - 2x_3 \\ -2x_3 & 3x_3^2 - 2x_2 \end{pmatrix}$$

$$\frac{\partial y}{\partial x'} = \begin{pmatrix} 2x_1 & 2x_2 & -2x_3 \\ -3x_2 & -3x_1 - 2x_3 & 3x_3^2 - 2x_2 \end{pmatrix}$$

$$\frac{\partial y_1}{\partial x} = \begin{pmatrix} 2x_1 \\ 2x_2 \\ -2x_3 \end{pmatrix}$$

$$\frac{\partial y}{\partial x_3} = (-2x_3 \quad 3x_3^2 - 2x_2).$$

The following simple matrix calculus results can be derived from our basic definitions.

Theorem
Let x be an $n \times 1$ vector and let A be a matrix of constants (i.e., the elements of A are not scalar functions of x). Then

$$\frac{\partial Ax}{\partial x} = A' \quad \text{for } A \text{ an } m \times n \text{ matrix}$$

$$\frac{\partial x'A}{\partial x} = A \quad \text{for } A \text{ an } n \times p \text{ matrix}$$

$$\frac{\partial x'Ax}{\partial x} = (A + A')x \quad \text{for } A \text{ an } n \times n \text{ matrix.}$$

Proof
The jth element of Ax is $\sum_k a_{jk}x_k$, and so the jth column of $\partial A/\partial x$ is $A'_{j\bullet}$, where $A_{j\bullet}$ is the jth row of A. Thus $\partial Ax/\partial x = A'$. Under our notation $\partial x'A/\partial x = \partial A'x/\partial x = A$. The jth element of $\partial x'Ax/\partial x$ is $\sum_i a_{ij}x_i + \sum_k a_{jk}x_k$ so $\partial x'Ax/\partial x = (A + A')x$.

Notice that if A is a symmetric matrix, as it often is in a quadratic form, then

$$\frac{\partial x'Ax}{\partial x} = 2Ax.$$

Example

Work out $\partial y' Bz / \partial y$ and $\partial y' Bz / \partial z$.

Applying the theorem we have $\partial y' Bz / \partial y = Bz$ and $\partial y' Bz / \partial z = (y'B)' = B'y$.

Suppose now we consider an $m \times n$ matrix X which we partition into its columns. We write

$$X = (x_1, x_2, \cdots, x_n)$$

where x_j is the jth column of X. We know that $x = \text{vec } X$ is the $mn \times 1$ vector given by stacking the columns of X under each other. That is,

$$x = \begin{pmatrix} x_1 \\ \vdots \\ x_n \end{pmatrix}.$$

Suppose y is a scalar function of x. Then by our definition

$$\frac{\partial y}{\partial x} = \begin{pmatrix} \dfrac{\partial y}{\partial x_1} \\ \vdots \\ \dfrac{\partial y}{\partial x_n} \end{pmatrix}.$$

That is, to obtain $\partial y / \partial x$ we stack the vectors $\partial y / \partial x_1 \cdots \partial y / \partial x_n$ under each other.

Example

Show that $\partial \text{tr } AX / \partial \text{vec } X = \text{vec } A'$.

Recall from Section 1.5 of Chapter 1 that $\text{tr } AX = (\text{vec } A')' \text{vec } X$. Applying the above theorem gives us the result.

Example

Suppose X is a nonsingular $n \times n$ matrix so its determinant $|X|$ is nonzero. Then

$$\frac{\partial |X|}{\partial \text{vec } X} = |X| \text{vec}(X^{-1'}).$$

If we expand the determinant of X using the jth column of X we have

$$|X| = \sum_{i=1}^{n} c_{ij} x_{ij}$$

where c_{ij} is the cofactor of x_{ij}, the (i, j)th element of X. Thus

$$\frac{\partial |X|}{\partial x_{ij}} = c_{ij}$$

and for the jth column of X, x_j, we have

$$\frac{\partial |X|}{\partial x_j} = \begin{pmatrix} c_{ij} \\ \vdots \\ c_{nj} \end{pmatrix}$$

which is the jth column of the adjoint of X'. Stacking these derivatives under each other we have

$$\frac{\partial |X|}{\partial \operatorname{vec} X} = \operatorname{vec}(\operatorname{Adj} X').$$

But $\operatorname{Adj} X' = |X| X^{-1'}$ which gives us our result.

In ordinary multivariate calculus we have a few general rules, such as the chain rule and the product rule that allow us to work out the derivatives of reasonably complicated expressions. The same is true with matrix calculus. Below we present two rules which are generalizations of the chain rule of ordinary calculus and a third rule which is a generalization of the product rule of ordinary calculus.

Theorem: the backward chain rule

Let $x = (x_i)$, $y = (y_j)$, and $z = (z_j)$ be $n \times 1$, $r \times 1$, and $m \times 1$ vectors respectively.

Suppose z is a vector function of y and y is a vector function of x so $z = z[y(x)]$. Then

$$\frac{\partial z}{\partial x} = \frac{\partial y}{\partial x} \frac{\partial z}{\partial y}.$$

Proof
The (i, j)th element of the matrix $\partial z / \partial x$ is

$$\left(\frac{\partial z}{\partial x} \right)_{ij} = \frac{\partial z_j}{\partial x_i} = \sum_{k=1}^{r} \frac{\partial y_k}{\partial x_i} \frac{\partial z_j}{\partial y_k}$$

$$= \left(\frac{\partial y}{\partial x} \right)_{i\bullet} \left(\frac{\partial z}{\partial y} \right)_{\bullet j}$$

$$= \left(\frac{\partial y}{\partial x} \frac{\partial z}{\partial y} \right)_{ij}.$$

Hence

$$\frac{\partial z}{\partial x} = \frac{\partial y}{\partial x}\frac{\partial z}{\partial y}.$$

If z is a vector function of two vectors, both of which are vector functions of x, then we have the following generalization of the chain rule.

Theorem: the generalized chain rule

Let $z = (z_j)$ be an $m \times 1$ vector function of two vectors $u = (u_q)$ and $v = (v_p)$, which are $r \times 1$ and $s \times 1$ respectively. Suppose u and v are both vector functions of an $n \times 1$ vector $x = (x_i)$, so $z = z[u(x), v(x)]$.

Then

$$\frac{\partial z}{\partial x} = \frac{\partial u}{\partial x}\frac{\partial z}{\partial u} + \frac{\partial v}{\partial x}\frac{\partial z}{\partial v} = \left.\frac{\partial z}{\partial x}\right|_{v \text{ constant}} + \left.\frac{\partial z}{\partial x}\right|_{u \text{ constant}}.$$

Proof

The (ij)th element of $\partial z/\partial x$ is

$$\left(\frac{\partial z}{\partial x}\right)_{ij} = \frac{\partial z_j}{\partial x_i}$$

$$= \sum_{q=1}^{r}\frac{\partial u_q}{\partial x_i}\frac{\partial z_j}{\partial u_q} + \sum_{p=1}^{s}\frac{\partial v_p}{\partial x_i}\frac{\partial z_j}{\partial v_p}$$

$$= \left(\frac{\partial u}{\partial x}\frac{\partial z}{\partial u}\right)_{ij} + \left(\frac{\partial v}{\partial x}\frac{\partial z}{\partial v}\right)_{ij}$$

and the result follows.

The generalized chain rule can be used to obtain a product rule for matrix calculus.

Theorem: the product rule

Let X be an $m \times n$ matrix and let Y be an $n \times p$ matrix and suppose the elements of both matrices are scalar functions of a vector δ.

Then

$$\frac{\partial \text{vec}\, XY}{\partial \delta} = \frac{\partial \text{vec}\, X}{\partial \delta}(Y \otimes I_m) + \frac{\partial \text{vec}\, Y}{\partial \delta}(I_p \otimes X').$$

Proof

From the generalized chain rule we have

$$\frac{\partial \text{vec}\, XY}{\partial \delta} = \left.\frac{\partial \text{vec}\, XY}{\partial \delta}\right|_{\substack{\text{vec}\, Y \\ \text{constant}}} + \left.\frac{\partial \text{vec}\, XY}{\partial \delta}\right|_{\substack{\text{vec}\, X \\ \text{constant}}}.$$

But from the chain rule

$$\frac{\partial \operatorname{vec} XY}{\partial \delta}\bigg|_{\substack{\operatorname{vec} Y \\ \text{constant}}} = \frac{\partial \operatorname{vec} XY}{\partial \delta} \frac{\partial \operatorname{vec} XY}{\partial \operatorname{vec} X}\bigg|_{\substack{\operatorname{vec} Y \\ \text{constant}}}$$

and as $\operatorname{vec} XY = (Y' \otimes I_m)\operatorname{vec} X$, we have $\partial \operatorname{vec} XY/\partial \operatorname{vec} X = (Y \otimes I_m)$, so

$$\frac{\partial \operatorname{vec} XY}{\partial \delta}\bigg|_{\substack{\operatorname{vec} Y \\ \text{constant}}} = \frac{\partial \operatorname{vec} X}{\partial \delta}(Y \otimes I_m).$$

Similarly,

$$\frac{\partial \operatorname{vec} XY}{\partial \delta}\bigg|_{\substack{\operatorname{vec} X \\ \text{constant}}} = \frac{\partial \operatorname{vec} Y}{\partial \delta}(I_p \otimes X').$$

These basic rules of matrix calculus allow us to derive matrix calculus results for more complicated vector functions and scalar functions as the following worked out examples show.

Example
Show that for a nonsingular $n \times n$ matrix X

$$\frac{\partial \operatorname{vec} X^{-1}}{\partial \operatorname{vec} X} = -(X^{-1} \otimes X^{-1'}).$$

As $XX^{-1} = I_n$ we have $\operatorname{vec} XX^{-1} = \operatorname{vec} I_n$. Differentiating with sides of this equation with respect to $\operatorname{vec} X$ we have by applying the Product Rule

$$\frac{\partial \operatorname{vec} X}{\partial \operatorname{vec} X}(X^{-1} \otimes I_n) + \frac{\partial \operatorname{vec} X^{-1}}{\partial \operatorname{vec} X}(I_n \otimes X') = 0.$$

But $\partial \operatorname{vec} X/\partial \operatorname{vec} X$ is the identity matrix, so solving for $\partial \operatorname{vec} X^{-1}/\partial \operatorname{vec} X$ we obtain

$$\frac{\partial \operatorname{vec} X^{-1}}{\partial \operatorname{vec} X} = -(X^{-1} \otimes I_n)(I_n \otimes X')^{-1} = -(X^{-1} \otimes X^{-1'}).$$

Example
If A and B are matrices of constants, show that

$$\frac{\partial \operatorname{vec} AX^{-1}B}{\partial \operatorname{vec} X} = -X^{-1}B \otimes X^{-1'}A'.$$

From the properties of the vec operator we have vec $AC^{-1}B = (B' \otimes A)$vec X^{-1}. Applying the Backward Chain rule we have

$$\frac{\partial \text{vec } AX^{-1}B}{\partial \text{vec } X} = \frac{\partial \text{vec } X^{-1}}{\partial \text{vec } X} \frac{\partial (B' \otimes A)\text{vec } X^{-1}}{\partial \text{vec } X^{-1}}$$

$$= -(X^{-1} \otimes X^{-1'})(B \otimes A')$$

$$= -X^{-1}B \otimes X^{-1'}A'.$$

Example
Show that

$$\frac{\partial u'(X^{-1'} \otimes I)u}{\partial \text{vec } X} = -(X^{-1} \otimes X^{-1'})\text{vec } U'U$$

where $u = \text{vec } U$.

Recall from Section 1.5 of Chapter 1 that

$$u'(X^{-1'} \otimes I)u = \text{tr } X^{-1}U'U.$$

By the chain rule,

$$\frac{\partial u'(X^{-1'} \otimes I)u}{\partial \text{vec } X} = \frac{\partial \text{vec } X^{-1}}{\partial \text{vec } X} \frac{\partial \text{tr } X^{-1}U'U}{\partial \text{vec } X^{-1}}$$

$$= -(X^{-1} \otimes X^{-1'})\text{vec } U'U.$$

Application of matrix calculus to econometrics

The matrix calculus results we have looked at in this section greatly facilitate the differentiation required in the application of classical statistical techniques to econometric models. We finish this chapter by considering a few examples. Recall from Section 3.3 of Chapter 3 that we can write the linear regression model in matrix notation as

$$y = X\beta + u.$$

Various statistical assumptions are usually placed on the disturbance vector, these need not concern us here, that give rise to what is known as the log likelihood function:

$$\ell(\beta, \sigma^2) = -\frac{n}{2} \log \sigma^2 - \frac{1}{2\sigma^2} u'u.$$

In this function we set u equal to $y - X\beta$. Maximum likelihood estimation is a classical statistical technique which obtains estimates for the unknown parameters by maximizing the likelihood function (or equivalently the log likelihood function) with respect to the parameters. Mathematically, the problem is

$$\max_{\beta, \sigma^2} \ell(\beta, \sigma^2).$$

The first order conditions for this maximization involve finding the derivatives $\partial\ell/\partial\beta$ and $\partial\ell/\partial\sigma^2$ and setting these equal to the null vector and zero respectively. It is at this point that matrix calculus comes into its own. By the chain rule of matrix calculus

$$\frac{\partial u'u}{\partial \beta} = \frac{\partial u}{\partial \beta}\frac{\partial u'u}{\partial u} = -2X'u.$$

So $\partial\ell/\partial\beta = 0$ implies that $X'(y - X\beta) = 0$.

Solving for β gives the maximum likelihood estimator

$$\tilde{\beta} = (X'X)^{-1}X'y,$$

which is also the ordinary least squares estimator.

A more complicated econometric model is the Seemingly Unrelated Regression Equations Model (SURE model). Again the statistical assumptions of this model need not concern us. It will suffice to say that the log likelihood function associated with this model is

$$\ell = -\frac{n}{2}\log|\Sigma| - \frac{1}{2}u'(\Sigma^{-1} \otimes I)u$$

$$= -\frac{n}{2}\log|\Sigma| - \frac{1}{2}\text{tr } U'U,$$

where in this function u is set equal to $y - X\beta$ and $u = \text{vec } U$. The application of maximum likelihood techniques involve working out the derivatives $\partial\ell/\partial\beta$ and $\partial\ell/\partial\text{vec }\Sigma$. Again matrix calculus makes this task relatively easy. The first derivative is, by the chain rule

$$\frac{\partial\ell}{\partial\beta} = -\frac{1}{2}\frac{\partial u}{\partial \beta}\frac{\partial u'(\Sigma^{-1} \otimes I)u}{\partial u}$$

$$= X'(\Sigma^{-1} \otimes I)(y - X\beta).$$

The second derivative is

$$\frac{\partial \ell}{\partial \text{vec } \Sigma} = -\frac{n}{2} \frac{\partial \log |\Sigma|}{\partial \text{vec } \Sigma} - \frac{1}{2} \frac{\partial \text{tr } \Sigma^{-1} U'U}{\partial \text{vec } \Sigma},$$

and we deal with each component in turn. First by the chain rule

$$\frac{\partial \log |\Sigma|}{\partial \text{vec } \Sigma} = \frac{\partial |\Sigma|}{\partial \text{vec } \Sigma} \frac{\partial \log |\Sigma|}{\partial |\Sigma|}$$

$$= |\Sigma| \text{vec } (\Sigma^{-1'}) / |\Sigma|$$

$$= \text{vec } (\Sigma^{-1'}).$$

Second, again by the chain rule

$$\frac{\partial \text{tr } \Sigma^{-1} U'U}{\partial \text{vec } \Sigma} = \frac{\partial \text{vec } \Sigma^{-1}}{\partial \text{vec } \Sigma} \frac{\partial \text{tr } \Sigma^{-1} U'U}{\partial \text{vec } \Sigma^{-1}}$$

$$= -(\Sigma^{-1} \otimes \Sigma^{-1'}) \text{vec } U'U$$

$$= -\text{vec } \Sigma^{-1'} U'U \Sigma^{-1}.$$

Combining, we have

$$\frac{\partial \ell}{\partial \text{vec } \Sigma} = (\text{vec } \Sigma^{-1} U'U \Sigma^{-1'} - n\text{vec } \Sigma^{-1'})/2.$$

Equating these two derivatives to the null matrices gives the maximum likelihood estimators

$$\tilde{\beta} = (X'(\Sigma^{-1} \otimes I)X)^{-1} X'(\Sigma^{-1} \otimes I)y \quad \text{and} \quad \tilde{\Sigma} = U'U/n.$$

Chapter 7

Comparative Static Analysis in Optimization Problems

7.1 Introduction

Associated with any optimization problem is a set of parameters or given constants which we may collect together in a vector a, say. The vector x contains the variables of the problem, whereas the vector a contains the parameters associated with the problem. When we carry out our optimization, we obtain an optimal point x^* whose elements will be functions of the parameters, so we write $x^* = x^*(a)$. Substituting this optimal point back into the objective function gives the optimal value of the objective function expressed in terms of the parameters of the problem.

To put our analysis in an economic context, the variables, represented by x are often the endogenous variables of the economic optimization problem, whereas the parameters, represented by a are often the associated exogenous variables. Comparative static analysis associated with economic optimization problems, is interested in answering two types of questions. First, how do the optimal values or equilibrium values $x_j^* = x_j^*(a)$ change when we change the value of one of the parameters or exogenous variables? Second, how does the optimal value of the objective function change when we change the value of one of the parameters or exogenous variables?

This chapter seeks to provide answers to these questions both in the context of unconstrained optimization and constrained optimization.

7.2 Unconstrained Optimization

We now write the objective function we are trying to optimize as

$$f(x; a),$$

where x is an $n \times 1$ vector of variables and a is an m $\times$ 1 vector of parameters associated with the problem. Alternatively, x can be regarded as containing the endogenous variables and a as containing the exogenous variables.

We carry out our optimization and obtain the optimal point x^*, where each element x_j^* is a function of the parameters a. We write $x_j^* = x_j^*(a)$ and $x^* = x^*(a)$, and say x is a **vector function** of a. The optimal value of the objective function is then given by

$$M(a) = \text{optimal } f(x; a) = f(x^*(a); a).$$

Definition

$M(a)$ is called the **optimal (maximum or minimum) value** function.

Notice that the optimal value function $M(a)$ is a function of the parameters or exogenous variables.

Example

Consider the competitive firm studied as an exercise at the end of Chapter 6. This firm seeks to maximize its total profit

$$\Pi = pL^{1/4}K^{1/2} - wL - rK.$$

In this problem the endogenous variables are the quantities of labor and capital, L and K, respectively. The parameters or exogenous variables are price of output p, the wage rate w, and the cost of capital r. So in our notation,

$$x = \begin{pmatrix} L \\ K \end{pmatrix} \quad \text{and} \quad a = \begin{pmatrix} p \\ w \\ r \end{pmatrix}.$$

Carrying out our optimization we obtained the optimal point

$$L^* = \frac{p^4}{64r^2w^2} \quad \text{and} \quad K^* = \frac{p^4}{32r^3w}.$$

Now L^* and K^* are functions of the exogenous variables. In fact they are the firm's demand functions for inputs.

Substituting these values back into the objective function gives us the maximum value function

$$M(p, r, w) = pL^{*1/4}K^{*1/2} - wL^* - rK^*$$

$$= \frac{p^4}{64r^2w}.$$

Returning to the first question posed in the introduction we now want to see how the optimal value of one of the endogenous variables x_j^* changes when there is a change in one of the exogenous variables a_i (say). An approximation to this change may be obtained by looking at the derivative $\partial x_j^*/\partial a_i$.

Example
In the above example suppose that we are interested in how the demand for labor changes when there is a small change in the cost of capital. Now

$$L^* = \frac{p^4}{64r^2w^2}$$

so

$$\frac{\partial L^*}{\partial r} = -\frac{p^4}{32r^3w^2}.$$

For small changes then

$$\Delta L^* \approx -\frac{p^4}{32r^3w^2}\Delta r.$$

In some optimization problems it is very difficult to obtain the optimal point x^*. The first order conditions may give rise to complicated nonlinear equations which are difficult to solve. Alternatively, we may not be given enough information to solve these conditions for x^*. Although in these cases we cannot obtain an explicit expression for x^* we may still be able to make noises about the derivatives $\partial x_j^*/\partial a_i$. What we are always able to do is totally differentiate the first order conditions with respect to a_i and then solve for $\partial x_j^*/\partial a_i$. Alternatively, instead of working with derivatives we could take the total differential of the first order conditions, allowing a_i to change and then solve for dx_j^*.

Probably the most famous example of such an analysis is that used to derive Slutsky's equation which we take up in Section 7.4 of this chapter. What we want to do now is consider the second question posed in the introduction and see how the optimal value function changes when we change the value of the exogenous variable a_i. Again using calculus we would look at

$$\frac{dM}{da_i},$$

the total derivative of M with respect to a_i.

Example
In the above example

$$M(p,\ r,\ w) = \frac{p^4}{64r^2w}.$$

Suppose we are interested in how this function changes when r changes, then we would look at

$$\frac{dM}{dr} = -\frac{p^4}{32r^3w}.$$

Notice that to answer this question, how M changes when r changes, really involved us in a lot of work. (As those of us who did the exercise know!)
We had to

(i) find the optimal point $L^*(p, w, r)$ and $K^*(p, w, r)$,
(ii) substitute the optimal point into the objective function to obtain the maximum value function $M(p, w, r) = \Pi^*(p, w, r)$,
(iii) differentiate M with respect to r.

If we only want to answer this comparative static question, all this work is quite unnecessary. We could in fact have obtained the answer a lot quicker by referring to an Envelope Theorem which we now consider.

The Envelope Theorem I
Consider again the optimal value function

$$M(a) = f(x^*(a); a).$$

When a_i changes we expect this change to affect $M(a)$ in two ways:

(i) directly as a_i is an element of a and a is contained in f,
(ii) indirectly through x^*.

The total derivative dM/da_i we know takes account of both these effects. But the Envelope Theorem says essentially that we need not worry about the indirect effect.

Theorem: The Envelope Theorem I

$$\frac{dM(a)}{da_i} = \left.\frac{\partial f(x; a)}{\partial a_i}\right|_{x^*}$$

Proof

$$\frac{dM(a)}{da_i} = \sum_{j=1}^{n} \frac{\partial f(x^*(a); a)}{\partial x_j^*} \frac{\partial x_j^*}{\partial a_i} + \frac{\partial f(x^*; a)}{\partial a_i}.$$

But

$$\frac{\partial f(x^*(a);a)}{\partial x_j^*} = \frac{\partial f(x;a)}{\partial x_j}\bigg|_{x^*} = 0,$$

by the first order conditions of the optimization process. So

$$\frac{dM(a)}{da_i} = \frac{\partial f(x^*;a)}{\partial a_i} = \frac{\partial f(x;a)}{\partial a_i}\bigg|_{x^*}.$$

Example

Above example. Using the Envelope Theorem to answer the question of how M changes when there is a small change in r we have

$$\frac{dM}{dr} = \frac{\partial \Pi}{\partial r}\bigg|_{L^*,K^*} = -K^* = -\frac{p^4}{32r^3w}.$$

In answering our question we need only compute K^*. In fact we need not compute the maximum value function at all.

Exercise for 7.2

For the Exercises for 6.2 compute how the maximum value function changes when there is a small change in (i) w, (ii) r, (iii) p. Do this without actually computing the maximum value function.

7.3   Constrained Optimization

We write the constrained optimization problem as

$$\text{Optimize} \quad f(x; a)$$
$$\text{subject to} \quad g(x; a) = b$$

where x is an $n \times 1$ vector of (endogenous) variables, a is an $m \times 1$ vector of parameters or exogenous variables and b is the parameter or exogenous variable which we have isolated on the right hand side of the constraint. The entire vector of parameters would be the $(m + 1) \times 1$ vector:

$$c = \begin{pmatrix} a \\ b \end{pmatrix}.$$

Notice that now the parameters can enter the problem through the objective function, through the constraint function, or from the right hand side of the constraint.

Example

Suppose a consumer seeks to maximize his or her utility function

$$U = x_1^{1/4} x_2^{1/2}$$

subject to

$$p_1 x_1 + p_2 x_2 = Y.$$

In this problem, no parameters enter through the objective function, whilst three, p_1, p_2, and Y, enter through the constraint. The entire vector of parameters is

$$c = \begin{pmatrix} p_1 \\ p_2 \\ Y \end{pmatrix}.$$

Again in our optimization we obtain an optimal point $x^* = x^*(c)$ and the optimal value function

$$M(c) = f(x^*(c); a).$$

Associated with the problem is of course the Lagrangian function.

$$Z = f(x; a) + \lambda(b - g(x; a)).$$

The Envelope Theorem generalizes to this problem in the following manner:

The Envelope Theorem II

$$\frac{dM}{dc_i} = \frac{\partial Z}{\partial c_i}\bigg|_{x^*, \lambda^*}$$

where x^* and λ^* form the critical point of the Lagrangian function.

Proof

The Lagrangian function is

$$Z(x, \lambda; c) = f(x; a) + \lambda(b - g(x)).$$

Suppose we evaluate this function at the optimal point $x^*(c)$, $\lambda^*(c)$ to obtain

$$Z^*(c) = Z(x^*(c), \lambda^*(c); c) = f(x^*(c); a) + \lambda^*(c)[b - g(x^*(c))].$$

But the optimal point x^* satisfies the constraint so $b = g(x^*(c))$ and

$$Z^*(c) = f(x^*(c); a) = M(c).$$

Totally differentiating both sides of this equation with respect to c_i we have

$$\frac{dM}{dc_i} = \sum_{j=1}^{n} \frac{\partial Z^*}{\partial x_j^*} \frac{\partial x_j^*}{\partial c_i} + \frac{\partial Z^*}{\partial \lambda^*} \frac{\partial \lambda^*}{\partial c_i} + \frac{\partial Z^*}{\partial c_i}.$$

But

$$\frac{\partial Z^*}{\partial x_j^*} = \frac{\partial Z}{\partial x_j} \text{ evaluated at } x^*, \lambda^*$$

$$= 0$$

by the first order conditions. Similarly,

$$\frac{\partial Z^*}{\partial \lambda^*} = \frac{\partial Z}{\partial \lambda} \text{ evaluated at } x^*, \lambda^*$$

$$= 0$$

by the first order conditions. Moreover,

$$\frac{\partial Z^*}{\partial c_i} = \frac{\partial Z}{\partial c_i} \bigg|_{x^*, \lambda^*}$$

yielding our result.

The Envelope Theorem, again, can be used to speed up comparative static analysis concerning changes in the optimal value function. Suppose, for example, in the above optimization problem for the consumer, we want to find out how maximum utility changes when the price of good 1 increases. We have two ways of proceeding:

1. Traditional analysis
   (i) Find the demand functions $x_1^* = x_1^*(p_1, p_2, Y), x_2^* = x_2^*(p_1, p_2, Y)$.
   (ii) Substitute into the utility function U to get the maximum value function $U^* = U^*(p_1, p_2, Y)$. (This function is called the indirect utility function).
   (iii) Compute dU^*/dp_1.

2. The Envelope Way
   The Lagrangian function associated with this problem is

$$Z = x_1^{1/4} x_2^{1/2} + \lambda(Y - p_1 x_1 - p_2 x_2);$$

so by the Envelope Theorem

$$\frac{dU^*}{dp_1} = \frac{\partial Z}{\partial p_1}\bigg|_{x^*\lambda^*} = -\lambda x_1|_{x^*,\lambda^*} = -\lambda^* x_1^*.$$

If we are sure the second order conditions hold for this problem, then our comparative static analysis need only involve us in computing λ^* and x_1^*.

The Lagrangian multiplier λ^* as a shadow price

In our constrained optimization problem, one of the parameters or exogenous variables is b, the parameter we have isolated on the right hand side of the constraint. Consider now the derivative dM/db. By the Envelope Theorem,

$$\frac{dM}{db} = \frac{\partial Z}{\partial b}\bigg|_{x^*,\lambda^*} = \lambda^*.$$

That is λ^* tells us how the optimal value of the objective function $f(x; a)$ changes when we change the right hand side of the constraint. In fact it gives the rate of change.

Suppose now we increase b by one unit and we ask how much would this change be worth to a person confronted by the optimization problem:

$$\text{Maximize} \quad f(x; a)$$
$$\text{subject to} \quad g(x; a) = b.$$

By increasing b by one unit, the constraint is less binding; so the maximum value of the objective function would go up. At most, the extra unit of b would be worth this increase in $M(c)$.

That is,

$$dM = \frac{dM}{db} db = \frac{dM}{db} = \lambda^*!$$

Economists say λ^* is a **shadow price.** In no way is this price associated with any market. It merely portrays how much an extra unit of b is worth in the problem.

Exercises for 7.3

1. For question 2 of the Exercises for 6.3 and the Exercise for 6.4, use the Envelope Theorem to determine how the indirect utility function changes for changes in (i) p_1, (ii) p_2, and (iii) Y. Do this without actually computing the indirect utility function.

2. For question 3 of the Exercises for 6.3, compute how the cost function changes with changes in (i) w, (ii) r, and (iii) Q_0, without actually computing this minimum value function.

3. For question 4 of the Exercises for 6.3, find how the minimum value function changes with small changes in (i) p_2, and (ii) u_0. Do this without first computing the minimum value function.

7.4   Slutsky's Equation

In this section we look at the most famous example of conducting the type of comparative static analysis involving $\partial x_j^* / \partial a_i$, where insufficient information is given to allow us to solve the first order conditions for x^*.

Slutsky was concerned with how price changes affect the consumer's demand for goods. He considered the traditional problem neoclassical economics assigns to the consumer, namely

$$\text{Maximize} \quad U(x_1, x_2)$$
$$\text{subject to} \quad p_1 x_1 + p_2 x_2 = Y.$$

In this problem, the endogenous variables are the quantities consumed of the two goods x_1 and x_2 and the parameters or exogenous variables are the prices p_1, p_2, and the consumer's income Y.

The Lagrangian function is

$$Z = U(x_1, x_2) + \lambda(p_1 x_1 + p_2 x_2 - Y),[1]$$

and the first order conditions are

$$Z_\lambda = p_1 x_1 + p_2 x_2 - Y = 0$$
$$Z_1 = U_1 \ + \lambda p_1 \qquad = 0$$
$$Z_2 = U_2 \ + \lambda p_2 \qquad = 0. \qquad (7.1)$$

---

[1] We have written this function slightly differently than is the usual case, in that the λ here is minus the usual λ! We have also concentrated on the two good cases though the analysis is easily generalized.

If we were given the utility function U, we could solve these conditions to get the Marshallian demand functions

$$x_1^* = x_1^*(p_1, p_2, Y) \quad \text{and} \quad x_2^* = x_2^*(p_1, p_2, Y)$$

and the associated value for the Lagrangian multiplier $\lambda^* = \lambda^*(p_1, p_2, Y)$. Of course the second order condition must hold for this critical point. This involves the bordered Hessian matrix

$$\bar{H} = \begin{pmatrix} 0 & p_1 & p_2 \\ p_1 & U_{11} & U_{12} \\ p_2 & U_{21} & U_{22} \end{pmatrix}$$

and requires that

$$|\bar{H}| > 0 \quad \text{at } x_1^*, x_2^*, \text{ and } \lambda^*.$$

The system of first order conditions given by (7.1) can be viewed as nonlinear equations which represent the equilibrium conditions of our model. Before we start further analysis we should check that it is in fact possible to solve for λ, x_1, and x_2 in terms of p_1, p_2, and Y. Using a straightforward generalization of the Implicit Function Theorem given in Section 5.4 of Chapter 5 we see that the Jacobian determinant is none other than the determinant of the bordered Hessian matrix, namely $|\bar{H}|$. The second order conditions for optimization ensure that such solutions do exist.

With x_1^* and x_2^* in hand we could answer Slutsky's concern by working out $\partial x_1^* / \partial p_1$ (say).

However we are not given the actual utility function, so this course of action is not open to us. We can still conduct such a comparative analysis using the tuuhniques we learn with respect to nonlinear economic models, discussed in Section 5.4 of Chapter 5. We regard the first order conditions (7.1) as equilibrium equations. If an exogenous variable changes, say p_1, we differentiate both sides of (7.1) with respect to p_1 remembering that x_1, x_2, and λ can be regarded as functions of the exogenous variables p_1, p_2, and Y. We get

$$x_1 + p_1 \frac{\partial x_1}{\partial p_1} + p_2 \frac{\partial x_2}{\partial p_1} = 0$$

$$U_{11} \frac{\partial x_1}{\partial p_1} + U_{12} \frac{\partial x_2}{\partial p_1} + \lambda + p_1 \frac{\partial \lambda}{\partial p_1} = 0$$

$$U_{21} \frac{\partial x_1}{\partial p_1} + U_{22} \frac{\partial x_2}{\partial p_1} + p_2 \frac{\partial \lambda}{\partial p_1} = 0,$$

or in matrix notation

$$
\begin{pmatrix} 0 & p_1 & p_2 \\ p_1 & U_{11} & U_{12} \\ p_2 & U_{21} & U_{22} \end{pmatrix}
\begin{pmatrix} \dfrac{\partial \lambda}{\partial p_1} \\[2ex] \dfrac{\partial x_1}{\partial p_2} \\[2ex] \dfrac{\partial x_2}{\partial p_1} \end{pmatrix}
= \begin{pmatrix} -x_1 \\ -\lambda \\ 0 \end{pmatrix}^{2},
$$

That is,

$$
\bar{H}
\begin{pmatrix} \dfrac{\partial \lambda}{\partial p_1} \\[2ex] \dfrac{\partial x_1}{\partial p_1} \\[2ex] \dfrac{\partial x_2}{\partial p_1} \end{pmatrix}
= \begin{pmatrix} -x_1 \\ -\lambda \\ 0 \end{pmatrix}.
$$

We could then use Cramer's rule to solve for the derivative that is of interest to us. For example, suppose we are interested in $\partial x_2 / \partial p_1$. Then by Cramer's rule

$$
\frac{\partial x_2^*}{\partial p_1} = \begin{vmatrix} 0 & p_1 & -x_1 \\ p_1 & U_{11} & -\lambda \\ p_2 & U_{21} & 0 \end{vmatrix} \Big/ |\bar{H}|.
$$

Alternatively, instead of using derivatives in our analysis, we could work with differentials, remembering always that the ratio of differentials is a derivative. Additionally, we want to conduct the most general comparative static analysis by allowing all the exogenous variables p_1, p_2, and Y to change at once.

We regard the left hand side of the first order conditions as functions in the endogenous variables x_1 and x_2, the exogenous variables p_1, p_2, and Y, and the Lagrangian multiplier λ. Recall that if

$$
y = f(x_1, \ldots, x_n)
$$

then

$$
dy = f_1 dx_1 + f_2 dx_2 + \cdots + f_n dx_n
$$

---

[2]Formally the xs should have stars on them to signify it is the equilibrium values of x_1 and x_2 being considered here. These are dropped for convenience though we shall put them back at the end of the analysis.

and this result is what we use in taking the differentials of both sides of equations in (7.1). We get

$$p_1 dx_1 + \quad x_1 dp_1 + p_2 dx_2 + x_2 dp_2 - dY = 0$$
$$U_{11} dx_1 + U_{12} dx_2 + p_1 d\lambda + \quad \lambda dp_1 \qquad = 0 \qquad (7.2)$$
$$U_{21} dx_1 + U_{22} dx_2 + p_2 d\lambda + \quad \lambda dp_2 \qquad = 0.$$

Isolating the differentials of the exogenous variables on the right hand side we have

$$p_1 dx_1 + p_2 dx_2 \qquad = dY - x_1 dp_1 - x_2 dp_2$$
$$p_1 d\lambda + U_{11} dx_1 + U_{12} dx_2 = -\lambda dp_1$$
$$p_2 d\lambda + U_{21} dx_1 + U_{22} dx_2 = -\lambda dp_2.$$

These are linear equations in the differentials of the endogenous variables x_1 and x_2 as well as the differential of λ. In matrix notation these equations can be written as

$$\bar{H} \begin{pmatrix} d\lambda \\ dx_1 \\ dx_2 \end{pmatrix} = \begin{pmatrix} dY - x_1 dp_1 - x_2 dp_2 \\ -\lambda dp_1 \\ -\lambda dp_2 \end{pmatrix}. \qquad (7.3)$$

All the comparative static results associated with this problem are summarized by these equations.

We now seek to analyze the effects of various changes in the exogenous variables:

1. p_1 changes, p_2 and Y remaining constant

We set $dp_2 = dY = 0$ in equations (7.3) to obtain

$$\bar{H} \begin{pmatrix} d\lambda \\ dx_1 \\ dx_2 \end{pmatrix} = \begin{pmatrix} -x_1 dp_1 \\ -\lambda dp_1 \\ 0 \end{pmatrix}.$$

Suppose we are interested in how the change in p_1 affects the equilibrium (optimal) value of x_1. Using Cramer's rule to solve for dx_1 we get

$$dx_1 = \begin{vmatrix} 0 & -x_1 dp_1 & p_2 \\ p_1 & -\lambda dp_1 & U_{12} \\ p_2 & 0 & U_{22} \end{vmatrix} \Big/ |\bar{H}|.$$

Expanding the determinant in the numerator using the second column we have

$$dx_1 = -x_1 dp_1 \frac{|\bar{H}_{12}|}{|\bar{H}|} - \lambda dp_1 \frac{|\bar{H}_{22}|}{|\bar{H}|},$$

where $|\bar{H}_{12}|$ and $|\bar{H}_{22}|$ are the cofactors of the $(1, 2)$ and $(2, 2)$ elements of $\bar{H}$, respectively.

Dividing through by dp_1 remembering the ratio of differentials is a derivative, and returning the stars, we have

$$\frac{\partial x_1^*}{\partial p_1} = -x_1^* \frac{|\bar{H}_{12}|}{\bar{H}} - \lambda^* \frac{|\bar{H}_{22}|}{|\bar{H}|}. \tag{7.4}$$

In essence this is Slutsky's equation. Slutsky's remarkable insight however, was to identify part of this equation as a "substitution effect" of the price change and the other part as the "income effect".

2. The income effect

Returning to equations (7.3) suppose now we let income change while holding prices fixed. That is we let

$$dp_1 = dp_2 = 0$$

in equations (7.3) to get

$$\bar{H} \begin{pmatrix} d\lambda \\ dx_1 \\ dx_2 \end{pmatrix} = \begin{pmatrix} dY \\ 0 \\ 0 \end{pmatrix},$$

Again using Cramer's rule to solve for dx_1 we get

$$dx_1 = \begin{vmatrix} 0 & dY & 0 \\ p_1 & 0 & U_{12} \\ p_2 & 0 & U_{22} \end{vmatrix} \Bigg/ |\bar{H}|$$

or

$$dx_1 = \frac{|\bar{H}_{12}|}{|\bar{H}|} dY.$$

Dividing through by dY and returning the star we get

$$\left(\frac{\partial x_1^*}{\partial Y} \right)_{\substack{\text{prices} \\ \text{constant}}} = \frac{|\bar{H}_{12}|}{|\bar{H}|}. \tag{7.5}$$

3. **The substitution effect**

Suppose now we insist that the consumer's utility remains the same. That is, any change in Y for example, is compensated by changes in p_1 and p_2 so the consumer remains at the old level of utility. Utility remaining constant implies

$$dU = U_1 dx_1 + U_2 dx_2 = 0$$

or

$$\frac{U_1}{U_2} dx_1 + dx_2 = 0$$

But from the first order conditions

$$\frac{U_1}{U_2} = \frac{p_1}{p_2}$$

in equilibrium; so holding utility constant implies

$$\frac{p_1}{p_2} dx_1 + dx_2 = 0$$

or

$$p_1 dx_1 + p_2 dx_2 = 0.$$

Finally from equation (7.2)

$$p_1 dx_1 + p_2 dx_2 = dY - x_1 dp_1 - x_2 dp_2.$$

Hence if utility is to remain the same, the exogenous variables p_1, p_2, and Y must change in such a way that

$$dY - x_1 dp_1 - x_2 dp_2 = 0.$$

If p_1 is the only price that is changing additionally we would require $dp_2 = 0$. Under these conditions equation (7.3) becomes

$$\bar{H} \begin{pmatrix} d\lambda \\ dx_1 \\ dx_2 \end{pmatrix} = \begin{pmatrix} 0 \\ -\lambda dp_1 \\ 0 \end{pmatrix}.$$

So using Cramer's rule to solve for dx_1 one last time gives

$$dx_1 = \begin{vmatrix} 0 & 0 & p_2 \\ p_1 & -\lambda dp_1 & U_{12} \\ p_2 & 0 & U_{22} \end{vmatrix} \Big/ |\bar{H}|$$

or

$$dx_1 = -\lambda dp_1 |\bar{H}_{22}| / |\bar{H}|.$$

Dividing both sides by the differential dp_1 and returning the stars gives

$$\left(\frac{\partial x_1^*}{\partial p_1}\right)_{\substack{\text{utility} \\ \text{constant}}} = -\lambda^* \frac{|\bar{H}_{22}|}{|\bar{H}|} \tag{7.6}$$

Substituting equations (7.5) and (7.6) in equation (7.4) gives **Slutsky's equation**:

$$\frac{\partial x_1^*}{\partial p_1} = -x_1^* \left(\frac{\partial x_1^*}{\partial Y}\right)_{\substack{\text{prices} \\ \text{constant}}} + \left(\frac{\partial x_1^*}{\partial p_1}\right)_{\substack{\text{utility} \\ \text{constant.}}}$$

$$\underbrace{\qquad\qquad}_{\substack{\text{Income} \\ \text{Effect}}} \qquad \underbrace{\qquad\qquad}_{\substack{\text{Substitution} \\ \text{Effect}}}$$

The signs of the substitution and income effects

The substitution effect is

$$\left(\frac{\partial x_1^*}{\partial p_1}\right)_{\substack{\text{utility} \\ \text{constant}}} = -\lambda^* |\bar{H}_{22}| / |\bar{H}|.$$

By the second order conditions $|\bar{H}| > 0$. Now

$$|\bar{H}_{22}| = (-1)^{2+2} \begin{vmatrix} 0 & p_2 \\ p_2 & U_{22} \end{vmatrix} = -p_2^2 < 0,$$

and in equilibrium from the first order conditions

$$U_1 = -\lambda^* p_1 \Rightarrow -\lambda^* = U_1/p_1.$$

The derivative U_1 is the marginal utility of good 1 and provided we make the assumption of nonsatiation as neoclassical economists do, we have $U_1 > 0$ so $-\lambda^*$ is positive. It follows that

$$\left(\frac{\partial x_1^*}{\partial p_1}\right)_{\substack{\text{utility}\\\text{constant}}} < 0.$$

The substitution effect is negative. Holding utility constant means that p_1 and x_1^* move in opposite directions. A fall in p_1 for example, by the substitution effect leads to an increase in x_1^* as illustrated by the following diagram:

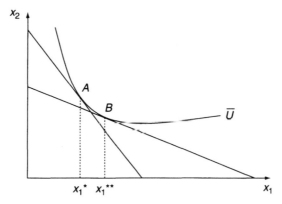

If we insist that we remain at the utility level given by the indifference curve $\bar{U}$ then the fall in price p_1 takes us from A to B, so the equilibrium value of x_1 increases. Notice that this must be the case if the indifference curve is convex. Essentially the second order conditions ensure this.

The income effect is

$$-x_1^*\left(\frac{\partial x_1^*}{\partial Y}\right)_{\substack{\text{prices}\\\text{constant}}} = -x_1^*|\bar{H}_{12}|/|\bar{H}|.$$

Now $|\bar{H}| > 0$ and $x_1^* > 0$ but

$$|\bar{H}_{12}| = (-1)^{1+2}\begin{vmatrix} p_1 & U_{12} \\ p_2 & U_{22} \end{vmatrix} = p_2 U_{12} - p_1 U_{22},$$

may be greater than zero or less than zero. Three cases present themselves:

Case 1: A normal good
In this case $|\bar{H}_{12}| > 0$ so

$$\left(\frac{\partial x_1^*}{\partial Y}\right)_{\substack{\text{prices}\\\text{constant}}} = \frac{|\bar{H}_{12}|}{|\bar{H}|} > 0.$$

Holding prices constant, income and x_1^* move in the same direction. An increase in income, for example, leads to an increase in x_1^*. Here the income effect reinforces the substitution effect. Diagrammatically we have the following:

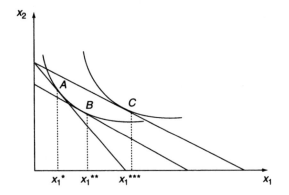

The income effect takes us from B to C reinforcing the substitution effect of a decrease in p_1.

Case 2: an inferior good
In this case $|\bar{H}_{12}|$ is less than zero so

$$\left(\frac{\partial x_1^*}{\partial Y}\right)_{\substack{\text{prices}\\\text{constant}}} < 0.$$

Income Y and x_1^* are moving in opposite directions now and the income effect moves in the opposite direction from the substitution effect. But for an **inferior** good the substitution effect outweighs the income effect so overall x_1^* and p_1 move in opposite directions. A fall in p_1 still leads to an increase in x_1^*.

Diagrammatically,

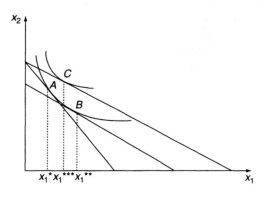

Case 3: a Giffen good
In this case too $|\bar{H}_{12}|$ is less than zero so

$$\left(\frac{\partial x_1^*}{\partial Y}\right)_{\substack{\text{prices} \\ \text{constant}}} < 0,$$

but now the income effect outweighs the substitution effect so overall p_1 and x_1^* move in the same direction. A fall in p_1 now leads to a fall in x_1^*. Diagrammatically,

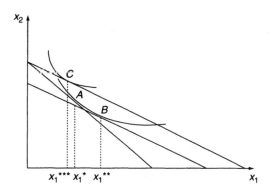

Exercises for 7.4
1. Consider the consumer's utility maximization problem:

$$\text{Max } U(x_1, x_2)$$

$$\text{s.t. } p_1 x_1 + p_2 x_2 = Y,$$

where x_1 and x_2 are the quantities of goods consumed, and p_1, p_2, and Y are the prices of the two goods and the consumer's income, respectively.
  (i) Obtain the first order conditions for utility maximization.
 (ii) Obtain the second order conditions for utility maximization.
(iii) By taking the total differential of both sides of the first order conditions obtain a system of equations that shows how (equilibrium) x_1, x_2, and λ change for small changes dp_1, and dp_2 and dY in prices and income, where λ is the Lagrangian multiplier.
     Hint: for convenience drop the equilibrium "stars" off the variables.
 (iv) Suppose only the price of good 2 changes. Using the system of equations obtained in (iii), find an expression for $\partial x_1/\partial p_2$ in terms of cofactors of the bordered Hessian matrix.
  (v) Suppose only income changes. Again using the system of equations in (iii) find an expression for $\partial x_1/\partial Y$.
 (vi) Using the utility function $U(x_1, x_2)$, the first order conditions, and the budget constraint $p_1 x_1 + p_2 x_2 = Y$, find an expression that the changes dp_1, dp_2, and dY must satisfy in order for the consumer's utility to remain constant.
(vii) Using the results of (iv), (v), and (vi) obtain Slutsky's equation:

$$\frac{\partial x_1}{\partial p_2} = \left(\frac{\partial x_1}{\partial p_2}\right)_{\substack{\text{Utility}\\\text{constant}}} - x_2 \left(\frac{\partial x_1}{\partial Y}\right)_{\substack{\text{Prices}\\\text{constant.}}} \tag{7.7}$$

Show that the substitution effect of a change in p_2 on good 1 is the same as the substitution effect of a change in p_1 on good 2.
2. (i) The elasticity of demand for the **compensated** or **Hicksian demand function** is defined by

$$\varepsilon_{12} = \left(\frac{\partial x_1}{\partial p_2}\right)_{\substack{\text{Utility}\\\text{constant}}} \frac{p_2}{x_1}.$$

Write Slutsky's equation (7.7) in terms of a compensated demand elasticity and other elasticities.
 (ii) Let A be a square matrix whose (i, j)th element is a_{ij} and let c_{ij} be the cofactor of this element. A well-known result to do with determination is that

$$\sum_j a_{ij} c_{kj} = 0 \quad i \neq k$$

$$\sum_i a_{ij} c_{ih} = 0 \quad i \neq h.$$

Use this result or otherwise to prove that

$$\varepsilon_{11} + \varepsilon_{12} = 0.$$

Hence prove that the sum of ordinary demand elasticities for good 1 is equal to the negative of the income elasticity.

7.5 Applications of the Envelope Theorems in Economics

Neoclassical economics, in the field of microeconomics in particular, has studied several optimization problems in detail. Associated with each of these problems is an optimal value function that invites the application of the appropriate Envelope Theorem. Indeed economists proved several results which are nothing else but simply applications of the Envelope Theorem. (They did not use the Envelope Theorem to obtain these proofs being unaware of its existence). In this section we look at these optimization problems and these applications of the Envelope Theorem.

As far as the theory of consumption is concerned, the traditional problem neoclassical economics assigns the consumer is one of maximizing utility subject to a budget constraint. In mathematical terms the problem can be formulated as

$$\text{Maximize} \quad U(x_1, \dots, x_n)$$
$$\text{subject to} \quad p_1 x_1 + p_2 x_2 + \cdots + p_n x_n = Y,$$

where x_j is the quantity of goods consumed, p_j is the price of that good, Y is the income of the consumer (or the amount available for consumption), and U is utility. We can write the problem more succinctly as

$$\text{Maximize} \quad U(x)$$
$$\text{subject to} \quad p'x = Y.$$

In this problem x represents the variables, or in economic terms the endogenous variables and p and Y represent the parameters or the exogenous variables. When we solve this problem for x, we get the optimal point as a function of p and Y:

$$x^* = x^*(p, Y).$$

These functions are called the **Marshallian demand functions**. Substituting x^* into the utility function $U(x)$ gives us the optimal value function

$$V(p, Y) = U(x^*(p, Y)).$$

This function is called the **indirect utility function**.

Example

Suppose the consumer's utility function is

$$U(x_1, x_2) = \log x_1 + \log x_2.$$

Find the consumer's Marshallian demand functions and his/her indirect utility function.

We consider the problem

$$\text{Maximize} \quad U(x_1, x_2) = \log x_1 + \log x_2$$
$$\text{subject to} \quad p_1 x_1 + p_2 x = Y.$$

The Lagrangian function associated with this problem is

$$L = \log x_1 + \log x_2 + \lambda(Y - p_1 x_1 - p_2 x_2)$$

and the first order conditions for maximization are

$$L_1 = 1/x_1 - \lambda p_1 = 0$$
$$L_2 = 1/x_2 - \lambda p_2 = 0$$
$$L_\lambda = Y - p_1 x_1 - p_2 x_2 = 0.$$

Solving the first two equations for λ gives

$$\lambda = \frac{1}{p_1 x_1} = \frac{1}{p_2 x_2}$$

so $p_1 x_1 = p_2 x_2$. Substituting into the third equation gives

$$2 p_2 x_2 = Y$$

so $x_2^* = Y/2p_2$. By symmetry

$$x_1^* = Y/2p_1.$$

These are the Marshallian demand functions. Substituting these into the utility function gives the indirect utility function

$$V(p, Y) = \log(Y/2p_1) + \log(Y/2p_2)$$
$$= 2 \log Y - \log p_1 - \log p_2 - \log 4.$$

Theorem: Roy's Identity
Our first application of the Envelope Theorem involves the maximum value function $V(p, Y)$. It is called Roy's Identity.

Theorem
If $x^*(p, Y)$ are the Marshallian demand functions then

$$x_i^*(p, Y) = -\frac{\partial V(p, Y)}{\partial p_i} \bigg/ \frac{\partial V(p, Y)}{\partial Y}, \quad i = 1, \ldots, n.$$

Proof
The Lagrangian function for our utility maximization problem is

$$L = U(x) + \lambda(Y - p'x).$$

By the Envelope Theorem then

$$\frac{\partial V}{\partial p_i} = \frac{\partial L}{\partial p_i} \bigg|_{x^*, \lambda^*} = -\lambda^* x_i^*$$

and

$$\frac{\partial V}{\partial Y} = \frac{\partial L}{Y} \bigg|_{x^*, \lambda^*} = \lambda^*.$$

The result follows immediately.

Example
Suppose the indirect utility function is given by $V(p, Y) = AY^{\alpha+\beta}/p_1^\alpha p_2^\beta$.
   Find the Marshallian demand functions.
   By Roy's Identity,

$$x_1^* = -\frac{\partial V}{\partial p_1} \bigg/ \frac{\partial V}{\partial Y} = \frac{\alpha V}{p_1} \bigg/ \frac{(\alpha + \beta)V}{Y} = \frac{\alpha}{\alpha + \beta} \frac{Y}{p_1}.$$

By symmetry,

$$x_2^* = \frac{\beta}{\alpha + \beta} \frac{Y}{p_2}.$$

A related problem that neoclassical economists have studied in detail is looking at the minimum expenditure required by the consumer to obtain a certain level of utility. That is

$$\text{Minimize} \quad p'x$$

$$\text{subject to} \quad u(x) = u^0,$$

where u^0 is the prescribed level of utility. Solving this problem will give an optimal point

$$\bar{x}(p, u^0).$$

These are called the **Hicksian demand functions**. Substituting $\bar{x}$ into the objective function $p'x$ gives a minimum value function

$$e(p, u^0) = p'\bar{x}(p, u^0).$$

This function is called the **expenditure function**.

Example
Suppose the consumer's utility function is $u(x_1, x_2) = x_1^\alpha x_2^{1-\alpha}$ for $0 < \alpha < 1$. Find the associated Hicksian demand functions and the expenditure function.
  We consider the problem

$$\text{minimize} \quad p_1 x_1 + p_2 x_2$$

$$\text{subject to} \quad x_1^\alpha x_2^{1-\alpha} = u^0$$

with the Lagrangian function

$$L = p_1 x_1 + p_2 x_2 + \lambda(u^0 - x_1^\alpha x_2^{1-\alpha}).$$

The first order conditions for this minimization are

$$L_1 = p_1 - \alpha \lambda x_1^{\alpha-1} x_2^{1-\alpha} = 0$$

$$L_2 = p_2 - (1-\alpha)\lambda x_1^\alpha x_2^{-\alpha} = 0$$

$$L_\lambda = u^0 - x_1^\alpha x_2^{1-\alpha} = 0.$$

From the first two equations we have

$$\frac{p_1}{p_2} = \frac{\alpha}{1-\alpha}\frac{x_2}{x_1},$$

so

$$x_1 = \frac{\alpha p_2}{(1-\alpha)p_1}x_2.$$

Substituting into the third equation gives

$$u^0 - \left(\frac{\alpha p_2}{(1-\alpha)p_1}\right)^\alpha x_2 = 0,$$

so

$$\bar{x}_2 = u^0 \left(\frac{(1-\alpha)p_1}{\alpha p_2}\right)^\alpha.$$

By symmetry,

$$\bar{x}_1 = u^0 \left(\frac{\alpha p_2}{(1-\alpha)p_1}\right)^{1-\alpha}.$$

These are the Hicksian demand functions. Substituting these in the objective function gives the expenditure function:

$$e(p, u^0) = p_1 u^0 \left(\frac{\alpha p_2}{(1-\alpha)p_1}\right)^{1-\alpha} + p_2 u^0 \left(\frac{(1-\alpha)p_1}{\alpha p_2}\right)^\alpha$$

$$= c u^0 p_1^\alpha p_2^{1-\alpha}$$

where c is a constant.

Again economists obtain results from the expenditure function which arise from a simple application of the Envelope Theorem.

Theorem: Shephard's Lemma

Let $\bar{x}_i(p, u^0)$ be the Hicksian demand function for good i. Then

$$\bar{x}_i(p, u^0) = \partial e(p, u^0)/\partial p_i$$

for $i = 1, \ldots, n$.

Proof

The Lagrangian function for our expenditure minimization problem is

$$L = p'x + \lambda(u^0 - u(x)).$$

By the Envelope Theorem

$$\frac{\partial e}{\partial p_i} = \frac{\partial L}{\partial p_i}\bigg|_{\bar{x},\bar{\lambda}} = \bar{x}_i.$$

Example

Suppose the expenditure function is given by $e(p, u^0) = u^0 p_1^\alpha p_2^{1-\alpha}$. Find the Hicksian demand functions.

By Shephard's Lemma

$$\bar{x}_1 = \frac{\partial e}{\partial p_1} = \alpha u^0 \left(\frac{p_2}{p_1}\right)^{1-\alpha}$$

$$\bar{x}_2 = \frac{\partial e}{\partial p_2} = (1-\alpha)u^0 \left(\frac{p_1}{p_2}\right)^\alpha.$$

Before we consider optimization problems in the theory of the firm it should be noted that the two problems assigned to the consumer are intimately related. This is best seen by considering the case involving two goods and solving the problems graphically, as is done in diagrams 1 and 2. In these diagrams the constraints we are given are shown in bold.

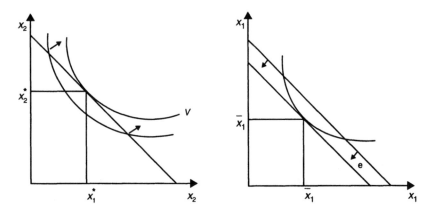

In problem 1 the prescribed level of income Y^0 fixes the budget line. We then move the indifference curve as high as we can and the optimal point x_1^*, x_2^* is obtained when the indifference curve becomes tangential to the fixed budget line. In problem 2 the prescribed level of utility u^0 fixes the indifference curve. We then try to lower the budget line as far as we can and the optimal point $\bar{x}_1$, $\bar{x}_2$ is obtained when the budget line becomes tangential to the fixed indifference curve.

Problem 1 clearly gives the same solution as problem 2 if we set the prescribed level of income Y^0 in problem 1 equal to e. Thus

$$V(p, e(p, u^0)) = u^0$$

$$x^*(p, e(p, u^0)) = \bar{x}(p, u^0).$$

Likewise, problem 2 clearly gives the same solution as problem 1 if we set the prescribed level of utility u^0 in problem 2 equal to V. Thus

$$e(p, V(p, Y^0)) = Y^0$$

$$\bar{x}(p, V(p, Y^0)) = x^*(p, Y^0).$$

These properties are known as the **consistency properties** and they allow us to derive the optimal value function of one of the problems from that of the other.

Example
Suppose the consumer's indirect utility function is

$$V(p, Y) = \frac{AY^{\alpha+\beta}}{p_1^\alpha p_2^\beta}.$$

Find the consumer's expenditure function.

From the consisting properties we have

$$V(p, e(p, u^0)) = u^0$$

so

$$\frac{Ae^{\alpha+\beta}}{p_1^\alpha p_2^\beta} = u^0.$$

Solving we get the required expenditure function

$$e = (p_1^\alpha p_2^\beta u^0 / A)^{1/\alpha+\beta}.$$

Example

Suppose the consumer's expenditure function is given by

$$e = -(\sqrt{p_1} + \sqrt{p_2})^2/u^0.$$

Find the consumer's indirect utility function.

By the consistency properties,

$$e(\boldsymbol{p}, V(\boldsymbol{p}, Y)) = Y;$$

thus

$$-(\sqrt{p_1} + \sqrt{p_2})^2/V = Y$$

so

$$V = -(\sqrt{p_1} + \sqrt{p_2})^2/Y.$$

Slutsky's equation again

The consistency properties present a neat way of achieving Slutsky's equation. We have for good i that

$$\bar{x}_i(\boldsymbol{p}, u^0) = x_i^*(\boldsymbol{p}, e(\boldsymbol{p}, u^0))$$

for any given level of utility u^0. Suppose we set u^0 equal to the maximum utility level given by $V(\boldsymbol{p}, y)$. That is, we take

$$u^0 = V(p, y) = u^*,$$

say. Then

$$\bar{x}_i(\boldsymbol{p}, u^*) = x_i^*(\boldsymbol{p}, e(\boldsymbol{p}, u^*)),$$

and differentiating we get

$$\frac{\partial \bar{x}_i}{\partial p_i} = \frac{\partial x_i^*}{\partial p_i} + \frac{\partial x_i^*}{\partial y}\frac{\partial e}{\partial p_i}(\boldsymbol{p}, u^*). \tag{7.8}$$

But from Shephard's Lemma

$$\frac{\partial e}{\partial p_i}(\boldsymbol{p}, u^*) = \bar{x}_i(\boldsymbol{p}, u^*) = \bar{x}_i(\boldsymbol{p}, V(\boldsymbol{p}, y)) \tag{7.9}$$

$$= x_i^*$$

where the last equality is obtained using the consistency properties again. Substituting equation (7.9) into equation (7.8) gives

$$\frac{\partial \bar{x}_i(p, u^*)}{\partial p_i} = \frac{\partial x_i^*}{\partial p_i} + x_i^* \frac{\partial x_i^*}{\partial y}$$

or

$$\frac{\partial x_i^*}{\partial p_i} = \frac{\partial \bar{x}_i(p, u^*)}{\partial p_i} - x_i^* \frac{\partial x_i^*}{\partial y}. \tag{7.10}$$

A little reflection reveals that this is Slutsky's equation, the first part of the right hand side of equation (7.10) being the substitution effect and the second part being the income effect.

Optimization problems abound in the theory of the firm as well. One of the problems neoclassical economics assigns to the competitive firm is minimizing the cost of producing a certain level of output. In mathematical terms we can formulate this problem as

$$\text{Minimize} \quad w_1 x_1 + w_2 x_2 + \cdots + w_n x_n$$

$$\text{subject to} \quad f(x_1, \ldots, x_n) = y$$

where x_j is the quantity of input j used in production, w_j is the price of input j, $f(x_1, \ldots, x_n)$ is the firm's production function and y is the prescribed level of output. In this problem the x_js are the variables, or in economic terms the endogenous variables; the input prices w_js and the level of output are the parameter or endogenous variables.[3]

Writing this problem more succinctly gives

$$\text{minimize} \quad w'x$$

$$\text{subject to} \quad f(x) = y.$$

Solving this problem gives an optimal point

$$\bar{x}(w, y).$$

These functions are called the firm's **conditional demand functions**. Substituting the optimal point into the objective function gives a minimum value function

$$c(w, y) = w'\bar{x}(w, y).$$

[3]This problem is the **long-run** problem facing the firm, where all inputs can vary. The **short-run** problem fixes the quantities of certain inputs.

This function is called the firm's **cost function**.

Example

Suppose a competitive firm has a Cobb-Douglas production function given by

$$f(x_1, x_2) = x_1^{\alpha} x_2^{\beta} \quad \alpha + \beta < 1.$$

Find the conditional demand functions and the cost function.

Our problem is

$$\text{Minimize} \quad w_1 x_1 + w_2 x_2$$

$$\text{subject to} \quad x_1^{\alpha} x_2^{\beta} = y,$$

and the associated Lagrangian function is

$$L = w_1 x_1 + w_2 x_2 + \lambda (y - x_1^{\alpha} x_2^{\beta}).$$

The first order conditions for our minimization are

$$L_1 = w_1 - \alpha \lambda x_1^{\alpha - 1} x_2^{\beta} = 0$$

$$L_2 = w_2 - \beta \lambda x_1^{\alpha} x_2^{\beta - 1} = 0$$

$$L_\lambda = y - x_1^{\alpha} x_2^{\beta} = 0.$$

From the first two equations we obtain

$$\frac{w_1}{w_2} = \frac{\alpha}{\beta} \frac{x_2}{x_1}$$

so

$$x_1 = \frac{\alpha w_2}{\beta w_1} x_2.$$

Substituting into the third equation gives

$$y - \left(\frac{\alpha w_2}{\beta w_1} \right)^{\alpha} x_2^{\alpha + \beta} = 0.$$

Thus

$$\bar{x}_2 = \left(\frac{\alpha w_2}{\beta w_1} \right)^{-\alpha/\alpha + \beta} y^{1/\alpha + \beta}.$$

By symmetry,

$$\bar{x}_1 = \left(\frac{\beta w_1}{\alpha w_2}\right)^{-\beta/(\alpha+\beta)} y^{1/(\alpha+\beta)}.$$

These are the conditional demand functions. The cost function then is

$$c(\boldsymbol{w}, y) = \left(w_1 \left(\frac{\beta w_1}{\alpha w_2}\right)^{-\beta/(\alpha+\beta)} + w_2 \left(\frac{\alpha w_2}{\beta w_1}\right)^{-\alpha/(\alpha+\beta)}\right) y^{1/(\alpha+\beta)}$$

$$= K w_1^{\alpha/(\alpha+\beta)} w_2^{\beta/(\alpha+\beta)} y^{1/(\alpha+\beta)}$$

where K is a constant.

Shephard investigated how one obtains a conditional demand function from a given cost function. The result represents another trivial application of the Envelope Theorem.

Theorem: Shephard's Lemma

Let $\bar{x}_i(\boldsymbol{w}, y)$ be the firm's conditional demand function for input i and let $c(\boldsymbol{w}, y)$ be the firm's cost function. Then

$$\bar{x}_i(\boldsymbol{w}, y) = \frac{\partial c(\boldsymbol{w}, y)}{\partial w_i}, \quad i = 1, \ldots, n.$$

Proof

The Lagrangian function for the cost minimization problem facing the firm is

$$L = \boldsymbol{w}'\boldsymbol{x} + \lambda(y - f(\boldsymbol{x})).$$

By the Envelope Theorem

$$\frac{\partial c}{\partial w_i} = \frac{\partial L}{\partial w_i}\bigg|_{\bar{\boldsymbol{x}}, \bar{\lambda}} = \bar{x}_i.$$

Notice that the same Envelope Theorem tells us that marginal cost is given by $\bar{\lambda}$. That is,

$$\frac{\partial c}{\partial y} = \frac{\partial L}{\partial y}\bigg|_{\bar{\boldsymbol{x}}, \bar{\lambda}} = \bar{\lambda}.$$

Example

Suppose the cost function of a competitive firm is given by

$$c(w, y) = w_1^\alpha w_2^\beta y.$$

Find the associated conditional demand functions.

By Shephard's Lemma the conditional demand functions are given by

$$\bar{x}_1 = \partial c / \partial w_1 = \alpha w_1^{\alpha-1} w_2^\beta y$$

$$\bar{x}_2 = \partial c / \partial w_2 = \beta w_1^\alpha w_2^{\beta-1} y.$$

The more traditional problem assigned to the competitive firm by neoclassical economics is one of profit maximization. As before, suppose $y = f(x_1, \ldots, x_n)$ is the production function of the firm and w be the given vector of input prices. Then this problem can be formulated as

$$\text{Maximize} \quad \pi = pf(x_1, \ldots, x_n) - w_1 x_1 - \cdots - w_n x_n,$$

or more succinctly in matrix terms as

$$\text{Maximize} \quad \pi = pf(x) - w'x.$$

The quantities of inputs used by the firm $x_1, \ldots, x_n$ are the variables, whereas the price of output p and the input prices $w_1, \ldots, w_n$ are the parameters. In economic terms the former are the endogenous variables whereas the latter are the exogenous variables. Solving this problem gives an optimal point, say

$$x^*(p, w).$$

These functions are called the firm's **demand functions** for inputs. Again, substituting this point into the objective function gives a maximum value function

$$\pi^*(p, w) = pf(x^*(p, w)) - w'x^*(p, w).$$

This is called the **profit function** of the firm.

Example

Suppose a competitive firm is faced with the following Cobb-Douglas production function

$$Y = Ax_1^\alpha x_2^\beta, \quad \alpha > 0, \beta > 0, \quad \alpha + \beta < 1.$$

Find the firm's demands for inputs.

Our unconstrained maximization problem is

$$\text{minimize} \quad \pi = pAx_1^{\alpha}x_2^{\beta} - w_1x_1 - w_2x_2.$$

The first order conditions are

$$\pi_1 = \alpha pAx_1^{\alpha-1}x_2^{\beta} - w_1 = 0$$

$$\pi_2 = \beta pAx_1^{\alpha}x_2^{\beta-1} - w_2 = 0$$

from which we obtain

$$\frac{\alpha}{\beta}\frac{x_2}{x_1} = \frac{w_1}{w_2}$$

or $x_1 = (\alpha w_2/\beta w_1)x_2$. Upon substitution into the second equation we get

$$\beta pA\left(\frac{\alpha w_2}{\beta w_1}\right)^{\alpha} x_2^{\alpha+\beta-1} - w_2 = 0$$

so

$$x_2^{\alpha+\beta-1} = \frac{\alpha^{-\alpha}}{A\beta^{1-\alpha}}\frac{w_1^{\alpha}w_2^{1-\alpha}}{p}.$$

Thus

$$x_2^* = c_2\left(\frac{w_1^{\alpha}w_2^{1-\alpha}}{p}\right)^{1/\alpha+\beta-1}$$

$$= c_2\left(\frac{p}{w_1^{\alpha}w_2^{1-\alpha}}\right)^{1/(1-\alpha-\beta)}$$

where c_2 is a constant.

By symmetry,

$$x_1^* = c_1\left(\frac{p}{w_2^{\beta}w_1^{1-\beta}}\right)^{1/(1-\alpha-\beta)}$$

where c_1 is a constant.

Substituting x_1^* and x_2^* into π gives the profit function.

If the firm's cost function is available, then the profit maximization problem can be reformulated as

$$\text{Maximize} \quad \pi = py - c(w, y).$$

The first order condition is

$$p = \frac{\partial c}{\partial y},$$

that is, price equals marginal cost and from this we obtain the optimal point

$$y^* = y^*(p, w).$$

This is called the firm's **supply function**. Again substituting this point into the objective function we get the profit function which can now be written as

$$\pi^*(p, w) = py^*(p, w) - c(w, y^*(p, w)).$$

Example

Suppose a competitive firm's cost function is

$$c(w, y) = w_1^{\alpha/(\alpha+\beta)} w_2^{\beta/(\alpha+\beta)} y^{1/(\alpha+\beta)}$$

(recall that such a cost function arises from a Cobb-Douglas production function). Find the supply function, and the total profit function.

Let $k(w) = w_1^{\alpha/(\alpha+\beta)} w_2^{\beta/(\alpha+\beta)}$ so total profit can be written as

$$\pi = py - k(w)y^{1/(\alpha+\beta)}.$$

The first order condition arising from maximizing π with respect to y is

$$p = \frac{1}{\alpha + \beta} k(w) y^{(1-\alpha-\beta)/(\alpha+\beta)}$$

so the supply function is

$$y^* = \left(\frac{(\alpha + \beta)p}{k(w)} \right)^{(\alpha+\beta)/(1-\alpha-\beta)}$$

and the total profit function is

$$\pi^*(p, w) = p \left(\frac{(\alpha + \beta)p}{k(w)} \right)^{(\alpha+\beta)/(1-\alpha-\beta)} - k(w) \left(\frac{(\alpha + \beta)p}{k(w)} \right)^{1/(1-\alpha-\beta)}.$$

Hotelling's lemma involves the total profit function and represents our last application of the Envelope Theorem.

Theorem: Hotelling's Lemma

Let $y^*(p, w)$ be a competitive firm's supply function, $x_i^*(p, w)$ be the firm's demand function for input i, and $\pi^*(p, w)$ be the firm's total profit function.

Then

$$y^*(p, w) = \partial \pi^*(p, w)/\partial p$$

$$x_i^*(p, w) = -\partial \pi^*(p, w)/\partial w_i \quad i = 1, \ldots, n.$$

Proof

Our profit maximizing problem can be reformulated as a constraint maximization problem namely

$$\text{Maximize} \quad \pi = py - w'x$$

$$\text{subject to} \quad y = f(x)$$

and $\pi^*(p, w)$ is the maximum value function associated with this problem. The Lagrangian function is

$$L = py - w'x + \lambda(y - f(x))$$

and by the Envelope Theorem

$$\frac{\partial \pi^*}{\partial p} = \left. \frac{\partial L}{\partial p} \right|_{x^*, y^*, \lambda^*} = y^*$$

$$\frac{\partial \pi^*}{\partial w_i} = \left. \frac{\partial L}{\partial w_i} \right|_{x^*, y^*, \lambda^*} = -x_i^*.$$

In conclusion, we have seen in this section, at the risk of mathematical repetitiveness that several of the results that economists have derived from the optimal value functions that crop up in neoclassical microeconomics are merely applications of the Envelope Theorem.

Exercises for 7.5

1. A consumer has a utility function given by

$$U(x_1, x_2) = x_1^\alpha x_2^\beta, \quad \alpha > 0, \beta > 0.$$

   (i) Compute the Marshallian demand functions.
   (ii) Compute the indirect utility function.

(iii) Using the consistency properties obtain the expenditure function.

(iv) Find the Hicksian demand functions.

2. Suppose a consumer has a utility function given by

$$U(x_1, x_2) = (x_1^p + x_2^p)^{1/p} \quad \text{where } p < 1.$$

(i) Find the Hicksian demand functions.

(ii) Find the expenditure function.

(iii) Using the consistency properties find the indirect utility function.

(iv) Find the Marshallian demand functions.

3. Suppose that a competitive firm has a CES production function of the form

$$y = (x_1^\rho + x_2^\rho)^{1/\rho}.$$

(i) Find the conditional demand functions for inputs.

(ii) Find the cost function.

(iii) Verify that Shephard's Lemma holds for this example.

4. Suppose a competitive firm has the following production function

$$y = 100 x_1^{1/2} x_2^{1/4}.$$

(i) Find the conditional factor demand functions.

(ii) Find the cost function.

(iii) Verify that $\bar{\lambda}$, the value of the Lagrangian multiplier that arises in this problem is equal to marginal cost.

(iv) Given the price of output p, find the factor demand functions and the profit function.

(v) Use Hotelling's lemma to derive the firm's supply function.

Part III

Dynamic Analysis

Chapter 8

Integration

8.1 Introduction

Most of the mathematics we have learnt to this stage is directed at comparative static analysis, be it in the context of linear economic models, nonlinear economic models, or optimization problems. In comparative static analysis we are basically comparing two equilibria, the first relating to the original set of values for the exogenous variables, the second relating to the new set of values for the exogenous variables. But in comparative static analysis in economics, nothing is said about how the endogenous variables involved in the study move from the old equilibrium to the new equilibrium. Nor are questions asked about the conditions required on the parameters of our economic model to ensure that our endogenous variables converge to the new equilibrium rather than diverge away from it. Nor is the possibility of cyclical behavior discussed.

All these matters belong to the realm of dynamic analysis rather than that of comparative static analysis. The essence of dynamic analysis is the explanation and characteristics of the time paths taken by economic variables, and it is this study that occupies the last section of this book.

Continuous versus discrete time

Time is dealt with in two ways by economists. First it is regarded as a **continuous variable.** Under this concept of time economic variables are viewed as changing continuously. The mathematical tools we use in our dynamic analysis, when time is viewed this way, are taken from the study of integration and differential equations.

The second way economists view time is as a **discrete variable**. Now economic variables are regarded as changing only at the end of discrete intervals of time. Here use is made of concepts taken from the study of difference equations.

Fortunately for us, the mathematics involved in the study of differential equations is very similar to that used in difference equations. Once we have come to grips with one of these areas it is very easy, with a few words of caution, to move to the other area.

In this chapter we first study integration, a mathematical subject which arose out of the investigation of certain types of sums associated with areas under the graph of a function. One of the most remarkable theorems of calculus links integration with the reverse of differentiation. Although integration is widely used in dynamic economic analysis when time is continuous, our economic applications at the end of this chapter do not all belong to this type of analysis. Instead the first application, measuring changes in consumers' welfare resulting from price changes, calls heavily on the indirect utility function, a maximum value function arising from the theory of the consumer. Likewise, the second application belongs to the field of social welfare. These applications are included at the end of this chapter for convenience.

The next chapter, Chapter 9 looks at the main mathematical tool used in continuous dynamic analysis, namely differential equations. As always, our economic applications are left to the end of this chapter. Chapter 10 deals with difference equations and their economic applications. The last chapter of the book deals with dynamic optimization, a branch of mathematics that has become very prevalent in modern macroeconomics.

8.2   Definite Integrals

Let $y = f(x)$ be a function of a single variable and suppose for the moment that this function is **monotonically increasing**. That is,

$$x_1 > x_2 \Rightarrow f(x_1) > f(x_2).$$

The graph of such a function is presented in the following diagram:

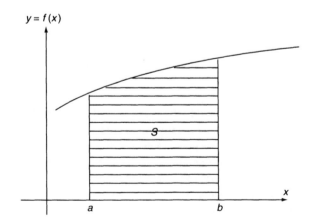

Suppose we set ourselves the task of finding that area under this graph between $x = a$ and $x = b$, that is on the **closed interval** $a \le x \le b$. Mathematically we represent this interval by $[a, b]$. The **open interval** $a < x < b$ is represented by (a, b). In the above diagram the area we are after is S. One way of doing this would be to divide the closed interval $[a, b]$ into n subintervals of length $\Delta x_1, \Delta x_2, \dots, \Delta x_n$ which need not be the same and consider the coordinates $y_1, y_2, \dots, y_{n+1}$ as in the following diagram:

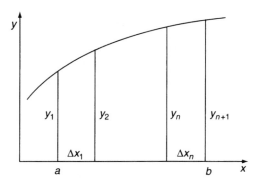

The area under the graph for the rth such subinterval clearly is between $y_r \Delta x_r$ and $y_{r+1} \Delta x_r$ as shown in the following diagram:

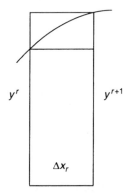

Let S_L be the sum of all such left inscribed areas and S_R be the sum of all such right inscribed areas, that is,

$$S_L = \sum_{r=1}^{n} y_r \Delta x_r, \quad S_R = \sum_{r=1}^{n} y_{r+1} \Delta x_r.$$

Then clearly

$$S_L \leq S \leq S_R,$$

and S_L and S_R come closer to the actual area the more subintervals we divide $[a, b]$ into. Suppose we then let the number of subintervals n increase indefinitely such that each $\Delta x_r \rightarrow 0$ and if when we do this

$$\lim_{n \to \infty} S_L = \lim_{n \to \infty} S_R$$

we would say that the common limit must be the area S under the graph. Moreover if this is the case we can use not only left hand heights y_r or right hand heights y_{r+1} to approximate the area, but any intermediate height $\bar{y}_r$ as well. As

$$y_r \leq \bar{y}_r \leq y_{r+1}$$

then

$$y_r \Delta x_r \leq \bar{y}_r \Delta x_r \leq y_{r+1} \Delta x_r;$$

so summing from $r = 1$ to $r = n$ we have

$$S_L \leq \bar{S} \leq S_R$$

where $\bar{S} = \sum_{r=1}^{n} \bar{y}_r \Delta x_r$. If $S_L \rightarrow S$ and $S_R \rightarrow S$ then by the **sandwich principle** $\bar{S} \rightarrow S$.

Definition
This common limit is called the **definite integral** of $f(x)$ with respect to x between the limits a and b and is denoted by

$$\int_a^b f(x)dx.$$

If such a limit exists, we say that $y = f(x)$ is **Rieman integrable** or just **integrable** over the closed interval $[a, b]$. The number a is called the **lower limit** of the definite integral and b is called the **upper limit**.

We have introduced the concept of a definite integral using, for convenience, a monotonically increasing function, but the analysis is perfectly general. If $y = f(x)$ is **monotonically decreasing**, that is

$$x_1 > x_2 \Rightarrow f(x_1) < f(x_2)$$

then all the above inequalities are reversed and our analysis still holds. Any general graph of a function of a single variable can be divided into sections where y is monotonically increasing and other sections where y is monotonically decreasing as the following figure shows:

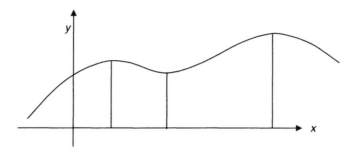

If over the interval $[a, b]$ the graph of $y = f(x)$ drops below the x axis, then areas above the x axis count positively, and areas below count negatively,

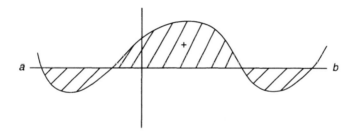

and the definite integral $\int_a^b f(x)dx$ gives the net effect.

All continuous functions are integrable. To see this, at least for the case where $y = f(x)$ is monotonically increasing, consider $S_R - S_L = \sum_{r=1}^{n} (y_{r+1} - y_r)\Delta x_r = \sum_{r=1}^{n} \Delta y_r \Delta x_r$, where $\Delta y_r = y_{r+1} - y_r$, which is nonnegative for y monotonically increasing. Let λ then be the largest of the Δy_r's. We have then

$$S_R - S_L \leq \lambda \sum_{r=1}^{n} \Delta x_r = \lambda(b - a).$$

If the function is continuous, then when $\Delta x_r \to 0$, $\Delta y_r \to 0$ for all r; so $\lambda \to 0$ as well. Thus

$$\lim_{n \to \infty} (S_R - S_L) = 0 \quad \text{or} \quad \lim_{n \to \infty} S_R = \lim_{n \to \infty} S_L, \text{ as required.}$$

From our definition of the definite integral given by

$$\int_a^b f(x)dx = \lim_{n \to \infty} \sum_{r=1}^n \bar{y}_r \Delta x_r$$

the following two properties are obvious:

(i) $\int_a^b f(x)dx = \int_a^c f(x)dx + \int_c^b f(x)dx$

(ii) For all a $\int_a^a f(x)dx = 0$.

From these two properties we can easily derive a third namely,

$$\int_a^b f(x)dx = -\int_b^a f(x)dx.$$

This property states that if we reverse the order of the limits of a definite integral we change the sign of that integral and this result is obtained by considering

$$0 = \int_a^a f(x)dx = \int_a^b f(x)dx + \int_b^a f(x)dx.$$

Hence

$$\int_a^b f(x)dx = -\int_b^a f(x)dx.$$

Definite integrals can be obtained from first principles but this requires considerable effort as the following simple example shows.

Example
Let $y = cx$ where c is a constant. Find $\int_a^b ydx$.

As y is a linear function of x it is continuous and therefore integrable. Moreover, in achieving the limit that is the definite integral, we can choose any division of the closed interval $[a, b]$ into subintervals, so let us divide the $b - a$ into n equal parts of length h. We have $nh = b - a$ and the ordinates are

$$y_1 = ca$$
$$y_2 = c(a + h)$$
$$\vdots \qquad \vdots$$
$$y_{n+1} = c(a + nh).$$

Consider the right hand sum

$$S_R = y_2h + y_3h + \cdots + y_{n+1}h = hc[(a+h) + (a+2h) + \cdots + (a+nh)]$$
$$= hc[na + h(1+2+\cdots+n)] = hc[na + hn(n+1)/2]$$
$$= c[hna + h^2n^2/2 + h^2n/2] = c[(b-a)a + (b-a)^2/2 + (b-a)h/2]$$
$$= c[ba - a^2 + b^2/2 - ab + a^2/2 + (b-a)h/2]$$
$$= c(b^2 - a^2)/2 + c(b-a)h/2.$$

Now let $n \to \infty$ so $h \to 0$. Then

$$I = \int_a^b cx\,dx = \lim_{n\to\infty} S_R = c(b^2 - a^2)/2.$$

Fortunately in the next section we show that obtaining definite integrals on the whole is a far easier process than illustrated by the above example. What is involved is essentially antidifferentiation.

Exercises for 8.2

1. Divide the closed interval $[0, 1]$ into n subintervals of length $1/n$. For each of the following functions find the Riemann sum S_R over this interval and the limit of this sum.
   (i)

   $$f(x) = x$$

   Hint: $1 + 2 + \cdots + n = \frac{1}{2}n(n+1)$.
   (ii)

   $$f(x) = x^2$$

   Hint: $1^2 + 2^2 + \cdots + n^2 = \frac{1}{6}n(n+1)(2n+1)$
   (iii)

   $$f(x) = x^3$$

   Hint: $1^3 + 2^3 + \cdots + n^3 = (1 + 2 + \cdots + n)^2$

8.3   Integration as Antidifferentiation

One of the most amazing theorems in mathematics is the so-called "Fundamental Theorem of Calculus." What the theorem does is link integration to differentiation in such a way that each process can be regarded as the reverse of the other. This theorem is best approached from another famous theorem called the Mean Value Theorem of Integral Calculus.

Suppose $y = f(x)$ is a continuous function of a single variable and suppose that on the closed interval $[a, b]$ y has a lower bound of m and an upper bound of M. Such a situation is illustrated in the following diagram:

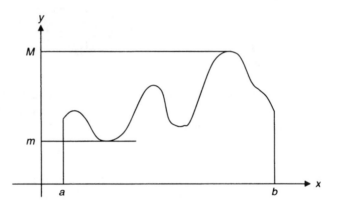

Then from our definition of I as the area under a graph it is clear that

$$m(b - a) \leq I \leq M(b - a).$$

It follows that there exists a $\bar{y}$ between m and M such that

$$I = \bar{y}(b - a)$$

and as the function is continuous, y must take on this value for some $x \in (a, b)$. Now let $\bar{y} = f(c)$ where $c \in [a, b]$. Then we have $f(c) = 1/(b - a) \int_a^b f(x)dx$.

We have proved the following theorem:

Mean value theorem
Let $y = f(x)$ be a continuous function defined on the closed interval $[a, b]$. Then there exists some $c \in [a, b]$ such that

$$f(c) = \frac{1}{b - a} \int_a^b f(x)dx.$$

The Mean Value Theorem, though interesting in its own right, is valuable to us in that it provides a simple proof for the Fundamental Theorem of Calculus.

Consider $I(u) = \int_a^u y\,dx$ and suppose we vary u to $u + \Delta u$. Then, using the properties of definite integrals

$$I(u + \Delta u) = \int_a^{u+\Delta u} y\,dx = \int_a^u y\,dx + \int_u^{u+\Delta u} y\,dx = I(u) + \Delta I$$

where $\Delta I = I(u + \Delta u) - I(u) = \int_u^{u+\Delta u} y\,dx$.

The situation we are confronted with here is illustrated in the following diagram:

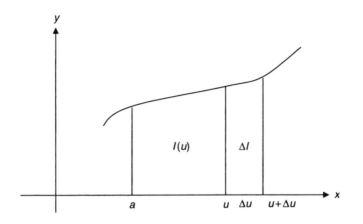

If $y = f(x)$ is continuous then by the Mean Value Theorem

$$\Delta I = \bar{y}\Delta u$$

where $\bar{y} = f(c)$ for some c between u and $u + \Delta u$. Thus

$$\frac{\Delta I}{\Delta u} = \bar{y}.$$

Now let $\Delta u \to 0$ so $\bar{y} \to y(u)$. We then have

$$\frac{dI}{du} = \lim_{\Delta u \to 0} \frac{\Delta I}{\Delta u} = y(u), \quad \text{or} \quad \frac{d}{du}\int_a^u f(x)\,dx = f(u). \qquad (8.1)$$

Note that it is of no importance which variable is used to signify the independent variable of a functional relationship. That is, we can write the functional relationship $y = f(\cdot)$ as $y = f(x)$ or $y = f(s)$, or use any other letter we like.

Given that this is the case, it is more conventional to write the relationship given by equation (8.1) as

$$\frac{d}{dx}\int_a^x f(s)ds = f(x).$$

Fundamental theorem of calculus

Let $I(x) = \int_a^x f(s)ds$, and suppose $y = f(s)$ is a continuous function of a single variable. Then

$$\frac{dI(x)}{dx} = f(x).$$

To show how this theorem helps us in the evaluation of definite integrals, suppose that we have a function $F(x)$ such that

$$\frac{d}{dx}F(x) = f(x)$$

for all x. But by the Fundamental Theorem of Calculus $dI(x)/dx = f(x)$.
Hence

$$\frac{d}{dx}(I(x) - F(x)) = 0$$

for all x so $I(x) = F(x) + c$ where c is a constant. Now $I(a) = \int_a^a f(s)ds = 0$ so $c = -F(a)$. We have then that

$$\int_a^x f(s)ds = F(x) - F(a).$$

If we change our notation somewhat by letting the upper limit be b instead of x and we replace s by x we have the standard form of this result, namely,

$$\int_a^b f(x)dx = F(b) - F(a) \quad \text{where} \quad \frac{dF(x)}{dx} = f(x).$$

We see then that the problem of evaluating a definite integral is fundamentally one of antidifferentiation: We need to find a function $F(x)$ such that $dF(x)/dx = f(x)$.

Moreover, any such $F(x)$ will do. Suppose we have found two such functions $F_1(x)$ and $F_2(x)$; so $(d/dx)F_1(x) = (d/dx)F_2(x) = f(x)$ for all x. It follows that $(d/dx)(F_1(x) - F_2(x)) = 0$; so $F_1(x) = F_2(x) + k$ where k is a constant.

If $F_1(x)$ is used to evaluate the definite integral we have $\int_a^b f(x)dx = F_2(b) + k - F_2(a) - k = F_2(b) - F_2(a)$ which is the same result if we used $F_2(x)$ to evaluate the integral.

A convenient notation that is often used when dealing with definite integrals is the following:

Notation

$$F(x)|_a^b = F(b) - F(a).$$

Examples
(i) Find the area between a and b under the graph of the linear function $y = cx$.
    This area is $\int_a^b cxdx$ and as $(d/dx)(cx^2/2) = cx$ we have $\int_a^b cx = (cx^2/2)|_a^b = (c/2)(b^2 - a^2)$.
    Finding this area is now considerably easier than before when we used first principles.
(ii) Graph the function $y = x^2 - 4x$, shading the areas between this graph and the x axis over the closed intervals $[0, 4]$ and $[4, 6]$. Show that these areas are $-32/3$ and $32/3$, respectively. Confirm that the area on the closed interval $[0, 6]$ is 0.

The function cuts the x axis at $x = 0$ and $x = 4$ and has a minimum at $x = 2$ as shown in the following diagram:

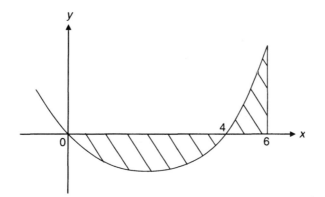

The area over the closed interval $[0, 4]$ is $\int_0^4 x^2 - 4xdx = (x^3/3) - 2x^2|_0^4 = -32/3$

The area over the closed interval $[4, 6]$ is $\int_4^6 x^2 - 4xdx = (x^3/3) - 2x^2|_4^6 = 32/3$

The area over the closed interval $[0, 6]$ is $\int_0^6 (x^3/3) - 2x^2|_0^6 = 72 - 72 = 0$

Exercises for 8.3
1. Find the area between the graph and the x axis for the function $y = 16 - x^2$.
2. Find the area between the graph and the x axis for each of the following functions over the indicated closed intervals.
    (i) $y = x^{1/2}$ $x \in [1, 9]$
    (ii) $y = 7 + x^4$ $x \in [0, 1]$
    (iii) $y = (x + 1)^{3/2}$ $x \in [-1, 0]$
    (iv) $y = x(5x^2 + 2)^3$ $x \in [1, 2]$
    (v) $y = (x + 1)^{-2}$ $x \in [0, 2]$.

8.4   Indefinite Integrals

We have seen in the previous section that in evaluating the definite integral $\int_a^b f(x)dx$ we use any function $F(x)$ such that $dF(x)/dx = f(x)$.

The indefinite integral denoted by $\int f(x)dx$ is defined as $F(x) + c$, where c is an arbitrary constant.

In obtaining the indefinite integral we are essentially performing antidifferentiation. We are looking for the class of functions $F(x) + c$ whose derivative is $f(x)$. Referring to the rules of differentiation yields the following table of results for indefinite integrals.

$$\int af(x)dx = a\int f(x)dx$$

$$\int [f(x) + g(x)]dx = \int f(x)dx + \int g(x)dx$$

$$\int x^n dx = \frac{x^{n+1}}{n+1} + c \quad n \neq -1$$

$$\int e^{f(x)}f'(x)dx = e^{f(x)} + c$$

$$\int \frac{1}{f(x)}f'(x)dx = \log f(x) + c$$

$$\int (f(x))^n f'(x)dx = \frac{1}{n+1}(f(x))^{n+1} \quad n \neq -1$$

Example
   (i) $\int (4x^3 + x^{2/3} + 4/x)dx = x^4 + 3/5x^{5/3} + 4\log x + c$.
   (ii) $\int e^{4x^2+6x}(4x + 3)dx = 1/2e^{4x^2+6x} + c$.
   (iii) $\int (x^4 + 3x^2 + 2)^2(2x^3 + 3x)dx = \frac{1}{6}(x^4 + 3x^2 + 2)^3 + c$.

The rules presented in the above table should not be learnt, as all they do is remind us of ways of looking for the antiderivative of a function. Certainly they accommodate many of the type of functions we encounter in economics. However, indefinite integrals can be difficult to find and many textbooks in undergraduate calculus contain chapters on tricks for doing this. Fortunately for us, most of these types of integrals rarely occur in economics. But two results that are useful for economists are studied in the next section.

Integration by substitution and by parts

Suppose $dy/dx = f(x)$. Then if we take the indefinite integral of both sides we have $\int (dy/dx)dx = \int f(x)dx$ or $y = \int f(x)dx$ which we know to be true.

Now consider the chain rule of differentiation. Let $y = y(x)$ and $x = x(u)$; so y is a function of u through x. The chain rule gives

$$\frac{dy}{du} = \frac{dy}{dx}\frac{dx}{du} = f(x(u))\frac{dx}{du}.$$

Taking the indefinite integral of both sides gives $y = \int f(x(u))(dx/du)du$. This rule is called **integration by substitution**.

Examples
(i) Compute $I = \int (1 + x^3)^5 x^2 dx$.

Let $u = 1 + x^3$ so $du/dx = 3x^2$ and treating the derivative as the ratio of differentials we have $du = 3x^2 dx$. Thus $I = \int (u^5/3)du = u^6/18 + c = (1 + x^3)^6/18 + c$.

(ii) Compute $I = \int \cos^3 x \, dx$.

Let $s = \sin x$ so $ds/dx = \cos x$ and $ds = \cos x \, dx$.

We can then write $I = \int \cos^2 x \cos x \, dx = \int (1 - s^2)ds$ as $\cos^2 x + \sin^2 x = 1$.

It follows that $I = s - s^3/3 + c = \sin x - (\sin x)^3/3 + c$.

This technique can also be used to evaluate definite integrals provided dx/du does not change sign over the range of integration given by the upper and lower limits.

Example
Compute the definite integral $I = \int_0^3 (x^2/\sqrt{1+x})dx$.

Let $u = \sqrt{1 + x}$; so $u^2 = 1 + x$, and $dx/du = 2u$ and $dx = 2udu$. As x ranges from 0 to 3, u ranges from 1 to 2 so dx/du does not change sign. Thus

$$I = \int_1^2 \frac{(u^2-1)^2}{u} 2u\,du = \int_1^2 (2u^4 - 4u^2 + 2)du = \left(\frac{2u^5}{5} - \frac{4}{3}u^3 + 2u\right)\Big|_1^2$$
$$= \frac{62}{5} - \frac{28}{3} + 2.$$

Suppose now instead of the chain rule we consider the product rule for two functions $u(x)$ and $v(x)$, which is $(uv)' = u'v + v'u$. Taking the indefinite integral of both sides we have $uv = \int u'v\,dx + \int v'u\,dx$ or $\int u'v\,dx = uv - \int v'u\,dx$. This result is called **integration by parts**.

Example
Find $I = \int xe^{-x}dx$
    Let $v = x$ and $u' = e^{-x}$. Then we have

$$I = -xe^{-x} + \int e^{-x}dx = -xe^{-x} - e^{-x}.$$

We finish this section with a last useful procedure. Suppose

$$\frac{dy}{dx} = f(x). \tag{8.2}$$

Then we know that

$$y = \int f(x)dx. \tag{8.3}$$

But from Section 5.5 of Chapter 5 we know that a derivative can be regarded as the ratio of differentials so we can write equation (8.2) as

$$dy = f(x)dx \tag{8.4}$$

Suppose we insert "$\int$" on both sides of equation (8.4). We get $\int dy = \int f(x)dx$ or $y = \int f(x)dx$. That is, starting with an equation involving differentials in y and x, we can solve for y by integrating.

Exercises for 8.4
1. Find the indefinite integral of each of the following functions:

(i) $9x^{-5} - 7x^2$ (ii) $(1 + x)^{-1/2}$

(iii) $3xe^{x^2}$ (iv) $(x^3 + 2)/x^6$

(v) $x^{1/2} - x^{-1/2}$ (vi) $(x^2 + 2x + 7)^{3/2}(x + 1)$

(vii) $(-10x^{3/2} + 6x^{1/2})/(x^{5/2} - x^{3/2})^2$ (viii) $x^4/(1 - x^5)^{1/2}$.

2. Use integration by substitution to work out the following integrals:

(i) $\int x^2 \sqrt{x + 1}\, dx$ (ii) $\int x^2/\sqrt{3x + 2}\, dx$ (iii) $\int_0^2 x/\sqrt{4x + 14}\, dx$.

3. Consider the definite integral

$$\int_{-1}^{1} 2x(x^2 + 1)\, dx.$$

Could we compute this integral by making the substitution $u = x^2 + 1$? What happens if we try?

4. Use integration by parts to evaluate the following integrals:

(i) $\int x \cos x\, dx$ (ii) $\int x \log 3x\, dx$

(iii) $\int xe^x\, dx$ (iv) $\int x(1 + x)^{1/2}\, dx$

(v) $\int \log x\, dx$ (vi) $\int x^3 e^{3x}\, dx$

(vii) $\int e^{ax} \sin bx\, dx$.

8.5   Further Considerations

Improper integrals

Our discussion of integration has been confined to the case where the function $y = f(x)$ is bounded over a finite interval $[a, b]$. Using limits however, we can extend our definition of a definite integral to the case where the upper bound and/or the lower bound is ∞ or $-\infty$, respectively.

Such integrals are called **improper** integrals. As an illustration consider

$$\int_a^\infty f(x)\, dx = \lim_{b \to \infty} \int_a^b f(x)\, dx.$$

Example

$$\int_a^\infty e^{-2x} dx = \lim_{b \to \infty} \int_a^b e^{-2x} dx = \lim_{b \to \infty} \left[-\frac{1}{2} e^{-2x} \Big|_a^b \right]$$

$$= \lim_{b \to \infty} \left[-\frac{1}{2} e^{-2b} + \frac{1}{2} e^{-2a} \right] = \frac{1}{2} e^{-2a}.$$

If $f(x)$ is continuous for $a \le x < \infty$[1] we say $\int_a^\infty f(x)dx$ **converges** to finite B if and only if $\lim_{b \to \infty} \int_a^b f(x)dx = B$. Otherwise we say the improper integral is **divergent**. Similarly if $f(x)$ is continuous for $-\infty < x \le b$, $\int_{-\infty}^b f(x)dx$ **converges** to finite A if $\lim_{a \to -\infty} \int_a^b f(x)dx = A$. If both $\int_a^\infty f(x)dx$ and $\int_{-\infty}^b f(x)dx$ are convergent then their sum is denoted by $\int_{-\infty}^\infty f(x)dx$.

Another type of improper integral occurs when the integrand becomes infinite in the range of integration. For example in the definite integral $\int_0^1 1/(1-x)^2 dx$ the integral is infinite at $x = 1$. If $f(x)$ is continuous for $a \le x < b$ and becomes infinite at $x = b$ we say $\int_a^b f(x)dx$ is **convergent** if and only if $\lim_{\varepsilon \to 0} \int_a^{b-\varepsilon} f(x)dx$ exists. Otherwise it is divergent. Similarly if $f(x)$ is continuous for $a < x \le b$ and become infinite at $x = a$, then the improper integral $\int_a^b f(x)dx$ is convergent if and only if $\lim_{\varepsilon \to 0} \int_{a+\varepsilon}^b f(x)dx$ exists. Finally if $f(x)$ is continuous for the closed interval $[a, b]$, but becomes infinite at $x = c$ for $a < c < b$, we consider $\int_a^b f(x)dx = \int_a^c f(x)dx + \int_c^b f(x)dx$ and our integral is convergent if the two integrals on the right hand side are convergent.

Examples

(i) Is $\int_0^1 1/(1-x)^2 dx$ convergent or divergent?

Consider

$$\int_0^{1-\varepsilon} \frac{dx}{(1-x)^2} = \frac{1}{1-x} \Big|_0^{1-\varepsilon} = \frac{1}{\varepsilon} - 1.$$

Therefore $\lim_{\varepsilon \to 0} \int_0^{1-\varepsilon} dx/(1-x)^2 = \infty$ and our integral is divergent.

(ii) Evaluate $\int_0^1 1/\sqrt{1-x}\, dx$.

We consider

$$\int_0^{1-\varepsilon} \frac{dx}{\sqrt{1-x}} = -2\sqrt{1-x} \Big|_0^{1-\varepsilon} = 2\sqrt{\varepsilon} + 2.$$

Thus $\int_0^1 dx/\sqrt{1-x} = \lim_{\varepsilon \to 0}(2\sqrt{\varepsilon} + 2) = 2$.

Multiple integration

Our discussion can also be generalized to the case where we are integrating functions of many variables. For example $\int_c^d \int_a^b f(x, y)dxdy = \int_c^d (\int_a^b f(x, y)dx)dy$ is an instruction to us to first integrate the function $f(x, y)$ with respect to x while holding y as a constant and then evaluate this integral between a and b.

[1] This interval is denoted by $[a, \infty)$. Likewise $-\infty < x \le b$ is denoted by $(-\infty, b]$.

This leaves us with a function in y. We now integrate this function with respect to y and evaluate the integral between c and d.

Example

$$\int_{2}^{3} \int_{1}^{2} 3x^2 y\, dx\, dy = \int_{2}^{3} x^3 y \Big|_{x=1}^{x=2} dy = \int_{2}^{3} 7y\, dy = 3.5y^2 \Big|_{2}^{3} = 17.5.$$

It is also possible for the limits of the first integration to involve functions of the second variable, as the following example illustrates.

Example

$$\int_{0}^{1/3} \int_{0}^{(1-3x)/2} (3x + 2y)^2 dy\, dx = \int_{0}^{1/3} (3x + 2y)^3 / 6 \Big|_{y=0}^{y=\frac{1-3x}{2}} dx$$

$$= \int_{0}^{1/3} \left(\frac{1}{6} - \frac{9}{2}x^3 \right) dx = \frac{1}{6}x - \frac{9}{8}x^4 \Big|_{0}^{1/3} = \frac{1}{24}.$$

Exercises for 8.5

1. Work out whether the following improper integrals are convergent or divergent.

   (i) $\int_{0}^{\infty} e^x\, dx$ (ii) $\int_{0}^{\infty} e^{-x}\, dx$

   (iii) $\int_{0}^{1} x^{-\frac{1}{2}}\, dx$ (iv) $\int_{0}^{1} x^{-2}\, dx$

   (v) $\int_{-1}^{2} x^{-2}\, dx$

2. Work out the following multiple integrals:

   (i) $\int_{1}^{2} \int_{0}^{1} x^2 + xy\, dx\, dy$ (ii) $\int_{0}^{1} \int_{1}^{2} x^2 + y^2\, dy\, dx$

   (iii) $\int_{0}^{1} \int_{0}^{x} x^2 + y^2 dy\, dx$ (iv) $\int_{0}^{1} \int_{0}^{y^2} (3x + 2y)^2 dx\, dy.$

8.6   Economic Applications

Although economic applications of integrations are less abundant than those of differentiation, they still abound and in this section we look at the more common examples.

Measures of changes in consumers' welfare resulting from price changes

Let $x(p, y)$ be a consumer's Marshallian demand function for a particular good. Here for convenience we have dropped the star off the x and we imagine the prices of all other goods remaining constant so we can regard this demand function as a function of price p and income y alone. Following the Walrasian tradition we can graph this function for a given y as in the following diagram:

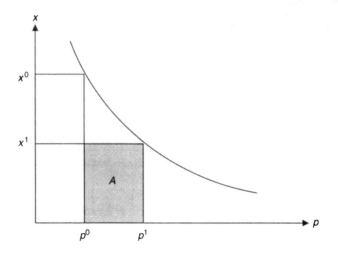

Suppose the price of the good rises from p^0 to p^1. Originally to buy x^1 units of the good, our consumer had to pay $x^1 p^0$. Now the expenditure required to buy this amount is $x^1 p^1$, so the area A represents a welfare loss accruing on these units to the consumer on a result of the price rise. Suppose we divide the price rise into a number of smaller rises say $\Delta p_1, \Delta p_2, \ldots, \Delta p_n$ and suppose after each rise the quantities demanded are $x_2, \ldots, x_{n+1}$ where $x_{n+1} = x^1$. Diagrammatically we have

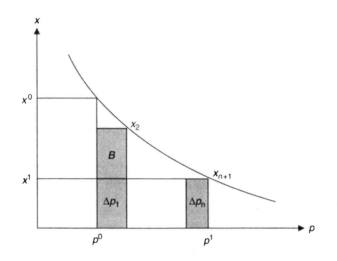

Then more accurately, the loss in consumer welfare resulting from the price rise is the sum of the areas like B generated by this process. That is $S_R = \sum_{r=1}^{n} x_{r+1} \Delta p_r$.

To get an even more accurate measure of the welfare loss we would continue to make these price rises increasingly smaller. From our work in Section 8.3 of this chapter we know that in the limit we obtain the definite integral

$$CS = \int_{p^0}^{p^1} x(p, y) dp.$$

This is called the **loss in consumer's surplus** resulting from the price rise.

Other measures can be used. The **compensation variation** C is the extra income the consumer needs to leave him or her just as well off in utility terms as before the price rise. Let $V(p, y)$ be the consumer's indirect utility function, remembering that we are holding all other prices constant. Then C is defined by

$$V(p^1, y + C) = V(p^0, y).$$

The **equivalence variation** E, is the amount of income we would have to take away from the consumer at the original price level p^0 to leave him or her at the new reduced utility level. That is, E is defined by

$$V(p^1, y) = V(p^0, y - E).$$

Definite comparisons can be made with regards to these three measures of welfare loss and again, integration is used in obtaining these comparisons. We start by appealing to the consistency properties discussed in Section 7.5 of Chapter 7 which allows us to write

$$e(p^1, V(p^1, y + C)) = y + C \quad \text{and} \quad e(p^0, V(p^0, y)) = y$$

where e is the consumer's expenditure function. It follows then that

$$C = e(p^1, V^0) - e(p^0, V^0)$$

where

$$V^0 = V(p^1, y + C) = V(p^0, y).$$

But by Shephard's Lemma

$$\frac{d}{dp}e(p,\,V^0) = \bar{x}(p,\,V^0),^2 \qquad (8.5)$$

where $\bar{x}$ is the Hicksian demand function for the good. Taking the definite integral of both sides of equation (8.5) we have

$$\int_{p^0}^{p^1} \bar{x}(p,\,V^0)dp = \int_{p^0}^{p^1} \frac{d}{dp}e(p,\,V^0)dp = e(p^1,V^0) - e(p^0,V^0) = C.$$

By a similar argument we obtain that

$$E = \int_{p^0}^{p^1} \bar{x}(p,\,V^1)dp$$

where

$$V^1 = V(p^1,y) = V(p^0,y - E).$$

To summarize what we have achieved so far, consumer surplus CS measures an area under the Marshallian demand function. Compensation variation C and Equivalence variation E measure the areas under the Hicksian demand functions evaluated at different utility levels. To complete our comparison, recall from Section 7.5 of Chapter 7 that Slutsky's equation can be expressed in terms of the Marshallian demand function and Hicksian demand function as follows:

$$\frac{\partial x}{\partial p} = \frac{\partial \bar{x}}{\partial p} - x\frac{\partial x}{\partial y}.$$

If the good in question is a normal good, then $\partial x/\partial y > 0$ and as x is greater than zero, $\partial x/\partial p < \partial \bar{x}/\partial p$. That is, the slope of the Marshallian demand function is less than that of the Hicksian demand function. For a non-Giffen good these slopes are negative, so diagrammatically we have the following

---

[2]We still insist that all other variables are held constant so the partial derivative of Shephard's Lemma becomes a total derivative.

situation:

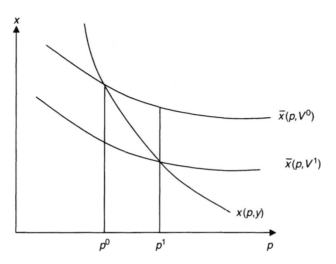

Clearly from this diagram

$$E < CS < C.$$

For a price **fall** from p^1 to p^o, the **gain** in consumer surplus is

$$CS = \int_{p^o}^{p^1} x(p, y)dp.$$

The compensation variation is the amount C we have to subtract from the consumer's income to leave him or her at the old level of maximum utility under the lower price, whereas the equivalence variation E is the amount we have to add to income to leave him or her at the new level of maximum utility, under the old price.

Lorenz Curve and the Gini coefficient

The Lorenz Curve is concerned with the inequality present in an income distribution. For a given family income level Y, let x be the proportion of families, expressed as a number between 0 and 1, whose income is less than or equal to Y. Similarly, let y be the proportion of total families income, again expressed as a number between 0 and 1, that these families earn. For example, according to the US Bureau of Statistics, in 1997 20 percent of families earned incomes annually less than $21,000 and these families received 4 percent of total family

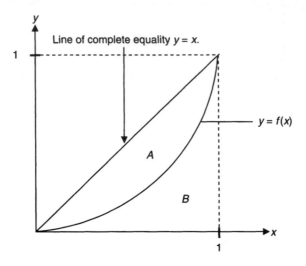

Figure 8.1　The Lorenz Curve.

incomes. For $Y = 21,000$, $x = 0.2$ and $y = 0.04$. If we consider all possible levels of family income, this gives us a sequence of x values with a corresponding sequence of y values. Suppose these two sequences can be expressed by the functional relationship $y = f(x)$. If we graph this function we obtain the **Lorenz Curve** as illustrated in Figure 8.1.

In this diagram, complete equality of income distributions is represented by the line $y = x$, and a measure of the inequality of the distribution would be how far the Lorenz curve deviates from this line. One such measure is the **Gini coefficient** G which is defined by

$$G = A/(A + B) = \frac{(A + B) - B}{A + B}.$$

As $A + B$ is the area of a right angled triangle with base 1 and height 1, $A + B = \frac{1}{2}$ so

$$G = 1 - 2B.$$

But B is the area under the Lorenz Curve between $x = 0$ and $x = 1$ so

$$B = \int_0^1 f(x)dx.$$

Present values

We have stressed that time in economics can be regarded in two ways, as a discrete variable or a continuous variable. In the first case we regard economic variables as changing only at the end of discrete integrals of time say $t = 0, 1, 2, 3, \ldots$. In the latter case we regard our variables as changing continuously. Integration is relevant to this second case but by way of contrast we consider both cases in this section.

Suppose that $x(t)$ is an economic variable where time t is regarded as a discrete variable. We say that $x(t)$ grows at a **constant proportionate rate** g if

$$\frac{x(t+1) - x(t)}{x(t)} = g, t = 0, 1, \ldots .$$

Let $x_0 = x(0)$. Then a little arithmetic shows that

$$x(1) = x_0(1 + g)$$
$$x(2) = x_0(1 + g)^2$$
$$\vdots \qquad \vdots$$

so in general

$$x(t) = x_0(1 + g)^t, \quad t = 0, 1, \ldots .$$

Suppose now an economic project promises cash flows given by $x(t)$, $t = 0, 1, \ldots$. The **present value** of the cash flow at period t, if an interest rate of g is applicable over the time horizon is

$$x_0(t) = \frac{x(t)}{(1 + g)^t}$$

and the present value of the entire project would be

$$PV = \sum_{t=0}^{T} \frac{x(t)}{(1 + g)^t}.$$

Consider next the case where $x(t)$ is an economic variable and we regard time as a continuous variable. We say that $x(t)$ is **growing exponentially** at growth rate g if

$$(dx/dt)/x = g.$$

Splitting the derivative into differentials we have

$$\frac{1}{x}dx = g\,dt$$

then taking the integral of both sides gives

$$\int \frac{1}{x}dx = \int g\,dt$$

so $\log x = tg + c$ which gives $x(t) = e^{tg+c}$.
Let $x_0 = x(0)$ then $x_0 = e^c$ and we can write

$$x(t) = x_0 e^{tg}.$$

Imagine an economic project that yields continuous returns given by $x(t)$ for $0 \le t \le T$. The **present value** of the flow at time t is

$$x_0 = x(t)e^{-tg}$$

and the present value of the entire project would be

$$PV = \int_0^T x(t)e^{-tg}\,dt.$$

Comparing the two cases we see that for continuous time a definite integral plays the same role as the summation of discrete time.[3]

Exercises for 8.6

1. Suppose the consumer seeks to maximize his or her utility function $U(x_1, x_2) = x_1\,x_2$ subject to the budget constraint $p_1\,x_1 + p_2\,x_2 = Y$.
   (i) Find the Marshallian demand functions.
   (ii) Find the indirect utility function.
   (iii) Suppose the price of good 1 rises from 1 to 1.2. Compute the resultant loss in consumer welfare using consumer surplus CS, compensating variation C, and equivalence variation E.
   (iv) Show that for this example

$$E < CS < C.$$

---

[3]We could expect this as we know that the definite integral is the limit of a Riemann sum.

2. Consider the indirect utility function

$$V(\boldsymbol{p}, y) = (y - \sum_{i=1}^{n} \gamma_i p_i) / \prod_{i=1}^{n} p_i^{\beta_i}$$

where $\sum_{i=1}^{n} \beta_i = 1$, $\beta_i > 0$ and we used the notation $\prod_{i=1}^{n} p_i^{\beta_i} = p_1^{\beta_1} p_2^{\beta_2} \cdots p_n^{\beta_n}$.

  (i) Use Roy's identity to obtain the Marshallian demand functions.
 (ii) Suppose that the price of good 1 increases by 10% while all other prices remain fixed. Using consumer surplus find the resultant loss in consumer welfare.
(iii) Use the indirect utility function to find two alternate measures of this welfare loss.

Chapter 9

Continuous Time: Differential Equations

9.1 Definitions

In dynamic economic analysis where time is regarded as a continuous variable the use of differential equations is pertinent.

A **differential equation** is one that involves derivatives. For example

$$\frac{dy}{dx} = x + 5 \tag{9.1}$$

$$\frac{d^2y}{dx^2} + 3x\frac{dy}{dx} + 2y = 0 \tag{9.2}$$

$$\frac{\partial^2z}{\partial x^2} + \frac{\partial^2z}{\partial y^2} = x^2 + y \tag{9.3}$$

If the derivatives involved are partial derivatives then the equation is a **partial differential equation,** otherwise it is called an **ordinary differential equation**. Equation (9.3) is a partial differential equation whereas equations (9.1) and (9.2) are ordinary differential equations. The **order** of a differential equation is the order of the highest derivative which occurs in the equation. Equation (9.1) has order 1, whereas equations (9.2) and (9.3) are of order 2. The differential equation is **linear** if the equation is linear in the derivatives and y. For example,

$$\left(\frac{d^2y}{dx}\right)^2 + 3\frac{dy}{dx} - y = 0$$

is a nonlinear differential equation, whereas equations (9.1), (9.2), and (9.3) are all linear. In general the **nth order linear ordinary differential equation** can be written as

$$\frac{d^ny}{dx^n} + a_1\frac{d^{n-1}y}{dx^{n-1}} + \cdots + a_{n-1}\frac{dy}{dx} + a_ny = f(x) \tag{9.4}$$

where $a_1, \ldots, a_n$ are constants or functions in x. If these coefficients are in fact constants, we say we have a **differential equation with constant coefficients.**

The **homogeneous form** of the differential equation given by equation (9.4) occurs when we put zero in place of $f(x)$ on the right hand side.

When we solve a differential equation, we find y as a function of x that satisfies the equation in the most general manner possible. Straightaway we have the following theorem concerning this general solution.

Theorem
The general solution of an ordinary differential equation of order n, linear or otherwise, gives y as a function of x involving exactly n arbitrary constants.

That is, $y = y(x; c_1, \ldots, c_n)$, where $c_1, \ldots, c_n$ are arbitrary constants.

The proof of this theorem is not given though it seems plausible enough. In the process of differentiation, a constant disappears with every derivative we take. When we solve the differential equation, we essentially reverse the process of differentiation but arbitrary constants now appear in place of those lost.

Sometimes in the problem we have in hand, we are given **initial conditions** which allow us to assign particular values to the arbitrary constants to obtain what is known as a **particular solution** to the differential equation.

In this course we mainly restrict our study to the class of differential equations most used in dynamic economic analysis. This class consists of ordinary linear differential equations of first and second order. The variable y will represent some economic variable and x will represent continuous time.

9.2   Linear Differential Equations

A convenient notation

Let $D, D^2, D^3 \ldots$ replace

$$\frac{d}{dx}, \frac{d^2}{dx}, \frac{d^3}{dx^3} \ldots$$

Under this notation, for example

$$D(x^3 - 5x^2 + x + 1) = 3x^2 - 10x + 1$$
$$D^2(x^3 - 5x^2 + x + 1) = 6x - 10,$$
$$D^3(x^3 - 5x^2 + x + 1) = 6.$$

D then is an instruction to differentiate whatever is to the right of it. It is called a **mathematical operator.** The convenience of introducing such an operator is that within certain limits we can treat them algebraically as we would do any other variable. Under this notation we can write the general nth order ordinary linear differential equation as

$$D^n y + a_1 D^{n-1} y + \cdots + a_{n-1} Dy + a_n y = f(x)$$

where $a_1, \ldots, a_n$ are constants or functions of x.

That is, $(D^n + a_1 D^{n-1} + \cdots + a_n)y = f(x)$ or

$$P(D)y = f(x)$$

where $P(D) = D^n + a_1 D^{n-1} + \cdots + a_{n-1}D + a_n$, is a new operator that is, a polynominal of degree n in the old operator D. This new operator, like the old one, is a **linear operator**. That is it satisfies the following conditions:

(i) $P(D)(y_1 + y_2) = P(D)y_1 + P(D)y_2$
(ii) $P(D)(cy) = cP(D)y$ where c is an arbitrary constant.

Using these properties we can prove the following:

Theorem
Let y_p be a particular solution to the linear differential equation $P(D)y = f(x)$ and let y_c be the general solution to the corresponding homogeneous form $P(D)y = 0$. Then the general solution to the nonhomogeneous equation $P(D)y = f(x)$ is $y = y_c + y_p$.

Proof
As $P(D)$ is a linear operator $P(D)(y_c + y_p) = P(D)y_c + P(D)y_p$. But $P(D)y_p = f(x), y_p$ being for particular solution of the nonhomogeneous equation, and $P(D)y_c = 0, y_c$ being the general solution of the homogeneous equation. Hence

$$P(D)(y_c + y_p) = f(x).$$

Moreover this is the most general solution as it has the proper number of arbitrary constants through y_c.

In what follows, we restrict our study, with one exception, to first and second order linear differential equations with constant coefficients.

9.3   First Order Linear Differential Equations with Constant Coefficients

This is the simplest differential equation we can study. It is of the form

$$\frac{dy}{dx} + ay = f(x), \tag{9.5}$$

where a is a constant. The homogeneous case is easily solved as follows: from

$$\frac{dy}{dx} + ay = 0,$$

we have

$$\frac{1}{y}\frac{dy}{dx} = -a$$

or

$$\frac{d \log y}{dx} = -a.$$

Integrating both sides gives

$$\log y = -ax + k,$$

with k an arbitrary constant. Taking antilogs gives the general solution

$$y = ce^{-ax},$$

where c is the arbitrary constant e^k.

Suppose at time $x = 0$ we are given the initial condition that $y(0) = y_0$ say. Then the particular solution that satisfies this initial condition is found with $y(0) = y_0 = ce^0 = c$.

That is,

$$y = y_0 e^{-ax}$$

The nonhomogeneous case takes a little more work. What we want is a particular solution to the nonhomogeneous equation. Adding this to the general solution of the homogeneous equation gives the general solution to the nonhomogenous equation. Finding a particular solution requires appealing to the Fundamental Theorem of Calculus studied in Section of 8.3 of Chapter 8.

Theorem

A particular solution to the nonhomogeneous equation given by equation (9.5) is

$$y(x) = e^{-ax} \int_0^x e^{as}f(s)ds.$$

Proof

Write $y(x) = e^{-ax}u(x)$ where $u(x) = \int_0^x e^{as}f(s)ds$.

Then

$$\frac{dy}{dx} = -ae^{-ax}u(x) + e^{-ax}\frac{du}{dx}$$
$$= -ay + e^{-ax}e^{ax}f(x),$$

by the Fundamental Theorem of Calculus.
Hence

$$\frac{dy}{dx} = -ay + f(x)$$

that is,

$$\frac{dy}{dx} + ay = f(x) \text{ as required.}$$

It follows then that the general solution to the differential equation

$$\frac{dy}{dx} + ay = f(x)$$

is

$$y(x) = ce^{-ax} + e^{-ax}\int_0^x e^{as}f(s)ds,$$

where c is an arbitrary constant.

Example
Find the general solution to

$$\frac{dy}{dx} + 6y = e^x$$

given the initial condition that $y = y_0$ at $x = 0$.
The general solution to the homogeneous form given the initial condition is

$$y = y_0 e^{-6x}.$$

A particular solution to the nonhomogeneous equation is found from

$$y = e^{-6x} \int_0^x e^{6s} ds$$

$$= e^{-6x} \left[\tfrac{1}{8} e^{8s} \right]_0^x$$

$$= \tfrac{1}{8} e^{-6x} (e^{8x} - e^0)$$

$$= \tfrac{1}{8} (e^{2x} - e^{-6x}).$$

The general solution to the nonhomogeneous equation is then

$$y = \left(y_0 - \tfrac{1}{8} \right) e^{-6x} + e^{2x}/8.$$

A second method that allows us to find a particular solution to the nonhomogeneous equation is the method of undetermined coefficients studied in Section 9.5.

A special case

A special case that deserves our particular attention because of its application in dynamic economic analysis is

$$\frac{dy}{dx} + ay = k, \quad \text{where } k \text{ is a constant.}$$

A particular solution to this equation is easily found by letting $y = \bar{y}$ a constant. We have $d\bar{y}/dx = 0$ and $a\bar{y} = k$. So

$$\bar{y} = \frac{k}{a}$$

is a particular solution.

Notice that when y reaches $\bar{y}$ it is no longer changing so in economic terms $\bar{y}$ represents a **potential equilibrium** value. We say potential as we are not sure whether the time path for y will converge to $\bar{y}$.

If we are given $y(0)$ then the general solution to the nonhomogeneous equation is

$$y(x) = \bar{y} + y(0)e^{-ax}.$$

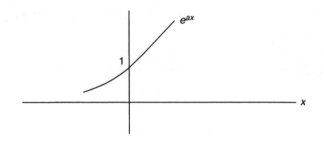

Figure 9.1   Graph of $y = e^{ax}$, $a > 0$.

The time path for y that results from this solution crucially depends on the behavior of e^{-ax}. Now the function e^{ax} with $a > 0$ is monotonically increasing in x as its graph demonstrates in Figure 9.1.

The function $e^{-ax} = 1/e^{ax}$ so with $a > 0$ $e^{-ax} \to 0$ as $x \to \infty$. We have then that $y(x) \to \bar{y}$ if and only if $e^{-ax} \to 0$, that is, $y(x) \to \bar{y}$ if and only if $a > 0$.

Definition
If $y(x) \to \bar{y}$ we say the y **converges** to $\bar{y}$ and the time path for y is **stable**.

Bernoulli equations

Certain nonlinear first order differential equations can be transformed into linear equations by a suitable change in variable. An equation of this sort is the **Bernoulli equation** which is important for one of our economic applications in the next section. It takes the form

$$\frac{dy}{dx} + ay = cy^m$$

where a and c are constants or functions of x, and m is any real number except, of course, 0 or 1. Dividing through by y^m yields

$$y^{-m}\frac{dy}{dx} + ay^{1-m} = c.$$

Now consider

$$z = y^{1-m}$$

so

$$\frac{dz}{dx} = \frac{dz}{dy}\frac{dy}{dx} = (1-m)y^{-m}\frac{dy}{dx}$$

and the differential equation can be written as

$$\frac{1}{1-m}\frac{dz}{dx} + az = c.$$

This is now a linear first order differential equation in z. If a and c are constants then it can be solved using the techniques discussed in this section.

Example
Solve the equation

$$\frac{dy}{dx} + 6y = 7y^3.$$

Dividing this equation through by y^3 gives

$$y^{-3}\frac{dy}{dx} + 6y^{-2} = 7.$$

Let $z = y^{-2}$ so $dz/dx = -2y^{-3}dy/dx$.
    Then in terms of z our equation becomes

$$-\frac{1}{2}\frac{dz}{dx} + 6z = 7$$

or

$$\frac{dz}{dx} - 12z = -14.$$

The solution to this equation is

$$z = c_1e^{12x} + \tfrac{7}{6}$$

where c_1 is an arbitrary constant. It follows that the solution for y is

$$y = \left(c_1e^{12x} + \tfrac{7}{6}\right)^{-1/2}.$$

9.4   Economic Dynamics Using First Order Differential Equations

The dynamics behind supply and demand models

Like many of the great intellectual achievements of mankind, supply and demand functions were invented at roughly the same time by two economists Walras and Marshall. But how they viewed these functions differed as did the dynamic hypothesis they presented to explain how the variables price and quantity moved toward equilibrium.

Walras regarded price P as the independent variable in the equations and quantity Q as the dependent variable so he wrote the functions as follows:

Demand function: $Q_D = Q_D(P)$

Supply function: $Q_S = Q_S(P)$.

His dynamic hypothesis was that price would change according to excess demand. Marshall on the other hand regarded Q as the independent variable in the functions and P as the dependent variable. He wrote the functions as follows:

Demand function: $P_D = P_D(Q)$

Supply function: $P_S = P_S(Q)$.

His dynamic hypothesis was that quantity adjusts according to the difference in the price buyers were prepared to pay P_D and the price sellers wanted P_S.

Both ways of doing things seem perfectly reasonable. Unfortunately for economics, they lead to conflicting results as we shall see.

Starting with Walras, if we assume linear functions for demand and supply we have

$$Q_D = \alpha + aP$$
$$Q_S = \beta + bP$$

and we have the following dynamic adjustment process

$$\frac{dP}{dt} = \lambda(Q_D - Q_S) \quad \text{with } \lambda > 0.$$

Substituting for Q_D and Q_S gives

$$\frac{dP}{dt} = \lambda(\alpha - \beta) + \lambda(a - b)P$$

or in our format

$$\frac{dP}{dt} - \lambda(a - b)P = \lambda(\alpha - \beta),$$

which is a first order linear ordinary differential equation with constant coefficients. Setting $P = \bar{P}$ and $dP/dt = 0$ gives the particular solution to the nonhomogeneous equation:

$$\bar{P} = \frac{\alpha - \beta}{b - a}.$$

This is the potential equilibrium value for P. The general solution to the nonhomogeneous equation is

$$P(t) = \bar{P} + ce^{-gt},$$

with c an arbitrary constant and $g = \lambda(b - a)$.

Note $P(t) \to \bar{P}$ if and only if $g > 0$. As $\lambda > 0$, the condition $g > 0$ is equivalent to $b > a$.

If the good in question is a normal good and there is no back bending supply, then we have $b > 0$ and $a < 0$ and the condition holds as Figure 9.2 illustrates.

At price P_1 there is excess demand which pushes price up toward P. Likewise at price P_2 there is excess supply which pushes price down toward $\bar{P}$.

Marshall would write the demand and supply function as

$$P_D = -\frac{\alpha}{a} + \frac{Q}{a}$$

$$P_S = -\frac{\beta}{b} + \frac{Q}{b},$$

which are the inverses of the original functions. Then he would assume the following dynamic adjustment process:

$$\frac{dQ}{dt} = \lambda(P_D - P_S) \quad \text{with } \lambda > 0.$$

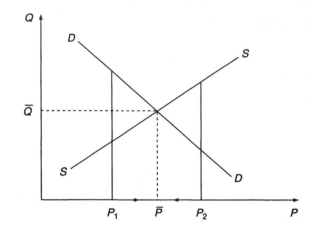

Figure 9.2   Walrasian equilibrium.

Substituting in for P_D and P_S gives the first order linear differential equation

$$\frac{dQ}{dt} + \lambda\left(\frac{1}{b} - \frac{1}{a}\right)Q = \lambda\left(\frac{\beta}{b} - \frac{\alpha}{a}\right).$$

A particular solution to this equation, which is our potential equilibrium value for Q is found by setting $Q = \bar{Q}$ and $dQ/dt = 0$ in this equation to obtain

$$\bar{Q} = \frac{\beta a - \alpha b}{a - b}.$$

The general solution to our equation is then

$$Q(t) = \bar{Q} + ce^{-ht},$$

where c is an arbitrary constant and

$$h = \lambda\left(\frac{1}{b} - \frac{1}{a}\right).$$

Now $Q(t) \to \bar{Q}$ if and only if $h > 0$. But with $\lambda > 0$ this requires

$$\frac{1}{b} > \frac{1}{a}.$$

Again in the usual case $b > 0$ and $a < 0$ so the condition holds as illustrated in Figure 9.3.

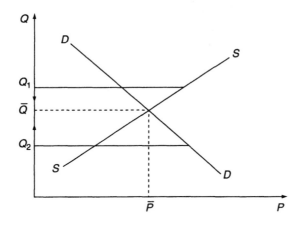

Figure 9.3 Marshallian equilibrium.

At Q_1 the price sellers want is higher than what buyers are prepared to pay and this forces quantity down toward $\bar{Q}$. At Q_2 the price buyers are prepared to pay is higher than what sellers require and this forces quantity up toward $\bar{Q}$.

If we take the theoretically possible but rather unlikely case where the good is a Giffen good so $a > 0$ and supply is backward bending $b < 0$, then both hypotheses would rate the market as dynamically unstable:

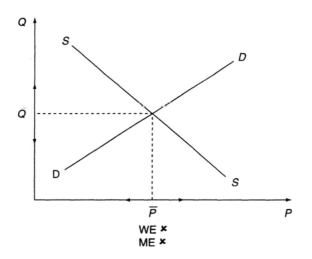

Where microeconomics runs into trouble is when we marry a Giffen good with the usual positive slope supply curve or a backward bending supply curve with a normal good. Now the two dynamic hypotheses conflict, one saying the time paths for price and quantity are stable the other saying they are unstable:

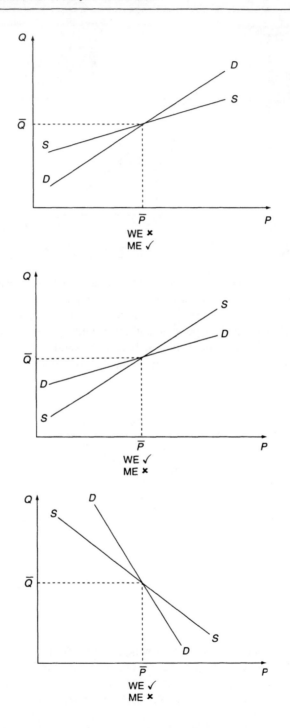

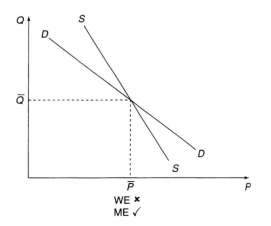

WE ✗
ME ✓

This situation is unfortunate to say the least. Both dynamic hypotheses seem perfectly reasonable but they lead to conflicting results in markets which are theoretically possible at least. Moreover, there is no other dynamic adjustment process in the offering that is preferable to either of these. As an aside it is worth noting that the two ways of looking at supply and demand functions have lead to considerable confusion in some undergraduate textbooks of economics. The supply and demand diagram originated from Marshall, and following the mathematical tradition, he placed his dependent variable P on the vertical axis and his independent variable Q on the horizontal axis. Most economic textbooks follow suit. But more often than not, in the main body of the text they use the Walrasian tradition which regards Q as the dependent variable and P as the independent variable. When one comes to computing slopes of our functions, as we do in evaluating elasticities, one then has to imagine swinging the supply and demand diagram around. In this book, more often than not, I follow the Walrasian tradition and when I graph supply and demand functions, I place Q on the vertical axis and P on the horizontal axis.

The Solow-Swan neoclassical growth model

The Solow-Swan model investigates the dynamics of an economy in which the factors of production are growing. It starts with a **neoclassical production function** for the economy of the form

$$Y = Y(K, L)$$

where K is the amount of capital available in the economy and L is the labor which is usually identified with the population of the economy. Such a production function is assumed to exhibit positive but diminishing marginal products, so for all positive K and L

$$\frac{\partial Y}{\partial K} > 0, \quad \frac{\partial^2 Y}{\partial K^2} < 0$$

$$\frac{\partial Y}{\partial L} > 0, \quad \frac{\partial^2 Y}{\partial L^2} < 0.$$

Also it is assumed that this function is homogeneous of degree one (often called **linearly homogeneous**). So

$$Y(\lambda K, \lambda L) = \lambda Y(K, L) \text{ for all } \lambda > 0,$$

and production is subject to constant returns to scale. Finally both inputs are considered essential for production so

$$Y(0, L) = Y(K, 0) = 0.$$

The condition of linear homogeneity implies that we can write

$$Y(K/L, 1) = \frac{Y}{L}$$

or

$$y = \phi(k),$$

where $k = K/L$ is the capital-labor ratio and $y = Y/L$ is per capita output. We assume that $\phi'(k) > 0$ and $\phi''(k) < 0$. The total output of the economy Y is allocated between consumption C and savings S and all savings goes into investment I. It is assumed that a constant proportion of output is saved so $S = sY$.

Let δ be the rate of depreciation of the capital stock. Net investment is then given by

$$K' = I - \delta K = S - \delta K = sY - \delta K$$

and dividing through by L renders

$$K'/L = sy - \delta k = s\phi(k) - \delta k. \tag{9.6}$$

Now

$$K' = \frac{dK}{dt} = \frac{d}{dt}(kL) = k\frac{dL}{dt} + L\frac{dk}{dt},$$

and assuming that the labor supply in the economy is growing at rate

$$\frac{dL/dt}{L} = n$$

we obtain

$$K' = knL + Lk'.$$

Substituting this expression into equation (9.6) yields

$$k' - s\phi(k) - (n + \delta)k$$

or

$$k' + (n + \delta)k = s\phi(k) \tag{9.7}$$

which is a first order nonlinear differential equation as the function $\phi(k)$ is non-linear. If $\phi(k) = k^m$, where m is a real number, then our equation is a Bernoulli equation and can be solved using the techniques discussed in Section 9.3. An example of this case is given in Exercise 4 at the end of this section.

The potential equilibrium in this model occurs when our variable is at rest, namely when $k' = 0$. This is often referred to as the **steady state**. Diagramatically the steady state occurs at the level of k where the concave function $s\phi(k)$ cuts the straight line $(n + \delta)k$ as shown in Figure 9.4.

Clearly referring to this diagram and equation (9.7) we have that if $k < k^*$ then $s\phi(k) > (n + \delta)k$ and $k' > 0$ and if $k > k^*$ then $s\phi(k) < (n + \delta)k$ and $k' < 0$.

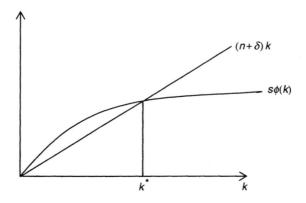

Figure 9.4   The steady state.

So plotting k' on the vertical axis and k on the horizontal axis we have the following figure

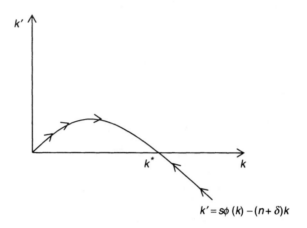

$$k' = s\phi(k) - (n + \delta)k$$

Such a diagram is often called a **phase** diagram.

At the steady state per capita consumption is given by

$$c^* = \phi(k^*) - (n + \delta)k^*.$$

Suppose now the proportion of output s going to savings and investment changes. Then the curve $s\phi(k)$ would move leading to a new steady state k^*. We can then regard k^* as a function of s. So we write

$$k^* = k^*(s), dk^*/ds > 0$$

and

$$c^*(s) = \phi(k^*(s)) - (n + \delta)k^*(s).$$

We now ask the question what level of savings should society choose in order to maximize the steady state level of consumption. The answer is found by differentiating $c^*(s)$ with respect to s to obtain

$$\frac{dc^*}{ds} = \frac{dc^*}{dk^*}\frac{dk^*}{ds} = (\phi'(k^*) - (n + \delta))\frac{dk^*}{ds}.$$

Setting this derivative equal to zero, remembering that $dk^*/ds > 0$ gives us the necessary condition that society should save at the level where

$$\phi'(k^*) = n + \delta.$$

This is often called the **golden rule of capital accumulation**. To maximize steady state consumption, society should save and invest at the level where the marginal product of capital $\phi'(k)$ is equal to the sum of the growth rate of the labor force and the depreciation rate.

Exercises for 9.4

1. Solve the following differential equations with the given initial conditions:
   (i) $dy/dx + 4y = e^{2x}$ if $y = 2$ when $x = 0$.
   (ii) $dy/dx + 7y = e^{-x}$ when $y(0) = 1$.
   (iii) $y' - y = -x^2$ given $y(1) = 1$.
2. The Harrod-Domar growth model consists of the following equations:

$$Y = C + I$$

$$I = v\frac{dY}{dt} + \bar{I} \quad \text{(Accelerator)}$$

$$C = \gamma Y. \quad \text{(Multiplier)}$$

   (i) By substituting into the definitional equation obtain a differential equation for Y.
   (ii) Solve this equation and obtain a stability condition on the parameters v and γ needed to ensure that $Y(t)$ tends to an equilibrium value.
   (iii) Is this condition likely to hold? If not what are the implications for the time path of Y?
3. Suppose that buyers take account not only of the price of the good but also how the price is changing. In particular assume that the demand and supply functions are

$$Q_d = a + bP(t) + c\frac{dP}{dt}, \quad a > 0, b < 0$$

$$Q_s = \alpha + \beta P(t), \quad \alpha < 0, \beta > 0$$

respectively, where $P(t)$ is the price at time t and a, b, c, α, and β are constants.
   (i) Provide a rationale for the demand equation. What sign would you expect c to have?

(ii) Solve the differential equation for $P(t)$ which results when we equate Q_s to Q_d.

(iii) The system obviously has an equilibrium if $P(t)$ tends to a finite limit as t tends to infinity. Determine the conditions on the parameters of the model needed to ensure this. What is the equilibrium value for P?

4. Consider the Solow-Swan growth model studies in the preceding section. Suppose that the economy has a production function given by

$$Y = K^\alpha L^{1-\alpha}, \quad 0 < \alpha < 1.$$

(i) Show that this function is linear homogeneous and satisfies the other requirements of a neoclassical production function.

(ii) Obtain the function $\phi(k)$ such that

$$y = \phi(k).$$

(iii) Obtain the differential equation corresponding to equation (9.7). Show that this is a Bernoulli equation and the solution is given by

$$k^{1-\alpha} = c_1 e^{-(1-\alpha)(n+\delta)t} + \frac{s}{n+\delta},$$

where c_1 is an arbitrary constant.

(iv) Show that

$$k^{1-\alpha} \rightarrow \frac{s}{n+\delta}$$

and hence find the steady state level of k.

(v) Find the steady state level of consumption, the golden rule level of k, and hence the golden rule level of s.

9.5 Second Order Linear Differential Equations with Constant Coefficients

Such an equation can be written as

$$\frac{d^2y}{dx^2} + p\frac{dy}{dx} + qy = f(x)$$

or

$$P(D)y = f(x)$$

where p and q are constants and $P(D) = D^2 + pD + q$. Again we proceed as we did for the first order equation. First we find the general solution to the corresponding homogeneous equation. Then we obtain a particular solution to the nonhomogeneous equation. Adding these together gives the required general solution to the nonhomogeneous equation.

General solution to the homogeneous equation

In this section our analysis relies heavily on the following theorem.

Theorem
Let y_1 and y_2 be particular solutions to the homogeneous equation

$$P(D)y = \frac{d^2y}{dx^2} + p\frac{dy}{dx} + qy = 0,$$

such that y_1 is not a constant times y_2. Then the general solution to this equation is $y = c_1 y_1 + c_2 y_2$, where c_1 and c_2 are arbitrary constants.

Proof
Consider

$$P(D)(c_1 y_1 + c_2 y_2) = P(D)c_1 y_1 + P(D)c_2 y_2$$
$$= c_1 P(D)y_1 + c_2 P(D)y_2,$$

as $P(D)$ is a linear operator. But as y_1 and y_2 are particular solutions to the homogeneous equation $p(D)y_1 = P(D)y_2 = 0$. Hence

$$P(D)(c_1 y_1 + c_2 y_2) = 0,$$

and as $c_1 y_1 + c_2 y_2$ contains two arbitrary constants it must be the general solution.

This theorem sets us the task of finding two particular solutions to the homogeneous equation and then combining these to give us the general solution of the homogeneous equation. In doing so, use is made of the following equation:

Definition
The equation $m^2 + pm + q = 0$ is called the **auxiliary equation**[1] associated with the second order linear differential equation.

---

[1] An alternative name is the **characteristic equation**

The auxiliary equation is a quadratic equation, so its roots may be real and unequal, real and repeated, or **conjugate complex roots.** The last case occurs when the roots are of the form

$$a + bi \quad \text{and} \quad a - bi,$$

where a and b are real numbers and i is the imaginary number $\sqrt{-1}$.

The particular solutions we obtain depends on which case we have in hand.

Case 1: Roots of the auxiliary equation are real and unequal

Theorem

If the roots m_1 and m_2 of the auxiliary equation are real and unequal then the general solution to the homogeneous equation is

$$y = c_1 e^{m_1 x} + c_2 e^{m_2 x},$$

where c_1 and c_2 are arbitrary constants.

Proof

We are required to show that $y_1 = e^{m_1 x}$ and $y_2 = e^{m_2 x}$ are particular solutions to the homogeneous equation. Consider $y_1 = e^{m_1 x}$. Then

$$Dy_1 = m_1 e^{m_1 x}, \quad D^2 y_1 = m_1^2 e^{m_1 x}$$

so

$$P(D)y_1 = (m_1^2 + pm_1 + q)e^{m_1 x} = 0,$$

as m_1 is a root of the auxiliary equation. Similarly for y_2.

Example

Solve

$$\frac{d^2 y}{dx^2} - \frac{dy}{dx} - 6y = 0.$$

The auxiliary equation is $m^2 - m - 6 = 0$ which has roots $m_1 = 3, m_2 = -2$. So the general solution is

$$y = c_1 e^{3x} + c_2 e^{-2x}.$$

Case 2: Roots of the auxiliary equation real and equal

Theorem

If the roots of the auxiliary equation are real and equal $m_1 = m_2 = r$ say, then the general solution to the homogeneous differential equation is

$$y = (c_1 + c_2 x)e^{rx}.$$

Proof

Clearly $y_1 = e^{rx}$ is a particular solution to the equation so we need to show that $y_2 = xe^{rx}$ is too. Now

$$Dy_2 = e^{rx} + rxe^{rx} = e^{rx}(1 + rx)$$

$$D^2 y_2 = e^{rx}(2r + r^2 x),$$

so

$$P(D)y_2 = e^{rx}[(r^2 + pr + q)x + 2r + p].$$

As r is a root of the auxiliary equation $r^2 + pr + q = 0$. For the auxiliary equation to have equal roots, $p^2 = 4q$ and $r = -p/2$ so $2r + p = 0$.
   Hence $P(D)y_2 = 0$ as required.

Example
Solve

$$\frac{d^2 y}{dx^2} + 6\frac{dy}{dx} + 9y = 0.$$

The auxiliary equation is $m^2 + 6m + 9 = 0$ which has repeated roots $m_1 = m_2 = -3$.
   The general solution is then $y = (c_1 + c_2 x)e^{-3x}$.

Case 3: Roots of the auxiliary equation conjugate complex

Theorem

If the roots of the auxiliary equation are conjugate complex, $m_1 = a + bi$ and $m_2 = a - bi$ then the general solution to the homogeneous equation is

$$y = e^{ax}(c_1 \cos bx + c_2 \sin bx).$$

Proof
Consider
$$y_1 = e^{ax} \cos bx.$$
Then
$$Dy_1 = e^{ax}(a \cos bx - b \sin bx)$$
$$D^2 y_1 = e^{ax}(a^2 \cos bx - b^2 \cos bx - 2ab \sin bx),$$
so
$$P(D)y_1 = e^{ax}[(a^2 - b^2 + pa + q) \cos bx - (2ab + pb) \sin bx].$$
Now as $a + bi$ is a root of the auxiliary equation
$$(a + bi)^2 + p(a + bi) + q = 0,$$
that is, $\quad (a^2 - b^2 + pa + q) + i(2ab + pb) = 0,$
so we must have $a^2 - b^2 + pa + q = 0$ and $2ab + pb = 0$. Thus y_1 is a particular solution and by a similar analysis so is $y_2 = e^{ax} \sin bx$.

Example
Solve $d^2y/dx^2 + 9y = 0$ when we are given the initial conditions $y = 0$ and $dy/dx = 5$, when $x = 0$. The auxiliary equation is $m^2 + 9 = 0$ so $m_1 = 3i$ and $m_2 = -3i$. The general solution is then
$$y = c_1 \cos 3x + c_2 \sin 3x.$$
Now $y(0) = 0 = c_1 \cos 0 + c_2 \sin 0 = c_1$ so $y(x) = c_2 \sin 3x$, with $dy/dx = 3c_2 \cos 3x$. Given our initial condition, $5 = 3c_2 \cos 0 = 3c_2$ so $c_2 = \frac{5}{3}$, and the required solution that satisfies the initial conditions is $y = \frac{5}{3} \sin 3x$.

A particular solution to the nonhomogeneous equation

The method of **undetermined coefficients** essentially makes an intelligent guess as to the particular solution, the guess made depending on the function $f(x)$. Table 9.1 gives the particular solution we try for various functions $f(x)$.

In the trial particular solutions, the cs represent undetermined coefficients whose values are determined by substituting the trial particular solution into the left hand side of the differential equation and equating the expression obtained to $f(x)$. Use is made of the table along with the following rules:

(i) If $f(x)$ is the sum of several different functions each should be treated separately and the particular solutions obtained summed.

Table 9.1   Trial particular solutions.

Trial particular solution	$f(x)$
ca^x	a^x
$c_1 \sin bx + c_2 \cos bx$	$\sin bx$ or $\cos bx$
$c_0 + c_1 x + \cdots + c_n x^n$	$a_0 + a_1 x + \cdots + a_n x^n$
$a^x(c_1 \sin bx + c_2 \cos bx)$	$a^x \sin bx$ or $a^x \cos bx$
$a^x(c_0 + c_1 x + \cdots + c_n x^n)$	$a^x(a_0 + a_1 x + \cdots + a_n x^n)$

(ii) If the trial particular solution includes a function which is in the general solution of the homogeneous equation, the trial particular solution should first be multiplied by x. If still confronted with this problem, multiply by x again.

Example
Solve the differential equation

$$\frac{d^2 y}{dx^2} + 2\frac{dy}{dx} + y = e^{-x} + 3x.$$

The auxiliary equation is $m^2 + 2m + 1 = 0$ which has repeated roots $m_1 = m_2 = -1$. The general solution to the homogeneous equations is

$$y = (c_1 + c_2 x)e^{-x}$$

where c_1 and c_2 are arbitrary constants. The function of the right hand side is the sum of two functions e^{-x} and $3x$, so we deal with each of these separately.

For e^{-x} we would try as a particular solution $y = ce^{-x}$, but this appears in the general solution in the homogeneous equation, so we try $y = cxe^{-x}$. But this too appears in this general solution, so we try $y = cx^2 e^{-x}$. Now

$$\frac{dy}{dx} = c(2x - x^2)e^{-x}$$

$$\frac{d^2 y}{dx^2} = c(2 - 2x)e^{-x} - c(2x - x^2)e^{-x}$$

$$= c(2 - 4x + x^2)e^{-x}.$$

The left hand side of our differential equation is

$$c(2 - 4x + x^2)e^{-x} + 2c(2x - x^2)e^{-x} + cx^2 e^{-x} = 2ce^{-x}.$$

Equating this to e^{-x} gives $c = \frac{1}{2}$ and a particular solution to this part of $f(x)$ given by $y = x^2 e^{-x}/2$.

Now for the $3x$ part. For a particular solution we try $y = c_1 + c_2 x$ which gives $dy/dx = c_2$ and $d^2y/dx^2 = 0$.

The left hand side of our differential equation becomes

$$2c_2 + c_1 + c_2 x.$$

Equating this to $3x$ gives $c_2 = 3$ and $c_1 = -6$, so the particular solution to this part of $f(x)$ is $y = -6 + 3x$. The required particular solution to the nonhomogeneous equation is then

$$y = -6 + 3x + x^2 e^{-x}/2$$

and the general solution to this equation is

$$y = (c_1 + c_2 x)e^{-x} - 6 + 3x + x^2 e^{-x}/2.$$

A special case

Again we consider the case where we have a constant on the right hand side of the equation:

$$\text{That is },\quad \frac{d^2y}{dx^2} + p\frac{dy}{dx} + qy = k, \quad \text{where } k \text{ is a constant.}$$

A particular solution to this equation is obtained by setting $y = \bar{y}, dy/dx = d^2y/dx^2 = 0$ to obtain

$$\bar{y} = \frac{k}{q}.$$

As in the case of the first order equation, $\bar{y}$ represents the potential equilibrium value for y. The general solution of the equation depends on the parameters in the equation and we know that three cases present themselves:

Case 1, $p^2 > 4q$

Here the roots of the auxiliary equation are real and unequal and the general solution is

$$y = \bar{y} + c_1 e^{m_1 x} + c_2 e^{m_2 x}.$$

The time path for y will be stable with y converging to $\bar{y}$ if and only if both roots (m_1 and m_2) are less than zero. If one or more roots is greater than zero the time path for y is explosive, diverging away from $\bar{y}$. In either case no cycles or fluctuations are possible.

Case 2, $p^2 = 4q$

Here the roots are real and equal $m_1 = m_2 = -p/2 = r$ say and the general solution is

$$y = \bar{y} + c_1 e^{rx} + c_2 x e^{rx}.$$

If $r < 0$ we know $e^{rx} \to 0$ as $x \to \infty$. But what about xe^{rx}? One part x is tending to infinity, the other part e^{rx} is tending to zero. It is this latter part that dominates as e^{rx} tends to zero at a faster rate than x tends to infinity. The net result is that

$$xe^{rx} \to 0 \text{ if and only if } r < 0.$$

In this case, y converges to $\bar{y}$ otherwise the time path for y is explosive. In either case no cycles are exhibited by this time path.

Case 3, $p^2 < 4q$

Here the roots are conjugate complex $m_1 = a + bi$ and $m_2 = a - bi$ and the general solution is

$$y = \bar{y} + e^{ax}(c_1 \cos bx + c_2 \sin bx).$$

The linear combination of a cos function and a sine function assures us that we get cycles in this case. If $a < 0$ then $e^{ax} \to 0$ as $x \to \infty$ and we get y converging to $\bar{y}$ with damped cycles. If $a = 0$ then $e^{ax} = 1$ and we get cycles of constant amplitude, and will never settle down to its potential equilibrium value $\bar{y}$. If $a > 0$ then $e^{ax} \to \infty$ as $x \to \infty$ and the time path of y is divergent with explosive cycles.

Notice that when dealing with the complex number $a + bi$, a is often called the **real part** of the complex number. Under this terminology we can say that the time path for y is convergent if and only if the real roots or the real part of the roots are all less than zero.

9.6   Economic Application: A Dynamic Supply and Demand Model

Consider the following dynamic supply and demand model:

$$Q_D = a + bP + cP' + dP''   \quad a > 0, b < 0$$
$$Q_S = \alpha + \beta P   \qquad\qquad \alpha < 0, \beta > 0,$$

where the dashes signify derivatives.

Equating demand to supply gives a second order linear differential equation in P. Show that

(i) if $d > 0$ then the roots of the auxiliary equation must be real and distinct and the time path for P is divergent,
(ii) if $d < 0$ nothing can be said about the roots of the auxiliary equation but if $c < 0$ also each case gives a convergent time path for P.

Equating demand to supply gives

$$dP'' + cP' + bP + a = \alpha + \beta P$$

or

$$dP'' + cP' + (b - \beta)P = \alpha - a.$$

A particular solution to this equation, which is also the potential equilibrium value for P is obtained by setting $P = \bar{P}, P' = P'' = 0$ to get

$$\bar{P} = \frac{\alpha - a}{b - \beta}.$$

The auxiliary equation is

$$dm^2 + cm + (b - \beta) = 0$$

whose roots are given by

$$m_1, m_2 = \frac{-c \pm \sqrt{c^2 - 4d(b - \beta)}}{2d}.$$

If d is positive then the sign of the number under the positive square root sign is given by

$$(+\text{ve}) - (+\text{ve})(-\text{ve}) = +\text{ve}$$

so we must have real distinct roots. Moreover, this positive square root is greater than $|c|$ as a positive number is added to c^2, so one of the roots is positive which means the time path for P is divergent.

If d is negative then we cannot put a sign to the number under the positive square root sign so nothing can be said about the roots of the auxiliary equation. However, if the roots are real and distinct and $c < 0$ then as

$$|c| > \sqrt{c^2 - 4d(b - \beta)}$$

both roots must be negative so the time path for P is convergent. If the roots are real and equal, $m_1 = m_2 = -c/d$ which is negative, again we get a convergent time path. Finally, if the roots are conjugate complex, the real part is $-c/d$ which is negative, again we get a convergent time path for P though this time with damped cycles.

Exercises for 9.6

1. Solve the following differential equations and find the particular solutions which correspond to initial conditions if these are given:
   (i) $y'' - 4y' + 4y = 0$, $y(0) = 2$, $y'(0) = 5$,
   (ii) $y'' - y' - 2y = 0$, $y = 1$, $y' = -5$ when $x = 0$,
   (iii) $\dfrac{d^2y}{dx^2} - \dfrac{2dy}{dx} - 3y = 9x^2$,
   (iv) $y'' - 2y' - 3y = 8e^{-x}$,
   (v) $\dfrac{d^2y}{dx^2} - \dfrac{dy}{dx} - 2y = 4e^{2x}$, $y = 5$ and $\dfrac{dy}{dx} = 1$ when $x = 0$,
   (vi) $2y'' - 2y' + y = 2$, $y = 4$, $y' = 2$ when $x = 0$,
   (vii) $\dfrac{d^2y}{dx^2} + \dfrac{dy}{dx} = x$, $y = 1$, $\dfrac{dy}{dx} = 0$ when $x = 0$,
   (viii) $\dfrac{d^2y}{dx^2} + \dfrac{2dy}{dx} + y = e^{-x}$.
2. Prove that if $y_1(x)$ is a solution to the linear differential equation $ay'' + by' + cy = f_1(x)$ and if $y_2(x)$ is a solution to $ay'' + by' + cy = f_2(x)$ then $y_1(x) + y_2(x)$ is a solution to $ay'' + by' + cy = f_1(x) + f_2(x)$ where a, b, and

c are constant coefficients. Use this result to find the general solution to the following differential equations:
  (i) $y'' - 3y' = 6 + 3e^{3x}$
  (ii) $y'' + 2y' + y = e^{-x} + 3x$
  (iii) $d^2y/dx^2 - dy/dx - 2y = 6x + 4e^{-x}$

9.7   Higher Order Linear Differential Equations

Although first and second order differential equations usually suffice the needs of economists in their dynamic analysis, occasionally a higher order equation is called for. Fortunately, our results generalize at least for the special case where we have a constant on the right hand side. Consider such an equation of the *n*th order

$$\frac{d^n y}{dx^n} + a_1 \frac{d^{n-1}}{dx^{n-1}} + \cdots + a_{n-1}\frac{dy}{dx} + a_n y = k$$

where $a_1, \ldots, a_{n-1}$ and k are constants. Again the general solution of this equation depends on the roots of the auxiliary equation

$$m^n + a_1 m^{n-1} + \cdots + a_{n-1}m + a_n = 0,$$

which is now an *n*th order polynomial equation. Such an equation has exactly *n* roots; these may be real, repeated, or complex, and of course this polynomial equation is a lot harder to solve than a quadratic equation. However, our main result still holds. The time path will be convergent if and only if all the real roots or real parts of the roots are all negative. Moreover, rather than solve the polynomial equation itself we can appeal to Routh's Theorem to see if this is the case.

Routh's Theorem
The real roots and real parts of all the roots of the *n*th degree polynomial equation

$$a_0 m^n + a_1 m^{n-1} + \cdots + a_{n-1}m + a_n = 0$$

are negative if and only if all the first *n* of the determinants

$$a_1, \quad \begin{vmatrix} a_1 & a_3 \\ a_0 & a_2 \end{vmatrix}, \quad \begin{vmatrix} a_1 & a_3 & a_5 \\ a_0 & a_2 & a_4 \\ 0 & a_1 & a_3 \end{vmatrix}, \quad \begin{vmatrix} a_1 & a_3 & a_5 & a_7 \\ a_0 & a_2 & a_4 & a_6 \\ 0 & a_1 & a_3 & a_5 \\ 0 & a_0 & a_2 & a_4 \end{vmatrix} \cdots$$

are all positive.

In applying this theorem, it is understood that we set $a_r = 0$ for all $r > n$ needed to obtain these determinants. For example, consider the third degree polynomial equation

$$a_0 m^3 + a_1 m^2 + a_2 m + a_3 = 0.$$

The determinants we need to look at are

$$a_1, \quad \begin{vmatrix} a_1 & a_3 \\ a_0 & a_2 \end{vmatrix}, \quad \begin{vmatrix} a_1 & a_3 & 0 \\ a_0 & a_2 & 0 \\ 0 & a_1 & a_3 \end{vmatrix}$$

where a_4 and a_5 have been set equal to zero.

Example
Without finding the roots of the auxiliary equation, determine whether the following differential equation will give rise to a convergent time path

$$y'''(x) + 11y''(x) + 34y'(x) + 24y = 5.$$

Consider the following determinants

$$11, \quad \begin{vmatrix} 11 & 24 \\ 1 & 34 \end{vmatrix}, \quad \begin{vmatrix} 11 & 24 & 0 \\ 1 & 34 & 0 \\ 0 & 11 & 24 \end{vmatrix}.$$

The first two are clearly positive whilst the third is equal to

$$24(-1)^{3+3} \begin{vmatrix} 11 & 24 \\ 1 & 34 \end{vmatrix},$$

which is also positive. Hence by Routh's Theorem the roots of the auxiliary equation all have real parts which are negative, so this equation gives rise to a convergent time path.

Exercises for 9.7

1. State Routh's Theorem. Use this theorem to prove that the time path for $y(x)$ in the equation $y''(x) + ay'(x) + b = c$ will be convergent if and only if a and b are both positive.

2. Without finding the roots of auxiliary equations determine whether the following equations give rise to a convergent path for y:

   (i) $y'''(t) - 21y''(t) + 29y'(t) + 20y(t) = 3$

   (ii) $y'''(t) + 21y''(t) + 36y'(t) + 20y(t) = 20$

   (iii) $y'''(t) + 8y''(t) - 7y'(t) + 4y(t) = 6$.

9.8   Descriptive Analysis of Nonlinear Differential Equations

Consider a first order differential equation system in two dependent variables y_1 and y_2 of the following form

$$y_1'(x) = f(y_1, y_2)$$
$$y_2'(x) = g(y_1, y_2).$$

Such a system is peculiar in that the derivatives $y_1'(x)$ and $y_2'(x)$ depends only on y_1 and y_2 without x appearing as a separate variable. The independent variable x enters these derivatives indirectly only through y_1 and y_2. Such a system of nonlinear equations is called an **autonomous system** and information about the time paths for y_1 and y_2 that result from this system can be gained descriptively using **phase diagrams**.

Suppose for the moment that we know the slopes of the nonlinear equations $f(y_1, y_2) = 0$ and $g(y_1, y_2) = 0$. We could then plot the graphs of $y_1'(x) = 0$ and $y_2'(x) = 0$. For example, we may get the following graphs:

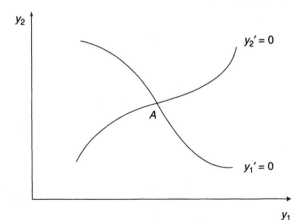

The point A represents a potential equilibrium for this system being the point where $y_1' = 0$ and $y_2' = 0$.

Suppose we also know the following information:

$$\text{To the right of } y_1' = 0 \text{ we have } y_1' < 0.$$

$$\text{To the left of } y_1' = 0 \text{ we have } y_1' > 0.$$

$$\text{Above } y_2' \text{ we have } y_2' < 0.$$

$$\text{Below } y_2' = 0 \text{ we have } y_2' > 0.$$

Then in the four quadrants defined by our graphs we could plot the following **directional arrows** indicating the movement of the two variables y_1, y_2 in each quadrant.

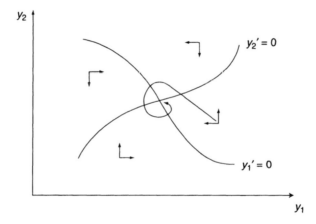

The directional arrows give rise to **stream lines** which in turn indicate the time paths of the two variables. In this case the stream lines dictate that the system is stable for the two variables, and that the variables converge to an equilibrium cyclically.

Other outcomes are of course possible. Suppose I change my a priori information so that for y_2 we have:

$$\text{Above } y_2' = 0 \text{ we have } y_2' > 0,$$

$$\text{Below } y_2' = 0 \text{ we have } y_2' < 0.$$

My directional arrows now are as follows:

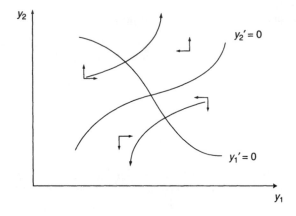

The streamlines now indicate divergent time paths without oscillations.

The slopes of the graphs may be of the same sign. We could for example have the following diagram:

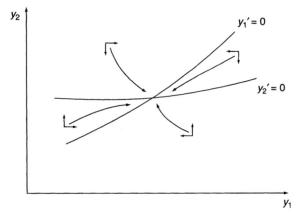

The streamlines here indicate convergent time paths for y_1 and y_2 without oscillations.

The a priori knowledge we needed to draw these diagrams consisted of the slopes of the nonlinear equation $f(y_1, y_2) = 0$ and $g(y_1, y_2) = 0$ together with the signs of the derivatives at either side of the graphs of $y_1' = 0$ and $y_2' = 0$. It turns out that if we know the signs of the partial derivatives

$$\frac{\partial f}{\partial y_1}, \frac{\partial f}{\partial y_2}, \frac{\partial g}{\partial y_1} \quad \text{and} \quad \frac{\partial g}{\partial y_2}$$

we have all this a priori information. Consider the slope of $y_1' = 0$. As $y_1' = f(y_1, y_2)$ we have

$$dy_1' = f_1 dy_1 + f_2 dy_2$$

where as always $f_1 = \partial f / \partial y_1$ and $f_2 = \partial f / \partial y_2$. But if $y_1' = 0$, then $dy_1' = 0$ so

$$\left. \frac{dy_2}{dy_1} \right|_{y_1'=0} = \frac{-f_1}{f_2}.$$

Similarly,

$$\left. \frac{dy_2}{dy_1} \right|_{y_2'=0} = \frac{-g_1}{g_2}.$$

Knowing the signs of the partial derivatives then gives us the required slopes. But such knowledge also gives us the directional arrows.

We know that $\partial y_1' / \partial y_1 = f_1$. Suppose now we also know that f_1 is negative. This means that y_1' and y_1 move in opposite directions. As we increase y_1, y_1' must decrease. But $y_1' = 0$ on the graph $f(y_1, y_2) = 0$. Hence in order for it to decrease as we increase y_1, y_1' must be positive to the left of this graph and negative to the right of it. In such a manner the required directional arrows can also be obtained if we are given the signs of the partial derivatives.

For an economic example of the applications of phase diagrams see Section 11.5 of Chapter 11.

Exercise for 9.8

1. Suppose the dynamic behavior of two economic variables $y_1(t)$ and $y_2(t)$ is given by the autonomous system

$$y_1'(t) = f(y_1, y_2)$$
$$y_2'(t) = g(y_1, y_2).$$

Draw the appropriate phase diagram(s) and determine the nature of the time paths of these two variables when we are given the following information:
  (i) $f_1 < 0, f_2 > 0, g_1 > 0, g_2 < 0$
  (ii) $f_1 < 0, f_2 < 0, g_1 < 0, g_2 > 0$
  (iii) $f_1 > 0, f_2 > 0, g_1 > 0, g_2 > 0$
  (iv) $f_1 > 0, f_2 > 0, g_1 > 0, g_2 < 0$

Chapter 10

Discrete Time: Difference Equations

10.1 Introduction and Definitions

Often it is unrealistic to think of economic variables as changing continuously. The classic example is the production of an agricultural product. Such production cannot be changed overnight. Instead a new crop has to be planted, tended, and harvested and all this takes time. In cases like this, it is more realistic to regard the economic variable as changing only at the end of discrete intervals of time and to view the independent variable x, representing time, as taking on the nonnegative integer values only. That is, $x = 0, 1, 2, \ldots$. The mathematical tool used in such economic dynamic analysis is difference equations.

A difference equation is one that involves a difference operator. Unlike the derivative operator in differential equations we are confronted with a choice of two difference operators: the forward difference operator, or the backward difference operator. Which one we use is largely irrelevant as the mathematical analysis of difference equations requires us to write the equation in terms of time period differences rather than in terms of difference operators.

Apart from this peculiarity, the analysis of difference equations is very similar to that of differential equations with the same general theorems applying and similar techniques used.

Difference operators

Consider a function $y = y(x)$ with the domain of this function being the set of nonnegative integers. Then we have the following definitions:

Definitions
The **first forward difference** of $y(x)$ is

$$\Delta y(x) = y(x + 1) - y(x).$$

The **second forward difference** of $y(x)$ is

$$\Delta^2 y(x) = \Delta(\Delta y(x)) = y(x+2) - 2y(x+1) + y(x)$$

and so on, successive forward differences being defined recursively by

$$\Delta^n y(x) = \Delta^{n-1} y(x) - \Delta^{n-1} y(x).$$

Notice that the nth order forward difference will involve $y(x+n)$, $y(x+n-1), \ldots, y(x)$.

Likewise the **first backward difference** of $y(x)$ is

$$\nabla y(x) = y(x) - y(x-1),$$

the **second backward difference** of $y(x)$ is

$$\nabla^2 y(x) = y(x) - 2y(x-1) + y(x-2),$$

and so on, successive backward differences being defined recursively by

$$\nabla^n y(x) = \nabla^{n-1} y(x) - \nabla^{n-1} y(x-1).$$

Notice that the nth order backward differences will involve $y(x), y(x-1), \ldots,$ $y(x-n)$.

The coefficients of the different period y's in the expansions of these differences can be readily obtained using **Pascal's triangle:**

$$
\begin{array}{ccccccccccc}
 & & & & & 1 & & & & & \\
 & & & & 1 & & 1 & & & & \\
 & & & 1 & & 2 & & 1 & & & \\
 & & 1 & & 3 & & 3 & & 1 & & \\
 & 1 & & 4 & & 6 & & 4 & & 1 & \\
1 & & 5 & & 10 & & 10 & & 5 & & 1
\end{array}
$$

For example

$$\nabla^4 y(x) = y(x) - 4y(x-1) + 6y(x-2) - 4y(x-3) + y(x-4).$$

Representation of a difference equation

An equation involving either $\Delta^n y(x)$ or $\nabla^n y$ is called a **nth order difference** equation. But as these operators involve $y(x+n), y(x+n-1), \ldots, y(x)$

or $y(x), y(x - 1), \ldots, y(x - n)$ respectively we can write the nth order difference equation as

$$\psi(x, y(x), y(x + 1), \ldots, y(x + n)) = 0$$

or

$$g(x, y(x), y(x - 1), \ldots, y(x - n)) = 0.$$

Both equations represent the same difference equation. All that has happened in moving from one to the other is that we shift the time origin (i.e. where $x = 0$) by n periods!

The **nth order linear difference** equation can be represented as

$$y(x + n) + a_1 y(x + n - 1) + \cdots + a_{n-1} y(x + 1) + a_n y(x) = f(x)$$

or

$$y(x) + a_1 y(x - 1) + \cdots + a_{n-1} y(x - n + 1) + a_n y(x - n) = f(x),$$

where we have changed the origin. The coefficients are constants or functions in x. If they are constants then the difference equations have **constant coefficients**. If $f(x) = 0$ we have a **homogeneous equation**.

In solving a difference equation we want y as the most general function of x that satisfies the equation. The same theorems apply here as did for the case of differential equations:

The general solution of an nth order difference equation involves exactly n arbitrary constants.

If y_p is a particular solution to the nonhomogeneous linear difference equation with constant coefficients and y_c is the general solution to the corresponding homogeneous equation, then $y_p + y_c$ is the general solution to the nonhomogeneous equation.

If y_1 and y_2 are particular solutions to the second order linear homogeneous difference equation with constant coefficients then the general solution to such an equation is $c_1 y_1 + c_2 y_2$ where c_1 and c_2 are arbitrary constants.

As in the case of differential equations we will concentrate on linear difference equations of first and second order with constant coefficients.

10.2 First Order Linear Difference Equations with Constant Coefficients

We concern ourselves only with the case where $f(x)$ is a constant and we write such an equation as

$$y(x + 1) + ay(x) = k.$$

Direct substitution shows that $y_c = c(-a)^x$ is the general solution to the homogeneous form of this equation and that

$$y_p = \frac{k}{1 + a} \quad a \neq -1$$
$$= kx \quad a = -1$$

is a particular solution to the nonhomogeneous equation. Adding y_c to y_p gives us the general solution to our equation, namely

$$y(x) = c(-a)^x + k/(1 + a) \quad a \neq -1$$
$$= c(-a)^x + kx \quad a = -1.$$

For the case $a \neq -1$, $y_p = k/(1 + a)$ represents a potential equilibrium for y as it is achieved by letting $y(x + 1) = y(x) = \bar{y}$ in the equation and then solving to get $\bar{y} = k/(1 + a)$. That is, it represents a value at which our economic variable is at rest.

Exercises for 10.2

1. Suppose the time path of a variable can be described by the nonlinear difference equation:

$$y_{t+1} = f(y_t), \quad y_t > 0.$$

Graph y_{t+1} on the vertical axis and y_t on the horizontal axis. The 45 degree line from the origin then represents points where $y_{t+1} = y_t$. Using this diagram what conditions do we need on the slope of the function $f(y_t)$ to get
  (i) a convergent time path for y with no oscillations,
  (ii) a convergent time path for y with oscillations,
  (iii) a divergent time path for y with no oscillations,
  (iv) a divergent time path for y with oscillations.

Apply your results to determine the nature of the time paths for y where

(a) $y_{t+1} = 10 + 5 \log y_t$ $0 < y_t < 1$
(b) $y_{t+1} = 3 - 8 \cos y_t$ $0 < y_t < \pi$
(c) $y_{t+1} = 10 + 8 y_t^5$ $y_t > 1$.

10.3   Second Order Linear Difference Equations with Constant Coefficients

We represent such an equation as

$$y(x + 2) + py(x + 1) + qy(x) = f(x),$$

where p and q are constants and proceed as we did for differential equations. The general solution to the homogeneous form of this equation is formed from two particular solutions, obtained by referring to the roots of the auxiliary equation. A particular solution to the nonhomogeneous equation can be obtained by the same method of undetermined coefficients. Adding the two gives the general solution we required.

The general solution of the homogeneous equation

The **auxiliary equation** associated with our difference equation is

$$m^2 + pm + q = 0.$$

Case 1: Roots of the auxiliary equation real and unequal, m_1, m_2

Theorem
The general solution to the homogeneous equation in this case is

$$y(x) = c_1 m_1^x + c_2 m_2^x,$$

where c_1 and c_2 are arbitrary constants.

Proof
Show by substituting that $y_1 = m_1^x$ and $y_2 = m_2^x$ are particular solutions to the homogeneous equation.

Example
Solve,

$$\Delta^2 y(x) - \Delta y(x) = 0.$$

We must first write our equation in terms of $y(x + 2)$, $y(x + 1)$, and $y(x)$ as follows:

$$\Delta^2 y(x) - \Delta y(x) = y(x + 2) - 2y(x + 1) + y(x) - y(x + 1) + y(x)$$
$$= y(x + 2) - 3y(x + 1) + 2y(x).$$

The auxiliary equation is $m^2 - 3m + 2 = 0$ which has roots $m_1 = 1$ and $m_2 = 2$. The general solution is then

$$y = c_1 1^x + c_2 2^x = c_1 + c_2 2^x.$$

Case 2: Roots of the auxiliary equation real and equal, $m_1 = m_2 = r$

Theorem
The general solution to the homogeneous equation in this case is

$$y(x) = (c_1 + c_2 x) r^x$$

where c_1 and c_2 arbitrary constants.

Proof
Show by substitution that $y_1 = r^x$ and $y_2 = xr^x$ are particular solutions.

Example
Find the general solution of

$$y(x + 2) - 6y(x + 1) + 9y(x) = 0$$

which corresponds to the initial conditions $y(0) = 0$ and $y(1) = 2$.
   The auxiliary equation is $m^2 - 6m + 9 = 0$ which has a repeated root $m_1 = m_2 = 3$.
The general solution is $y(x) = (c_1 + c_2 x) 3^x$.
   From the initial conditions

$$y(0) = c_1 = 0$$
$$y(1) = c_2 3 = 2 \text{ so } c_2 = 2/3.$$

The required solution is then

$$y = \tfrac{2}{3} x 3^x.$$

Case 3: Roots of the auxiliary equation conjugate complex numbers, $m_1 = a + bi$, $m_2 = a - bi$

Theorem
The general solution to the homogeneous equation for this case is

$$y(x) = \rho^x (c_1 \cos \theta x + c_2 \sin \theta x),$$

where $\rho = \sqrt{a^2 + b^2}$, θ is defined by $\tan \theta = a/b$, and c_1 and c_2 are arbitrary constants.

The proof requires knowledge of the workings of complex numbers not needed in this book, so it is not given.

Example
Solve the following difference equation

$$2\nabla^2 y(x) - 2\nabla y(x) + y(x) = 0.$$

Substituting in for the backward difference operator the equation becomes

$$y(x) - 2y(x - 1) + 2y(x - 2) = 0,$$

which has an auxiliary equation

$$m^2 - 2m + 2 = 0.$$

The roots of this equation are the following conjugate complex number

$$m_1 = 1 + i \quad \text{and} \quad m_2 = 1 - i,$$

so $\rho = \sqrt{1 + 1} = 2^{1/2}$ and $\tan \theta = 1$ implying that $\theta = \pi/4$.
The general solution then is

$$y(x) = 2^{x/2} \left(c_1 \cos \frac{\pi x}{4} + c_2 \sin \frac{\pi x}{4} \right),$$

c_1 and c_2 being arbitrary constants.

A particular solution for the nonhomogeneous equation

The method of undetermined coefficients discussed in the corresponding section on differential equations works perfectly here as well.

Example

Solve the difference equation

$$\Delta^2 y(x) - 2\Delta y(x) + y(x) = 3x + 2^x.$$

Our first step is to substitute in for the forward operator so that the equation becomes

$$y(x + 2) - 4y(x + 1) + 4y(x) = 3x + 2^x.$$

The auxiliary equation is

$$m^2 - 4m + 4 = 0$$

which has repeated roots $m_1 = m_2 = 2$ so the general solution to the homogeneous equation is

$$y = (c_1 + c_2 x)2^x.$$

In obtaining a particular solution to the nonhomogeneous equation we separate the two functions on the right hand side. For $3x$ we try as a particular solution $c_0 + c_1 x$. Substituting the left hand side of the equation and equating to $3x$ gives

$$c_0 + c_1(x + 2) - 4[c_0 + c_1(x + 1)] + 4(c_0 + c_1 x) = 3x.$$

Collecting and equating coefficients gives

$$c_1 = 3$$

and

$$c_0 + 2c_1 - 4(c_0 + c_1 - c_0) = 0$$

which gives

$$c_0 = 6.$$

The particular solution for this part of $f(x)$ is then

$$y = 6 + 3x.$$

For 2^x we try initially $y = c2^x$, but this appears in the general solution of the homogeneous equation, as does $cx2^x$, so we try $y = cx^2 2^x$. Substituting in the left hand side of the equation and equating to 2^x gives

$$c(x+2)^2 2^{x+2} - 4c(x+1)^2 2^{x+1} + 4cx^2 2^x = 2^x.$$

The coefficients of the $x^2 2^x$ and $x2^x$ terms are both zero and equating the coefficient of the 2^x term to 1 gives

$$8c = 1 \text{ or } c = 1/8.$$

The particular solution derived from this part then is

$$y = x^2 2^x / 8$$

and the required particular solution as a whole is

$$y = 6 + 3x + x^2 2^x / 8.$$

The general solution to the nonhomogeneous equation is

$$y = (c_1 + c_2 x)2^x + 6 + 3x + x^2 2^x / 8.$$

A special case

As with differential equations a case that deserves special attention, given the use made of this equation in dynamic economic analysis, is where the function on the right hand side of the equation consists merely of a constant. Namely

$$y(x+2) + py(x+1) + qy(x) = k$$

where p, q, and k are constants. A particular solution to this equation is easily obtained by letting $y(x) = y(x+1) = y(x+2) = \bar{y}$ in this equation to obtain

$$\bar{y} = \frac{k}{1+p+q}.$$

As y is at rest at $\bar{y}$, $\bar{y}$ represents a potential equilibrium. Whether the actual time path for y converges to $\bar{y}$ or diverges away from $\bar{y}$ and whether it does this with oscillations or not, depends on the nature of the coefficients p and q.

We know we have three cases to look at depending on the nature of the roots of the auxiliary equation

$$m^2 + pm + q = 0.$$

Case 1   Real and distinct roots, $p^2 > 4q$
Our general solution is

$$y(x) = \bar{y} + c_1 m_1^x + c_2 m_2^x.$$

Now $m^x \to 0$ if and only if the absolute value of m is less than one. So if $|m_1| < 1$ and $|m_2| < 1$, the time path is convergent.

Suppose now one of the roots, say m_1, has absolute value greater than one, that is

$$|m_1| > 1 \quad \text{and} \quad |m_2| < 1.$$

As x increases m_2^x gets smaller in absolute size, whilst m_1^x gets larger in absolute size so m_1 dominates and we get a divergent time path.

Convergence requires then that both the roots of the auxiliary equation have absolute values less than one. Notice that unlike differential equations it is now possible to experience oscillations in this case. If m is negative then m^x is positive if x is even but negative if x is odd. Suppose $|m_1| > |m_2|$ but m_1 is negative. Then m_1^x dominates and we get oscillations for our time path.

Case 2   Real and equal roots, $p^2 = 4q$
The general solution is

$$y(x) = \bar{y} + (c_1 + c_2 x) r^x$$

where r is the common root.
Now $xr^x \to 0$ as $x \to \infty$ if and only if $|r| < 1$.
If r is negative then the time path exhibits oscillations.

Case 3   Conjugate complex roots, $p^2 < 4q$
The general solution in this case is

$$y(x) = \bar{y} + \rho^x (c_1 \cos \theta x + c_2 \sin \theta x)$$

and as this involves a linear combination of sine and cos functions we must get oscillations. If $\rho > 1$ then $\rho^x \to \infty$ as $x \to \infty$ and we get explosive oscillations. If $\rho < 1$ then $\rho^x \to 0$ as $x \to \infty$ and the time path exhibits damped oscillations with y converging to $\bar{y}$. In dealing with this case we should note the following definition:

Definition
The absolute value of a complex number

$$a + bi \text{ or } a - bi \text{ is } \sqrt{a^2 + b^2}.$$

With this definition we can summarize this special case as follows.

Unlike differential equations it is possible that the time path of our economic variable will exhibit oscillations in all three cases.

The time path of our economic variables will be convergent if and only if the absolute value of every root of the auxiliary equation is less than one.

Exercises for 10.3

1. Solve the following difference equations:
   (i) $\Delta^2 y(x) - 2\Delta y(x) = 0$
   (ii) $\nabla^2 y(x) - 2\nabla y(x - 1) + y(x - 2) = x^2$
   (iii) $\Delta^2 y(x) + y(x) = x^2 + 6x$
   (iv) $y(x) - 4y(x - 1) + 4y(x - 2) = 2^x + 8x$
   (v) $2y(x + 2) - 6y(x + 1) + 4y(x) = 2^x + 5$, when $y(0) = 0$ and $y(1) = 5/8$.
2. In a model designed to study the nature and stability of inventory cycles, Metzler came up with the following differential equation for output:

$$y(t) = (2 + \alpha)\beta y(t - 1) - (1 + \alpha)\beta y(t - 2) + v$$

where β is the marginal property to consume, α is the accelerator and v is a constant. We know that $0 < \beta < 1$ and $\alpha \geq 0$.
   (i) Find the condition on the parameters required to give real and distinct roots of the underlying auxiliary equation. Show that this condition implies $\beta > 2/(2 + \alpha)$. Hence show that for this case the time path of output is divergent and nonoscillatory.

   Hint: For the second part show that both roots are positive but the implied condition on β requires the sum of the roots to be greater than two.
   (ii) Find the conditions on the parameters for the roots to be real and equal. Show that for this case the time path for output is also divergent and nonoscillatory.
   (iii) Find the condition on the parameters for the time path of output to be subject to cycles. When will these cycles be (a) convergent, (b) divergent?

(iv) Draw a graph with β on the vertical axis and α on the horizontal axis and delineate the various regions of these parameters which give rise to different time paths for output.

3. Distinguish between discrete time and continuous time. Explain why the analysis of the time path of an economic variable arising from a second order linear difference equation is more complex than that arising from a second order linear differential equation.

10.4 Investigating the Nature of the Roots of a Quadratic Equation

We have just seen that the analysis of a second order linear difference equation is more complicated than the corresponding case for differential equations, in that for the former it is possible to get oscillations in all three cases if one of the roots is negative. It pays us to consider a mathematical aside that investigates ways of determining the nature of the roots of a quadratic equation. Consider the general quadratic equation

$$am^2 + bm + c = 0$$

where a, b, and c are constants. Then the roots of this equation are given by

$$m_1, m_2 = \frac{-b \pm \sqrt{b^2 - 4ac}}{2a}.$$

It follows then that

$$m_1 + m_2 = -b/a$$

and

$$m_1 m_2 = c/a.$$

If we have a priori information on a, b, and c this information may help us in determining whether the roots m_1 and m_2, are

(i) both positive
(ii) both negative
(iii) one positive and one negative

The following relationships are important:

(i) If $m_1 m_2 > 0$ then m_1 and m_2 must have the same sign. It follows that if $m_1 + m_2 > 0$ as well, then m_1 and m_2 are both positive, whereas if $m_1 + m_2 < 0$ then m_1 and m_2 are both negative.

(ii) If $m_1 m_2 < 0$ then one root is negative whereas the other is positive.

In determining whether the time path of the variable of our difference equation is convergent or divergent, we need to know whether one of the roots has absolute value greater than one. Sometimes looking at the relationship

$$(1 - m_1)(1 - m_2) = 1 - (m_1 + m_2) + m_1 m_2$$

may help in determining this. For example, suppose we have already established that one root m_2 is negative while the other m_1 is positive and that $m_1 > |m_2|$. (Showing that $m_1 m_2 < 0$ and $m_1 + m_2 > 0$ would establish this). Then we would only have divergence if $m_1 > 1$ which in turn would imply that $(1 - m_1)(1 - m_2)$ must be less than zero. If this is not the case then $m_1 \not> 1$, and we must have convergence.

Suppose we focus our attention more specifically on the auxiliary equation

$$f(m) = m^2 + pm + q = 0$$

and consider the case where we have two real and unequal roots. Then such an equation has a critical point that is a minimum so its graph must look like this:

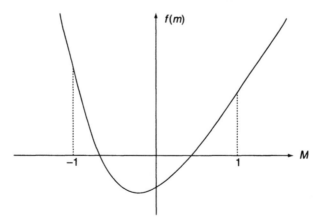

A necessary condition for the roots to have absolute values less than one, is that $f(1) > 0$ and $f(-1) > 0$, but this is not sufficient, as both roots could be larger than +1 or less than −1, and we would still have $f(1) > 0$ and $f(-1) > 0$ as the following diagram shows

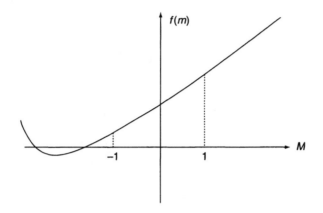

But in these latter two cases $m_1 m_2 = q$ would be greater than one. The absolute values of both roots of the auxiliary equation are less than one then, if and only if

(i) $f(1) = 1 + p + q > 0$
(ii) $f(-1) = 1 - p + q > 0$
(iii) $q < 1$.

Our investigation is helpful for differential equations as well. For our special case we know that we get convergence if and only if real roots are less than zero. If either c or a is negative whilst the other is positive, $m_1 m_2$ will be negative, and one root must be positive making the time path divergent. If c and a are both positive or both negative then $m_1 m_2$ is positive, and m_1 and m_2 are either both positive or both negative. If as well $b > 0$ with $a > 0$, then $m_1 + m_2$ is negative and both will be negative, resulting in a convergent time path. Other possibilities are left to the reader.

10.5 Economic Applications

Cobweb models

We started this chapter by noting that agriculture production takes time to alter involving as it does seeding, tending, and harvesting. Economists have highlighted this point in developing dynamic microeconomic models designed to explain the fluctuations in prices and quantities often experienced in agricultural markets. Such models are often called Cobweb models, after the pattern that results from the time path in our variables.

The basic Cobweb model

Consider the following dynamic supply and demand model

$$\text{Demand}: \quad Q_D(t) = \alpha + aP(t), \qquad a < 0$$
$$\text{Supply}: \quad Q_S(t) = \beta + bP(t - 1), \quad b > 0.$$

Supply highlights the fact that the supply of the agricultural product at time t is based on decisions made in the previous period, the intervening time being taken up with seeding, tending, and harvesting. Equating demand to supply gives a first order difference equation with constant coefficients.

$$\alpha + aP(t) = \beta + bP(t - 1)$$

or

$$aP(t) - bP(t - 1) = \beta - \alpha.$$

A particular solution to this equation is obtained by letting $P(t) = P(t - 1) = \bar{P}$ in the equation, to obtain our potential equilibrium given by

$$\bar{P} = \frac{\beta - \alpha}{a - b}.$$

The general solution is

$$P(t) = \bar{P} + k \left(\frac{b}{a}\right)^t,$$

where k is an arbitrary constant. The a priori information we are given about the parameters is $a < 0$ and $b > 0$ so b/a is negative and the time path for P must exhibit oscillations. These oscillations will be convergent if and only if $|b|/|a| < 1$. That is if and only if $b < |a|$.

If we graph our supply and demand functions following the mathematical tradition and plotting Q on the vertical axis then this condition states that the slope of the supply curve must be less than the absolute slope of the demand curve (Figure 10.1).

This basic model certainly gives rise to oscillations but the behavior it implies for farmers is unrealistic. Presumably farmers will only go to the trouble of

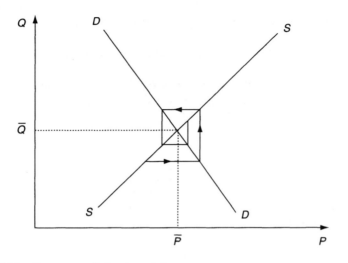

Figure 10.1 Convergent Cobweb model.

changing the amount of crops they seed if they believe the price of the output confronting them will persist in the future. But in each period the price changes again and the farmers follow suit in changing their production. In other words, the basic model implies that farmers never learn.

In any case, a more realistic approach would have farmers basing their seeding decisions at time $t - 1$, not on the price prevailing then, but on their expected price. Formulating expectations in economics is a tricky business, but one way of doing it is to base expected price at any given period not only on the price prevailing in the previous period but also on the price changes that took place in the previous period. That is

$$P^e(t) = P(t - 1) - \rho \nabla P(t - 1), \quad 0 < \rho < 1$$
$$= (1 - \rho)P(t - 1) + \rho P(t - 2),$$

where $P^e(t)$ is the price farmers expect at time t. The supply function is now formulated in terms of this expected price, so our model becomes

Demand : $\quad Q_D(t) = \alpha + aP(t), \quad a < 0$

Supply : $\quad Q_S(t) = \beta + bP^e(t) \quad b > 0, \, 0 < \rho < 1.$

Equating supply to demand gives

$$\alpha + aP(t) = \beta + b(1 - \rho)P(t - 1) + b\rho P(t - 2),$$

or

$$P(t) + c(1 - \rho)P(t - 1) + c\rho P(t - 2) = (\beta - \alpha)/a,$$

where $c = -b/a > 0$. We are now confronted with a second order linear difference equation with constant coefficients. The particular solution to this equation is found by setting $P(t) = P(t - 1) = P(t - 2) = \bar{P}$ in this equation to obtain

$$\bar{P} = \frac{\beta - \alpha}{a - b}.$$

The general solution to the homogeneous equation depends on the roots of the auxiliary equation:

$$m^2 + c(1 - \rho)m + c\rho = 0$$

All three cases need to be considered.

Case 1: Roots real and unequal
This case occurs when $c^2(1 - \rho)^2 > 4c\rho$
or

$$c > \frac{4\rho}{(1 - \rho)^2}.$$

The roots are given by

$$m_1, m_2 = \frac{-c(1 - \rho) \pm \sqrt{c^2(1 - \rho)^2 - 4c\rho}}{2}.$$

We now have two ways of proceeding. We could argue that as $c > 0$ and $\rho > 0$, what is under the positive square root sign is less than $c^2(1 - \rho)^2$, and as $(1 - \rho) > 0$ this means that both roots must be negative. Alternatively, we could look at

$$m_1 m_2 = c\rho > 0$$

and

$$m_1 + m_2 = -c(1 - \rho) < 0.$$

The first inequality assures us that both roots are either positive or negative. The second inequality assures us that they are in fact both negative.

Either way this process leads to the conclusion that for this case we must have oscillations.

Convergence requires both roots to have absolute values less than one and from our discussion in the previous section this is the case if and only if

(i) $1 + c(1 - \rho) + c\rho > 0$,

that is, $1 - b/a > 0$, which is the same condition derived from the basic model

(ii) $1 - c(1 - \rho) + c\rho > 0$,

that is, $1 > c(1 - 2\rho)$

(iii) $c\rho < 1$,

that is, $c < 1/\rho$.

Case 2: Real and equal roots

This occurs when $c = 4\rho/(1 - \rho)^2$, and the common root is

$$m_1 = m_2 = -c(1 - \rho)/2 < 0.$$

Again we must have oscillations. These oscillations will be convergent if

$$\frac{c(1 - \rho)}{2} < 1$$

or

$$c(1 - \rho) < 2.$$

Case 3: Conjugate complex roots

This case occurs when $c < 4\rho/(1 - \rho)^2$, and we know that it always leads to oscillations. These oscillations will be convergent if the absolute value of the roots is less than 1.

That is,

$$\sqrt{\frac{c^2(1 - \rho)^2 + 4c\rho - c^2(1 - \rho)^2}{4}} < 1,$$

that is,

$$\sqrt{c\rho} < 1$$

or

$$c\rho < 1.$$

Samuelson's multiplier accelerator model

Agricultural products may be subject to fluctuations in prices. But the economy as a whole seems to be subject to the oscillations of a business cycle. Samuelson, in a famous 1939 article in the *Review of Economic Statistics*, combines two concepts that were prevalent in macroeconomics at the time to produce a dynamic model capable of exhibiting cycles. These two concepts were the multiplier and the accelerator.

The multiplier arises in Keynesian economics when we relate aggregate consumption C to national income Y. The accelerator in turn relates investment I to the increase in national income or equivalently to the increase in aggregate consumption. The models starts with the definitional equation for national income at time t

$$Y_t = C_t + I_t + G, \tag{10.1}$$

where for simplicity we assume government expenditure G is constant through time. The multiplier is represented in the model by relating consumption at time t to the previous years income

$$C_t = \gamma Y_{t-1} \quad 0 < \gamma < 1, \tag{10.2}$$

where γ is the marginal propensity to consume. The accelerator is portrayed in the model by

$$\begin{aligned} I_t &= \alpha(C_t - C_{t-1}) \quad \alpha > 0. \\ &= \alpha\gamma(Y_{t-1} - Y_{t-2}) \end{aligned} \tag{10.3}$$

Substituting equations (10.2) and (10.3) into the definitional equation (10.1) we have

$$Y_t = \gamma Y_{t-1} + \alpha\gamma(Y_{t-1} - Y_{t-2}) + G$$

or

$$Y_t - \gamma(1 + \alpha)Y_{t-1} + \alpha\gamma Y_{t-2} = G$$

which is a second order linear difference equation with constant coefficients. A particular solution to this equation is found by letting $Y_t = Y_{t-1} = Y_{t-2} = \bar{Y}$ in the equation to yield

$$\bar{Y} = \frac{G}{1 - \gamma}$$

which is the usual Keynesian equilibrium level of national income. The general solution to the homogeneous equation depends on the roots of the auxiliary equation

$$m^2 - \gamma(1 + \alpha)m + \alpha\gamma = 0,$$

which are given by

$$m = \frac{\gamma(1 + \alpha) \pm \sqrt{\gamma^2(1 + \alpha^2) - 4\alpha\gamma}}{2}.$$

All three cases are possible and are studied in turn.

Case 1: Real distinct roots $\gamma^2(1 + \alpha^2) > 4\alpha\gamma$

The nature of the two distinct roots can be ascertained from

$$m_1 + m_2 = \gamma(1 + \alpha) > 0$$

and

$$m_1 m_2 = \alpha\gamma > 0.$$

Thus both roots are positive and no cycles arise from this case. Whether the time path is divergent or convergent depends on whether the roots are greater than one or less than one respectively. Let m_1 be the larger root. Then we have the following possibilities:

(i) $0 < m_2 < m_1 < 1$
(ii) $0 < m_2 < m_1 = 1$
(iii) $0 < m_2 < 1 < m_1$
(iv) $1 = m_2 < m_1$
(v) $1 < m_2 < m_1$.

To determine which of these possibilities are acceptable to the model given that it specifies $\alpha > 0$ and $0 < \gamma < 1$ we consider

$$(1 - m_1)(1 - m_2) = 1 - (m_1 + m_2) + m_1 m_2$$
$$= 1 - \gamma(1 + \alpha) + \gamma\alpha$$
$$= 1 - \gamma$$

and

$$m_1 m_2 = \alpha\gamma.$$

Now

 (i) $\Rightarrow (1 - m_1)(1 - m_2) > 0$
   $\Rightarrow 1 - \gamma > 0$
   $\Rightarrow 1 > \gamma$
   which is acceptable.
   Also
 (ii) $\Rightarrow (1 - m_1)(1 - m_2) = 0 > \gamma = 1$ which is unacceptable as we must have $\gamma < 1$.
 (iii) $\Rightarrow (1 - m_1)(1 - m_2) < 0 \Rightarrow \gamma > 1$ which is unacceptable.
 (iv) $\Rightarrow \gamma = 1$ which is unacceptable.
 (v) $\Rightarrow (1 - m_1)(1 - m_2) > 0 \Rightarrow 1 > \gamma$ and $m_1 m_2 > 1 \Rightarrow \alpha\gamma > 1$. Both these implications are acceptable.

Two possibilities are left.

Subcase 1C:
This subcase gives rise to a convergent non-oscillating time path which is convergent. The subcase implies that

$$\gamma < 1 \quad \text{and} \quad \alpha\gamma < 1.$$

Subcase 1D:
This subcase gives rise to a divergent non-oscillating time path which is divergent and implies that

$$\gamma < 1 \quad \text{and} \quad \alpha\gamma > 1.$$

Case 2: Real and equal roots $\gamma^2(1 + \alpha^2) = 4\alpha\gamma$
Here

$$m_1 = m_2 = \frac{\gamma(1 + \alpha)}{2} > 0.$$

Again, no cyclical behavior for Y arises from this case. By conducting an analysis similar to the previous case we obtain two possible regimes which are acceptable to our model.

Subcase 2C: $0 < m < 1$
This case leads to a convergent time path for Y and implies the same conditions on α and γ as subcase 1C, namely

$$\gamma < 1 \text{ and } \alpha\gamma < 1.$$

Subcase 2D: $m > 1$
This subcase leads to divergent time path for Y and implies the same conditions as α and γ as subcase 1D.

Case 3: Conjugate complex roots $\gamma^2(1 + \alpha^2) < 4\alpha\gamma$

We know that this case must give us oscillations in the time path for Y, and whether these are convergent or divergent depends on the absolute value of the complex roots

$$R = \sqrt{\frac{\gamma^2(1 + \alpha)^2 + 4\gamma\alpha - \gamma^2(1 + \alpha)^2}{4}} = \sqrt{\gamma\alpha}.$$

Again two possibilities present themselves and these are both acceptable to the model.

Subcase 3C: Convergent Oscillations.
    Here

$$R < 1 \Rightarrow \gamma\alpha < 1$$

Subcase 3D: Divergent oscillations.
    Here

$$R \geq 1 \Rightarrow \gamma\alpha \geq 1.$$

The following diagram delineates the various regions that are possible for our parameters and the subcases that arise from these regions:

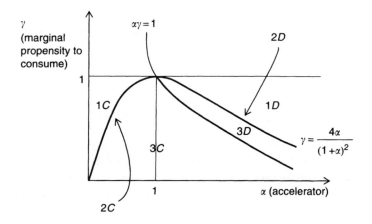

Exercises for 10.5
Consider the following version of the multiplier accelerator model:

$$Y_t = C_t + I_t$$

$$C_t = a + bY_t$$

$$I_t = v(Y_{t-1} - Y_{t-2})$$

where a and v are positive and $0 < b < 1$.

(i) Obtain a difference equation in Y, the auxiliary equation of this difference equation, and a potential equilibrium value for Y.
(ii) Let $c = v/(1 - b)$. What conditions do we need on c to obtain real and distinct roots of the auxiliary equation? Show that for this case we must have explosive growth for Y. Do we also have oscillations for Y?
(iii) Find the conditions on c needed to obtain real and equal roots of the auxiliary equation. What are the characteristics of the time path for Y in this case?
(iv) Find the condition on c needed to ensure cycles. What about for explosive or damped cycles?
(v) Give an economic interpretation of your conditions.

10.6   Higher Order Linear Difference Equations

The solution to the nth order linear difference equation

$$y(x + n) + a_1 y(x + n - 1) + \cdots + a_n y(x) = k,$$

where $a_1, \ldots, a_n$, and k are constants depends on the roots of the auxiliary equation

$$m^n + a_1 m^{n-1} + \cdots + a_{n-1} m + a_n = 0.$$

Such an nth order polynominal equation is a lot harder to solve than a quadratic equation, but like the latter, the former can have roots which are real, repeated, or complex. Regardless of the nature of these roots the time path for $y(x)$ will converge if and only if every root has absolute value less than one. As in the case for differential equations, we can determine whether this is the case or not, without solving for the roots, by appealing to an appropriate theorem.

Schur's theorem

The roots of the nth order polynomial equation

$$a_0 m^n + a_1 m^{n-1} + \cdots + a_{n-1} m + a_n = 0$$

will all have absolute value less than one if and only if the following n determinants

$$\begin{vmatrix} a_0 & a_n \\ a_n & a_0 \end{vmatrix}, \begin{vmatrix} a_0 & 0 & a_n & a_{n-1} \\ a_1 & a_0 & 0 & a_n \\ a_n & 0 & a_0 & a_1 \\ a_{n-1} & a_n & 0 & a_0 \end{vmatrix}, \ldots,$$

$$\begin{vmatrix} a_0 & 0 & \cdots & 0 & a_n & a_{n-1} & \cdots & a_1 \\ a_1 & a_0 & \cdots & 0 & 0 & a_n & \cdots & a_2 \\ \vdots & \vdots & & \vdots & \vdots & \vdots & & \vdots \\ a_{n-1} & a_{n-2} & \cdots & a_0 & 0 & 0 & \cdots & a_n \\ a_n & 0 & \cdots & 0 & a_0 & a_1 & \cdots & a_n \\ a_{n-1} & a_n & \cdots & 0 & 0 & a_0 & \cdots & a_{n-2} \\ \vdots & \vdots & & \vdots & \vdots & \vdots & & \vdots \\ a_1 & a_2 & \cdots & a_n & 0 & 0 & \cdots & a_0 \end{vmatrix}$$

all are positive.

Example

Using Schur's theorem, test for convergence in the time path of the solution of the following difference equation:

$$y(x + 3) + 6y(x + 1) + \frac{1}{2}y(x) = 7.$$

$$\begin{vmatrix} 1 & \frac{1}{2} \\ \frac{1}{2} & 1 \end{vmatrix} = \frac{3}{4} > 0$$

$$\begin{vmatrix} 1 & 0 & \frac{1}{2} & 6 \\ 0 & 1 & 0 & \frac{1}{2} \\ \frac{1}{2} & 0 & 1 & 0 \\ 6 & \frac{1}{2} & 0 & 1 \end{vmatrix} = 1(-1)^{2+2}\begin{vmatrix} 1 & \frac{1}{2} & 6 \\ \frac{1}{2} & 1 & 0 \\ 6 & 0 & 1 \end{vmatrix} + \frac{1}{2}(-1)^{4+2}\begin{vmatrix} 1 & \frac{1}{2} & 6 \\ 0 & 0 & \frac{1}{2} \\ \frac{1}{2} & 1 & 0 \end{vmatrix}$$

$$= 6(-1)^{3+1}\begin{vmatrix} \frac{1}{2} & 6 \\ 1 & 0 \end{vmatrix} + 1(-1)^{3+3}\begin{vmatrix} 1 & \frac{1}{2} \\ \frac{1}{2} & 1 \end{vmatrix}$$

$$+ \frac{1}{4}(-1)^{3+2}\begin{vmatrix} 1 & \frac{1}{2} \\ \frac{1}{2} & 1 \end{vmatrix}$$

$$= -36 + \frac{3}{4} - \frac{3}{16}$$

$$< 0.$$

The second determinant being less than zero, Schur's theorem ensures that the time path will be divergent.

Exercises for 10.6

1. Use Schur's theorem to test the convergence of the time paths that result from the following difference equations.
   (i) $\Delta^2 y(x) - \Delta y(x) = 6$
   (ii) $\nabla^2 y(x) - 3\nabla y(x) + y(x) = -7$
   (iii) $3y(x+2) - 2y(x+1) + y(x) = 10$
2. In the case of the third order difference equation:

$$\Delta^3 y(x) + a_1 \Delta^2 y(x) + a_2 \Delta y(x) + a_3 y(x) = c$$

what are the exact forms of the determinants involved in Schur's theorem?

Chapter 11

---

*Dynamic Optimization

*11.1   Introduction

The constrained optimization problems studied in Chapters 6 and 7 may be referred to as **static** optimization problems. In them time plays no crucial role. Instead the decision maker seeks to choose the point that optimizes the value of an objective function which is subject to an equality constraint. We saw that the Lagrangian function played an essential role in the solution to these problems, with the Lagrangian multiplier associated with the optimal point having a shadow price or imputed value interpretation.

In this last chapter we want to look at **dynamic** optimization problems, optimization problems that take place over time. We shall see in the next section that these problems are very different from the familiar static problems, and the mathematics involved is decidedly more complicated. However, similarities remain. In dynamic problems the Hamiltonian plays a role similar to the Lagrangian function in the static problems, while the costate variable plays a role similar to the Lagrangian multiplier.

When time is treated as a continuous variable dynamic optimization involves minimizing or maximizing the value of an integral. Originally such a problem was tackled by a branch of mathematics called the **calculus of variations**, but the work done by Russian mathematicians, L.S. Pontryagin and his colleagues in the 1950s, generalized this theory when they developed what is now known as **optimal control theory**. At the same time an American mathematician Bellman developed **dynamic programming**, a different tack to the problem that is particularly suited to the case where time is treated as a discrete variable.

In this chapter we will be contented with an introduction to optimal control theory for the case where time is treated as a continuous variable. The mathematics involved is well outside the scope of this book, so instead of proofs I will provide a few heuristic arguments. For a more formal discussion the reader is referred to such advanced books as Lambert (1985), or Sydsaeter, Hammond, Seierstand, and Strom (2005).

*11.2   Dynamic Optimization Versus Static Optimization

In this section we wish to highlight how optimal control problems differ from static optimization problems. The salient features of an optimal control problem may be introduced by considering a problem from resource economics, namely the optimal management of a fishery. Suppose a fishing operator has the rights to harvest fish from a given lake from the present time designated by $t = 0$ to some terminal date say $t = T$. Let $x(t)$ be the stock of fish in the lake at time t and suppose $u(t)$ is the amount of fish harvested at time t. All fish caught can be sold at price p. The cost of fishing C depends positively on the harvest $u(t)$ and negatively on the stock of fish, as it is easier to catch fish when they are abundant. Thus $C = C(u(t), x(t))$. The cash flow for the operator at time t is then

$$pu(t) - C(u(t), x(t)).$$

The value of the operator's fishing rights is the present value of the stream of cash flow namely

$$V = \int_0^T [pu(t) - C(u(t), x(t))]e^{-rt} dt.$$

The operator wishes to maximize V but he or she is constrained by the effect the harvest has on the stock. Suppose in the lake a biological renewal function $f(x(t))$ operates for the fish. Then at each point in time the growth rate of the fish stock is given by

$$x'(t) = f(x(t)) - u(t).$$

The initial stock of fish in the lake say $x(0) = x_0$, provides the starting point. It may also be the case that the license requires that a stock of fish $x(T) = x_T$ must be present in the lake when operations cease.

The problem facing the fishing operator is

$$\text{Max } V = \int_0^T [pu(t) - C(u(t), x(t))] e^{-rt} dt \qquad (11.1)$$

subject to

$$x'(t) = f(x(t)) - u(t) \tag{11.2}$$

and end conditions

$$x(0) = x_0, \quad x(T) = x_T. \tag{11.3}$$

This example typifies an optimal control problem. It differs from the static optimization problem in the following ways:

(i) Optimization takes place over a **planning horizon**, in this case from time $t = 0$ to $t = T$. In our example the time of termination T is fixed. In other examples, T could be infinite or the time of termination itself could be variable of the optimization problem.

(ii) The integrand that is maximized is a **functional** rather than a function. That is, instead of being a function of variables it is a function of functions $x(t)$ and $u(t)$. In maximizing V we seek to find functions $x^*(t)$ and $u^*(t)$ that represent the optimal time paths for $x(t)$ and $u(t)$ for t ranging from 0 to T.

(iii) Unlike static optimization our problem contains two sorts of variables, a stock variable $x(t)$ and a flow variable $u(t)$. At any time period our operator chooses the harvest rate $u(t)$ but this choice in turn affects future values of the stock variable. In optimal control theory jargon, $x(t)$ is called the **state variable** and $u(t)$ is called the **control variable**.

(iv) One of the constraints of our dynamic problems is a differential equation which tells us how the choice of the control variable $u(t)$ affects a change in the state variable $x(t)$. This constraint is called the **state equation**.

(v) The second set of constraints in the dynamic problem concerns conditions on the initial and terminal values of the state variable. In our fishing example these values are specified. Although this is usually the case for the initial value of the state variable, the terminal condition on state variable may be more flexible. For example the fishing license may require that the stock of fish in the lake at the termination of the license must be at least as great as x_T, in which case the terminal conditions would be

$$x(T) \geq x_T.$$

Alternatively, no condition may be placed on the terminal value of the state variable, so $x(T)$ is a free variable like all the other $x(t)$s except of course $x(0)$.

Our fishery example typifies our basic optimal control problem. In the next section we present an heuristic argument for the maximum principle which represents a set of necessary conditions for the optimal solution to our problem. We then show how these conditions can be used to obtain a solution for the basic problem. Generalizations of this problem such as the terminal time being infinite or variable, the control variable being constrained to a control region, or more flexible terminal conditions will be dealt with in the section following.

*11.3   The Basic Optimal Control Problem and Pontryagin's Maximum Principle[1]

Our basic optimal control problem can be formulated as

$$\text{Max} \int_0^T f(x(t), u(t), t)dt \tag{11.4}$$

subject to the state equation

$$\frac{dx}{dt} = g(x(t), u(t), t) \tag{11.5}$$

and the end point conditions

$$x(0) = x_0, \quad x(T) = x_T. \tag{11.6}$$

An American mathematician Richard Bellman studying dynamic optimization in the 1950s came up with a basic principle that the optimal solution must satisfy.

The principle of optimality[2]

"An optimal policy has the property that whatever the initial state and the initial decision are, the remaining decisions must constitute an optimal policy with regard to the state resulting from the first decision."

Although this principle is best suited to dynamic optimization problems where time is treated as a discrete variable, it can be adapted to the continuous case to give some insight into the necessary conditions for achieving an optimal solution $x^*(t)$, $u^*(t)$ to our basic problem.

---

[1] This section is adapted from Eugene Silberg, "The Structural of Economics: A Mathematical Analysis," second edition, McGraw-Hill 1990, pp 617–620.

[2] Richard Bellman and Stuart Dreyfus "Applied Dynamic Programming", Princeton University Press 1962, p. 15.

Suppose for the moment we have such an optimal solution $x^*(t)$, $u^*(t)$. Like all other optimization problems, these optimal values will depend on the parameters of the problem namely x_0 and x_T and any other parameters appearing in functions. Moreover, a maximum value function for our problem would be given by

$$M(x_0, x_T, \ldots) = \int_0^T f(x^*(t), u^*(t), t) dt.$$

From our work in Section 7.3 of Chapter 7 we know that the shadow price or an imputed value of an extra unit of say x_0 would be

$$\frac{\partial M}{\partial x_0} = \lambda(0) \text{ say.}$$

Suppose now we are at time t in our planning horizon having made optimal decisions up to that time and we contemplate the decision we should make for an (infinitesimally) small period of time $t + \Delta t$. Bellman's 'Principle of Optimality' says that our decision must be optimal when we take $x^*(t)$ as the initial condition for the state variable at the beginning of this period. Choosing $u^*(t)$ as the value for the control variable for our (infinitesimal) small period of time means an immediate benefit of $f(x^*(t), u^*(t), t)$. But we must also take into consideration how $u^*(t)$ affects the imputed value of our stock. Suppose that $\lambda(t)$ is the imputed value for one unit of our stock. Then as $x^*(t)$ is being regarded as an initial condition for our period we must have $\partial M / \partial x^*(t) = \lambda(t)$ say where M is the appropriate maximum value function. The imputed value of the entire stock at the beginning of our period is then $\lambda(t) x^*(t)$ and the change in this imputed value would be

$$\frac{d}{dt} \lambda x^* = \frac{d\lambda}{dt} x^* + \lambda \frac{dx^*}{dt}.$$

Thus the net benefit derived from $x^*(t)$ and $u^*(t)$ for our infinitesimal period would be

$$f(x^*(t), u^*(t), t) + \frac{d\lambda}{dt} x^* + \lambda \frac{dx^*}{dt}.$$

Suppose now we take a step back and ask what characteristics must our optimal solution $x^*(t)$ and $u^*(t)$ display. Surely it must be that for each t they optimize this expression.

Dropping the stars, our heuristic argument leads us to conclude that for each t in the planning horizon the optimal solution must satisfy

$$\max_{u,x} f(x,u,t) + \lambda x' + \lambda' x, \tag{11.7}$$

where for convenience we have suppressed the dependence of u and x on t. Finally using the state equation we write problem (11.7) as

$$\max_{u,x} f(x,u,t) + \lambda g(x,u,t) + \lambda' x. \tag{11.8}$$

This problem is traditionally written in terms of the Hamiltonian, which we now define.

Definition
The **Hamiltonian** is the function

$$H(x,u,\lambda,t) = f(x,u,t) + \lambda g(x,u,t).$$

Note that the Hamiltonian is a function of four variables: x, u, λ, and t. The variable $\lambda(t)$ is called the **costate** or **adjoint** variable.

The maximization problem given by equation (11.8) can then be written as

$$\max_{u,x} H(x,u,\lambda,t) + \lambda' x.$$

Our discussion leads us to conclude the following famous principle.

Pontryagin's maximum principle

If a solution $x^*(t), u^*(t)$ exists to our problem, then for each t there exists a $\lambda(t)$ such that $x^*(t)$ and $u^*(t)$ maximize

$$H(x(t),u(t),\lambda(t),t) + \lambda(t)'x(t).$$

The above discussion suggests that $\lambda(t)$ represents the imputed value or shadow price of the state variable at time t and this is indeed true. In our basic problem, no constraints are placed on the control variable $u(t)$. Moreover $x(t)$ is unconstrained (except for $t = 0$ and $t = T$) so we can freely optimize with respect to both these variables. Assuming differentiability of our functions, the first order conditions for maximizing $H + \lambda' x$ with respect to u and x are

$$\frac{\partial H}{\partial u} = 0$$

$$\lambda' = \frac{-\partial H}{\partial x}. \tag{11.9}$$

Equation (11.9) is called the **costate equation**. A further condition

$$x' = \frac{\partial H}{\partial \lambda}$$

ensures that the state equation holds.

The above discussion can be summarized in the following theorem:

Theorem 1[3]

Consider the basic optimal control problem as presented by equations (11.4), (11.5), and (11.6). Form the Hamiltonian

$$H(x, u, \lambda, t) = f(x, u, t) + \lambda g(x, u, t).$$

A set of necessary conditions for an optimal solution are that for each t

(i)	u maximizes $H(x, u, \lambda, t)$	Maximizing with respect to u.
(ii)	$\lambda' = -\dfrac{\partial H}{\partial x}$	Costate Equation
(iii)	$x' = \dfrac{\partial H}{\partial \lambda}$	State Equation
(iv)	$x(0) = x_0, x(T) = x_T$	End Point Conditions.

In our work on unconstrained optimization in Section 6.7 of Chapter 6 we saw that necessary conditions for optimization become sufficient with the additional condition that the object function has the right curvature (i.e. that it is convex or concave). A similar result for optimal control theory was proved by Mangasarian.

---

[3]Our heuristic argument does not represent a formal mathematical proof of this theorem. Some authors refer to condition (i) as the maximum principle.

Theorem 2 (Mangasarian 1966)[4]

If the Hamilton $H(x, u, \lambda, t)$ is concave in x and u for each t then the conditions of Theorem 3 are necessary and sufficient for a solution.

Theoretically, Theorems 1 and 2 give the following procedure for solving our basic problem. First we check that the Hamiltonian H is concave in x and u. Next we maximize H with respect to u by solving $\partial H / \partial u = 0$ in terms of x and λ and ensuring that at this point $\partial^2 H / \partial u^2$ is less than zero. Substituting for u in the costate and state equations gives two differential equations in λ and x which we solve. The general solutions to these equations will involve arbitrary constants, which can be assigned particular values using the end point conditions. The optimal paths $x^*(t)$ for the state variable and the corresponding imputed values $\lambda^*(t)$ are thus obtained. Finally substituting back into the solution for u gives us the optimal time path $u^*(t)$ for the control variable.

Example

Solve the following problem:

$$\text{Maximize } \int_0^1 (-x - 5u^2)dt$$
$$\text{subject to } \quad x' = u$$
$$x(0) = 5, \quad x(1) = 10.$$

The Hamiltonian for this problem is

$$H = -(x + 5u^2) + \lambda u.$$

This function is concave in x and u being the sum of concave functions, so the conditions of Theorem 1 become necessary and sufficient. Now

$$\frac{\partial H}{\partial u} = -10u + \lambda = 0$$

and

$$\frac{\partial^2 H}{\partial u^2} = -10,$$

[4] Mangasarian, O.L. (1966) "Sufficient conditions for the optimal control of non-linear systems". SIAM Control Journal, 4, 139–52.

so the value of u that maximizes H is $u = \lambda/10$. The costate and state equations are

$$\lambda' = -\frac{\partial H}{\partial x} = 1$$

$$x' = \frac{\partial H}{\partial \lambda} = u,$$

and substituting for u we are left with two differential equations in x and λ:

$$\lambda' = 1$$

$$x' = \lambda/10.$$

The first of these yields $\lambda = t + c_1$, where c_1 is an arbitrary constant. Substituting into the second equation and solving gives

$$x = (t^2/2 + tc_1)/10 + c_2,$$

where c_2 is another arbitrary constant. As $x(0) = 5$, we get $c_2 = 5$ and as $x(1) = 10$, $c_1 = 99/2$ so our optimal solutions are

$$x^*(t) = (t^2/2 + 99t/2)/10 + 5$$

$$u^*(t) = (t + 99/2)/10$$

with imputed values

$$\lambda^*(t) = t + 99/2.$$

Note

Before we leave this section it should be noted that minimization problems are easily accommodated. Suppose the problem confronting us is to

$$\text{Minimize} \quad \int_0^T h(x(t), u(t), t) dt$$

$$\text{subject to} \quad \frac{dx}{dt} = g(x(t), u(t), t)$$

the end point conditions

$$x(0) = x_0, \quad x(T) = x_T.$$

Minimizing $\int_0^T h(x(t), u(t), t)dt$ is equivalent to

Maximizing $\int_0^T -h(x(t), u(t), t)dt$

or

Maximizing $\int_0^T f(x(t), u(t), t)dt,$

where $f(x(t), u(t), t) = -h(x(t), u(t), t)dt$. With this change, the minimization problem is changed into our basic maximization problem.

Exercises for 11.3

1. In the following problems $x(t)$ is the state variable and $u(t)$ is the control variable. Find the optimal paths for these variables together with the optimal path of the costate variable.

(i)

Maximize $\int_0^1 (u - u^2)dt$

subject to $\quad x' = u$

$$x(0) = 4, \quad x(1) = 2.$$

(ii)

Maximize $\int_0^1 -(4u + u^2)dt$

subject to $\quad x' = x - 2u$

$$x(0) = 2, \quad x(1) = 10.$$

(iii)

Maximize $\int_0^1 x - u^2 dt$

subject to $\quad x' = u - 3x$

$$x(0) = 1, \quad x(1) = 4.$$

2. Consumer's endowment problem

Suppose a person inherits $1 million. He decides to retire and take as his income the interest payments he gets from investing this money. Let $W(t)$ be his wealth at time t and suppose the rate of return on invested money is 5%. His income at time t is then

$$Y(t) = 0.05W(t).$$

This income can either be consumed or reinvested so

$$W'(t) = Y(t) - C(t) = 0.05W(t) - C(t).$$

Suppose the consumer's utility function is $U(t) = \log C(t)$ and his personal rate of time preference is 2%. He expects to live another 40 years and wants to leave a bequest of half a million dollars to his children.

(i) Set up the dynamic optimization problem facing this consumer. What is the state variable? What is the control variable?

(ii) What are the necessary conditions for an optimal solution? Are these conditions sufficient?

(iii) Find the optimal time paths for consumption and the accompanying time path for his wealth.

3. Calculus of variations problem

A Calculus of variations problem is of the form

$$\text{Maximize} \quad \int_a^b f(x'(t), x(t), t)dt$$

$$\text{subject to} \quad x(a) = x_a, \quad x(b) = x_b.$$

(i) Reformulate this problem as an optimal control problem by letting

$$x'(t) = u(t).$$

(ii) Form the Hamiltonian of this problem and obtain the necessary conditions for an optimal solution.

(iii) By differentiating $\partial H / \partial u$ with respect to t, show that these conditions imply Euler's equation which is

$$\frac{\partial f(x'(t), x(t), t)}{\partial x(t)} = \frac{d}{dt}\left(\frac{\partial f(x'(t), x(t), t)}{\partial x'(t)}\right).$$

*11.4   Extensions to the Basic Problem[5]

Different terminal conditions

We have seen that when we come to solve the state equation, and the costate equation, two arbitrary constants of integration appear in the general solutions. In the basic problem the end point conditions $x(0) = x_0$ and $x(T) = x_T$ are used as initial conditions to assign particular values to these arbitrary constants and thus obtain our optimal time paths.

The end point condition on $x(0)$ seems perfectly reasonable. It tells us that at the start of our planning horizon a certain amount of the state variable is available. For example in our fishery problem this end point condition tells us that there is a certain amount of fish in the lake at the commencement of the license period. The terminal end point condition in the basic problem appears however, unnecessarily restrictive. Specifying $x(T) = x_T$ in our fishery example means that at the end of the license period there must be a certain stock of fish left in the lake. A less restrictive terminal condition might be

$$x(T) \geq x_T.$$

That is, in our example the stock of fish left in the lake must be at least as great as a specified amount. Alternatively, the fishing license may be such that the operator is free to exploit the lake as much as he likes, in which case $x(T)$ would be subject to no restrictions. We say here that $x(T)$ is **free** (i.e. free from any restriction).

For the terminal conditions

$$x(T) \text{ free}$$

and

$$x(T) \geq x_T,$$

no end point condition on $x(T)$ is available as an initial condition that we can use to assign a particular value to one of the arbitrary constants in the solutions of our differential equations. Fortunately for us the mathematics of the problem for these two cases throw up implied conditions on the values of $\lambda(T)$. These conditions are called **transversality conditions**, and are used in place of a specified value for $x(T)$ to assign values to our arbitrary constants.

---

[5] For details of the mathematics behind these extensions, refer to specialist texts such as Kamien, M. and Schwartz, N. "Dynamic Optimization" North Holland, NY 1981 or Chiang, A.C. "Dynamic Optimization" McGraw-Hill NY, 1992.

If our problem is such that $x(T)$ is free then the transversality condition is $\lambda(T) = 0$ and condition iv of Theorem 1 is replaced by

$$\text{(iv)} \quad x(0) = x_0, \quad \lambda(T) = 0.$$

In the case that $x(T) \geq x_T$, the transversality condition is

$$\lambda(T) \geq 0 \quad x(T) \geq x_T, \quad (x(T) - x_T)\lambda(T) = 0, ^6$$

and condition (iv) of Theorem 1 is replaced by

$$\text{(iv)} \quad x(0) = x_0, \quad \lambda(T) \geq 0, \quad x(T) \geq x_T, \quad (x(T) - x_T)\lambda(T) = 0.$$

The condition $(x(T) - x_T)\lambda(T) = 0$ means that at least one of $x(T) - x_T$ and $\lambda(T)$ must equal zero. One way of handling this condition would be to try $\lambda(T) = 0$ as a possibility first, and test if the resultant $x^*(T)$ satisfies the restriction $x^*(T) \geq x_T$. If it does, then we have found the optimal solution. If not then we rerun the problem with $x(T) = x_T$ as an end point condition.

Example 1
Solve the problem

$$\text{Maximize} \quad \int_0^2 2x + 3u - \frac{1}{2}u^2 dt$$

$$\text{subject to} \quad x' = x + u$$

$$x(0) = 5, \quad x(2) \text{ free.}$$

The Hamiltonian is

$$H = 2x + 3u - \tfrac{1}{2}u^2 + \lambda(x + u)$$

which is clearly concave in x and u.

Moreover

$$\frac{\partial H}{\partial u} = 3 - u + \lambda, \quad \frac{\partial^2 H}{\partial u^2} = -1$$

so the value of u that maximizes H is

$$u = \lambda + 3.$$

---

[6] If the reader is familiar with Kuhn-Tucker theory this condition resembles "complementary slackness".

The costate and state equations are

$$\lambda' = -\frac{\partial H}{\partial x} = -(2 + \lambda)$$

$$x' = \frac{\partial H}{\partial \lambda} = x + u = x + \lambda + 3.$$

The solution to the first of these differential equations is

$$\lambda = -2 + c_1 e^{-t}$$

where c_1 is an arbitrary constant. As $x(2)$ is free the implied transversality condition is $\lambda(2) = 0$ so $c_1 = 2e^2$ and $\lambda = 2(e^2 e^{-t} - 1)$. Substituting this solution into the second differential equations yields

$$x' - x = 2e^2 e^{-t} + 1$$

which is a first order nonhomogeneous linear differential equation which has a particular solution given by

$$e^t \int_0^t e^{-s}(2e^2 e^{-s} + 1)ds = e^t \int_0^t 2e^2 e^{-2s} + e^{-s}ds$$

$$= e^t\big[-e^2 e^{-2s} - e^{-s}\big]_0^t$$

$$= e^t\big[-e^{2-2t} - e^{-t} + e^2 + 1\big].$$

The general solution for x is then given by

$$x = c_2 e^t - e^{2-t} - 1 + e^{t+2} + e^t.$$

Finally as $x(0) = 5$ we have $c_2 = 5$.
Our optimal solutions are then

$$x^*(t) = 6e^t - e^{2-t} + e^{t+2} - 1$$

$$\lambda^*(t) = 2(e^{2-t} - 1)$$

$$u^*(t) = 2e^{2-t} + 1.$$

Example 2
Solve the problem

$$\text{Maximize } \int_0^1 1 - x^2 - u^2 dt$$

$$\text{subject to } x' = u$$

and

$$x(0) = 1, \quad x(1) \geq 2.$$

The Hamiltonian is

$$H = 1 - x^2 - u^2 + \lambda u,$$

which is concave in x and u. Moreover as

$$\frac{\partial H}{\partial u} = -2u + \lambda \quad \text{and} \quad \frac{\partial^2 H}{\partial u^2} = -2$$

the value of u that maximizes H is $u = \lambda/2$.
    The costate and state equations are

$$\lambda' = -\frac{\partial H}{\partial x} = 2x, \quad x' = \frac{\partial H}{\partial \lambda} = u = \lambda/2,$$

so $\lambda'' = 2x' = \lambda$ which is a second order linear differential equation whose general solution is

$$\lambda = c_1 e^t + c_2 e^{-t} \tag{11.10}$$

where c_1 and c_2 are arbitrary constants.
    Moreover

$$x = \lambda'/2 = (c_1 e^t - c_2 e^{-t})/2. \tag{11.11}$$

As the terminal condition is $x(1) \geq 2$, the transversality condition is

$$\lambda(1) \geq 0, \quad x(1) \geq 2, \quad [x(1) - 2]\lambda(1) = 0.$$

Try $\lambda(1) = 0$. Then from equation (11.10) we have

$$0 = c_1 e + c_2 e^{-1}. \tag{11.12}$$

Moreover as $x(0) = 1$ we have equation (11.11)

$$c_1 - c_2 = 2. \tag{11.13}$$

Solving equations (11.12) and (11.13) yields

$$c_2 = \frac{-2e}{e + e^{-1}}, \quad c_1 = \frac{2e^{-1}}{e + e^{-1}}.$$

This case would then give

$$\lambda = \frac{2}{e + e^{-1}} (e^{t-1} - e^{1-t}).$$

and

$$x = \frac{1}{e + e^{-1}} (e^{t-1} + e^{1-t}).$$

But

$$x(1) = \frac{2}{e + e^{-1}}$$

which is less than 2 so the condition $x(1) \geq 2$ is violated and setting $\lambda(1)$ equal to zero does not yield the optimal solution. We rerun the problem with $x(1) = 2$ as an end point condition. From equation (11.11) we have

$$x(1) = (c_1 e - c_2 e^{-1})/2 = 2,$$

so

$$c_1 e - c_2 e^{-1} = 4.$$

Combining this with $c_1 = c_2 + 2$ gives

$$c_2 = \frac{4 - 2e}{e - e^{-1}}, \quad c_1 = \frac{4 - 2e^{-1}}{e - e^{-1}}.$$

Thus the optimal solution is

$$\lambda^*(t) = \frac{1}{e - e^{-1}}[(4 - 2e^{-1})e^t + (4 - 2e)e^{-t}]$$

$$x^*(t) = \frac{1}{2(e - e^{-1})}[(4 - 2e^{-1})e^t - (4 - 2e)e^{-t}]$$

$$u^*(t) = \lambda^*(t)/2.$$

Different planning horizons

In the basic problem the terminal T is regarded as fixed. That is, we are given that the planning horizon runs from $t = 0$ to $t = T$. Sometimes the problem involves an infinite planning horizon from $t = 0$ into an infinite future. The appropriate transversality conditions are modified for this case by inserting $\lim_{T \to \infty}$ in the appropriate place. For example if the terminal condition is $x(\infty) \geq \bar{x}$, then the appropriate transversality condition is

$$\lim_{T \to \infty} \lambda(T) \geq 0, \quad \lim_{T \to \infty} x(T) \geq \bar{x} \quad \text{and} \quad \lim_{T \to \infty} (x(T) - \bar{x})\lambda(T) = 0.$$

In other problems an end point condition $x(T) = x_T$ may be specified but T itself may be regarded as a free variable. Here it does not matter how long it takes for the state variable $x(T)$ to reach x_T so long as the optimal path is chosen.

Alternatively, we may specify that x_T is reached within a certain time frame say $T \leq T_{\max}$. In these more complicated cases the implied transversality conditions are on the Hamiltonian H rather than the costate variable λ. A further complication is that concavity of the Hamiltonian H in x and u is no longer sufficient for optimality. For the details the reader is referred to a specialist text such as Seierstad and Sydsaeter (1987).

A control region

In our basic problem we have assumed that the control variable $u(t)$ is a free variable. Accordingly, we used differential calculus to find the u that maximizes the Hamiltonian. In more general problems $u(t)$ may be constrained to belonging to a subset of real numbers U say. Such a set is called the **control region**. If U is a closed set then we have the possibility that the optimal value of u occurs at the boundary of U rather than at an interior point of U. If this is the case, then differential calculus may not be applicable in detecting the optimal point.[7]

Example

$$\text{Maximize} \quad \int_0^1 (5x - 9u)dt$$

$$\text{subject to} \quad x' = x + u$$

$$x(0) = 8, \quad x(1) \text{ free}$$

$$u(t) \in [0, 10].$$

The Hamiltonian is

$$H = 5x - 9u + \lambda(x + u) = (5 + \lambda)x + (\lambda - 9)u$$

which is an increasing function in u if λ is greater than 9 but a decreasing function in u if λ is less than 9. In order to maximize H with respect to u we would choose, u as large as possible in the former case and as small as possible in the latter case. Thus the optimal value of u is

$$u^* = 10 \quad \text{if } \lambda > 9$$

$$u^* = 0 \quad \text{if } \lambda < 9.$$

From the costate equation

$$\lambda' = -\frac{\partial H}{\partial x} = -5 - \lambda$$

which is a first order differential equation in λ whose general solution is

$$\lambda(t) = -5 + c\,e^{-t}$$

where c is an arbitrary constant. But the transversality condition is $\lambda(1) = 0$ so $c = 5e$ and

$$\lambda^*(t) = -5 + 5e\,e^{-t}.$$

---

[7]Differential calculus is only helpful when an optimum occurs at the boundary, if the optimal point also happens to be a critical point that occurs at the boundary. See Section 11.5.

This is a decreasing function in t, starting from $\lambda^*(0) = -5 + 5e = 8.5914$ so the optimal solution for $u(t)$ is

$$u^*(t) = 0.$$

From the state equation

$$x' = x$$

whose solution is $x(t) = c_1 e^t$ where c_1 is an arbitrary constant. Using the terminal end point $x(0) = 8$ we get $c_1 = 8$ and the optimal for the state variable

$$x^*(t) = 8e^t.$$

When a control region is specified it is also possible for the optimal control function $u^*(t)$ to switch from one boundary point of the control region to another during the planning horizon. Such functions are called **bang-bang** optimal control functions and they are **piecewise continuous**, being continuous everywhere except at a point of discontinuity where a **finite jump** is made. In this case the graph of $x^*(t)$ will have a 'kink' in it corresponding to the jump in $u^*(t)$.

Example
Solve the following dynamic optimization problem

$$\text{Maximize} \quad \int_0^1 (5x - 6u)dt$$
$$\text{subject to} \quad x' = x + u$$
$$x(0) = 9, \quad x(1) \text{ free}$$
$$u(t) \in [0, 10].$$

Graph the optimal solution $u^*(t), x^*(t)$.

Proceeding as we did in the previous example the optimal value of u is

$$u^* = 10 \quad \text{if } \lambda > 6$$
$$u^* = 0 \quad \text{if } \lambda < 6,$$

and

$$\lambda^*(t) = -5 + 5e\, e^{-t}.$$

As $\lambda^*(t)$ is a decreasing function in t starting from $\lambda^*(0) = 8.5641$, $\lambda^*(t)$ must pass through $\lambda^* = 6$ at some time in the planning horizon thus causing u^* to switch from $u^* = 10$ to $u^* = 0$. Let $\bar{t}$ denote this critical time. Then

$$\lambda^*(\bar{t}) = -5 + 5e^{1-\bar{t}} = 6$$

so

$$1 - \bar{t} = \log_e 2.2 = 0.7884 \Rightarrow \bar{t} = 0.2116.$$

Thus our optimal control function is

$$u^*(t) = 10 \quad 0 \le t \le 0.2116$$
$$u^*(t) = 0 \quad\;\; 0.2116 < t \le 1.$$

The state equation is

$$x' = x + u^*$$

so for the first time interval $[0, 0.2116]$

$$x^*(t) = -10 + ce^t$$

where c is an arbitrary constant.

But $x^*(0) = 9$ so $c = 19$ and $x^*(t) = -10 + 19e^t$. However for the second time interval $(0.2116,\ 1]$, $u^* = 0$, so from the state equation

$$x' = x$$

whose solution is

$$x^* = c_2 e^t$$

where c_2 is an arbitrary constant. But

$$x(0.2116) = -10 + 19e^{0.2116} = 13.4774$$

so

$$c_2 = 13.4774/e^{0.2116} = 10.9071.$$

The solution for our state variable is

$$x^*(t) = -10 + 19e^t \quad 0 \le t \le 0.2116$$
$$x^*(t) = 10.9071e^t \quad\quad 0.2116 < t \le 1.$$

Graphing $x^*(t)$ and $u^*(t)$ we have

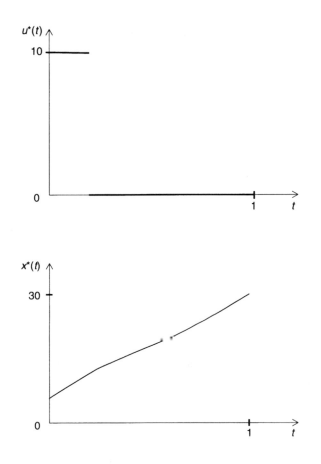

Autonomous problems

In the examples we have presented to date the costate and state equations give rise to linear first order differential equations which are easy to solve. However, this may not be the case in more realistic problems where the costate and state equations present us with nonlinear first order differential equations. In

Section 9.8 of Chapter 9 we saw that phase diagrams could be used to characterize the solutions arising from an autonomous system of nonlinear differential equations, even where it was difficult to obtain the actual solutions to such a system.

If t does not enter the function f of the objective function or the function g in the state equation, then we are assured that the state and costate equations give rise to an autonomous system of first order differential equations which are therefore amenable to phase diagram analysis. Such a dynamic programming problem is called, naturally enough, an **autonomous problem**. The Hamiltonian of an autonomous problem does not contain t as a separate argument and is of the form

$$H(x, u, \lambda) = f(x, u) + \lambda g(x, u).$$

Often in economic problems we are concerned with maximizing the present value of future cash flows and t enters through the discount factor e^{-rt} only. The objective function is of the form

$$\int_0^T F(x, u) \, e^{-rt} dt,$$

and the Hamiltonian is

$$H(x, u, \lambda, t) = F(x, u)e^{-rt} + \lambda g(x, u)$$

where λ is the usual costate variable.

Such problems can be transformed into autonomous problems by use of the **current value Hamiltonian**.

$$H_c(x, u, \mu) = He^{rt} = F(x, u) + \mu g(x, u)$$

where $\mu = \lambda e^{rt}$ now represents the **current value** imputed price.

As e^{rt} with $r > 0$ is a monotonically increasing function, maximizing H with respect to u is equivalent to maximizing H_c with respect to u.

Condition (ii) of Theorem 1 can be rewritten in terms of μ as

$$(\text{ii}) \quad \mu' = -\frac{\partial H_c}{\partial x} + r\mu.$$

Exercises for 11.4

1. Find the optimal time paths for the state, costate, and control variables of the following problems:

(i)

$$\text{Maximize} \quad \int_0^{10} 2x - u - \frac{u^2}{2} \, dt$$

$$\text{subject to} \quad x' = x - u,$$

$$x(0) = 5, \quad x(10) \text{ free.}$$

(ii)

$$\text{Maximize} \quad \int_0^1 4x - 3u - 2u^2 \, dt$$

$$\text{subject to} \quad x' = x + u$$

$$x(0) = 2, \quad x(1) \text{ free}$$

(iii)

$$\text{Maximize} \quad \int_0^1 x - u^2 \, dt$$

$$\text{subject to} \quad x' = u - 3x$$

$$x(0) = 1, \quad x(1) \geq 3.$$

(iv)

$$\text{Maximize} \quad \int_0^1 tu + x - u^2 \, dt$$

$$\text{subject to} \quad x' = u + x$$

$$x(0) = 1, \quad x(1) \geq 2.$$

(v)

$$\text{Maximize} \quad \int_0^1 10x - 20u \, dt$$

$$\text{subject to} \quad x' = x + u$$

$$x(0) = 2, \quad x(1) \text{ free}$$

$$u \in [0, 3].$$

(vi)

$$\text{Maximize} \quad \int_0^2 10x - 50u \, dt$$

$$\text{subject to} \quad x' = x + u$$

$$x(0) = 1, \quad x(2) \text{ free}$$

$$u \in [2, 4].$$

2. Consumer's endowment problem in general

Suppose a consumer's income is derived from his/her wealth according to

$$Y = rW.$$

This income is either consumed or invested, investments adding to the stock of wealth so

$$W' = I = Y - C = rW - C.$$

The consumer's initial wealth is $W(0) = W_0$ and at the end of his/her expected lifetime at $t = T$, we must have $W(T) \geq 0$.

The consumer's initial utility function is $U(C(t))$ and the consumer seeks to maximize

$$\int_0^T U(C(t)) e^{-\delta t} \, dt$$

where δ is the consumer's personal rate of time preference.

Suppose that $U(C(t)) = \log C(t), C(t) > 0$.

(i) Formulate the problem facing the consumer.
(ii) Show that the Hamiltonian is concave in W and C.
(iii) Write down the necessary conditions for an optimal solution. Are these conditions also sufficient?
(iv) Show that optimal consumption is given by

$$C^*(t) = \frac{1}{\lambda_0} e^{t(r-\delta)}$$

where λ_0 is a constant of integration.

(v) Show that the transversality condition requires that $\lambda_0 > 0$ and this condition requires that $\lambda(T) > 0$ and $W(T) = 0$.

(vi) What condition do we need for optimal consumption to rise (fall) over time?

Exhaustible resource problem

Let $x(t)$ denote the stock of a limited resource which at time t is being extracted at the rate of $u(t)$ so

$$x' = -u.$$

This resource is then transformed into a consumption good via the production function

$$c = c(u) \quad \text{with} \quad c' > 0, \ c'' < 0,$$

and the consumption good in turn yields utility for the community given by

$$u = u(c), \quad u' > 0, \quad u'' < 0.$$

At reasonable extraction rates, the resource is calculated to last the community at least one hundred years. The community seeks to find the extraction rate that maximizes utility over that period.

Suppose

$$
\begin{aligned}
c(u) &= au^\alpha \quad 0 < \alpha < 1 \\
U(c) &= \log c \\
x(0) &= 1000.
\end{aligned}
$$

(i) Formulate the problem facing the community.
(ii) Form the Hamiltonian and write down a set of conditions which are necessary and sufficient for this problem.
(iii) Find the optimal rate of extraction and the accompanying time path of the resource.

*11.5 Economic Application: Ramsey/ Solow Model

The model

Modern macroeconomics uses dynamic optimization extensively. A model that is commonly presented is one that imposes a social welfare function on the

Solow-Swan growth model which we studied in Section 9.3. From our point of view, the resultant dynamic macroeconomic model is interesting as it encompasses several of the extensions covered in the previous section. Further a number of mathematical intricacies arise in the analysis of the model.

As with the Solow-Swan growth model we start with a neoclassical production function for the economy of the form

$$Y = Y(K, L)$$

where K is the amount of capital available to the economy and L is the labor supply usually identified with the population of the economy. In per capita terms, we write this function as

$$y = \phi(k)$$

where $y = Y/L$ and $k = K/L$ and we assume that $\phi'(k) > 0$ and $\phi''(k) < 0$. The total output of the economy is allocated between consumption C and investment I.

Let δ be the rate of depreciation of the capital stock K. Then net investment is given by

$$K' = I - \delta K = Y - C - \delta K. \tag{11.14}$$

In Section 9.4 we showed that we could write

$$K' = knL + Lk'$$

where n is the growth rate of the labor supply in the economy. Substituting this expression for K' in equation (11.14) yields

$$k' = y - c - (n + \delta)k = \phi(k) - c - (n + \delta)k$$

where $c = C/L$ is per capita consumption.

Let $U(c)$ be a social welfare function such that $U'(c) > 0$ and $U''(c) < 0$, so marginal utility is positive and diminishing. The function $U(c)$ can be thought of as the utility function of a representation family from the economy. Let θ denote the social discount rate or society's rate of time preference. Then the objective function facing an economic planner would be

$$V = \int_0^\infty U(c)e^{-\theta t}dt.$$

Imposing this on the neoclassical growth model we are presented with the following dynamic programing problem:

$$\text{Maximize} \quad V = \int_0^\infty U(c)e^{-\theta t}dt$$

$$\text{subject to} \quad k' = \phi(k) - c - (n + \delta)k$$

$$k(0) = k_o, \quad k(\infty) \geq 0$$

$$0 \leq c(t) \leq \phi(k).$$

In this problem k is the state variable and c is the control variable.

Necessary and sufficient conditions

The Hamiltonian for this problem is

$$H = U(c)e^{\theta t} + \lambda[\phi(k) - c - (n + \delta)k]$$

and the current value Hamiltonian is

$$H_c = He^{-\theta t} = U(c) + \mu[\phi(k) - c - (n + \delta)k],$$

where $\mu = \lambda e^{\theta t}$.

Using Theorem 1 and the extensions of Section 11.4, for each t the optimal solution must satisfy:

(i)

$$\frac{\partial H_c}{\partial c} = U'(c) - \mu = 0. \tag{11.15}$$

As

$$\frac{\partial^2 H_c}{\partial c^2} = U''(c) < 0,$$

equation (11.15) defines the value of c that maximizes H_c.

(ii)

$$\mu' = -\frac{\partial H_c}{\partial k} + \theta\mu$$

$$= -\mu[\phi'(k) - (n + \delta)] + \theta\mu = -\mu[\phi'(k) - (n + \delta + \theta)]$$

(iii)

$$k' = \frac{\partial H_c}{\partial \mu} = \phi(k) - c - (n + \delta)k$$

(iv)

$$k(0) = k_o, \quad \lim_{T \to \infty} \lambda(T) \geq 0, \quad \lim_{T \to \infty} k(T) \geq 0, \quad \lim_{T \to \infty} \lambda(T)k(T) = 0.$$

As we have assumed that $U(c)$ and $\phi(k)$ are concave function and as $\mu = U'(c)$ is positive and therefore λ is positive, the Hamiltonian is concave in c and k so these conditions are sufficient as well as necessary.

Interpretations of these conditions

We have just noted that $\mu = U'(c)$ so $\lambda = U'(c)e^{-\theta t}$ and we can write the transversality condition (iv) as

$$\lim_{T \to \infty} k(T)U'(c(T))e^{-\theta T} = 0. \tag{11.16}$$

To get an insight into what this condition means, suppose instead of an infinite planning horizon, T represents the terminal time. If the present value of marginal utility at time T is positive, it would not be optimal to retain any capital stock in the last period. Instead the entire capital stock would be consumed. If this were the case we would expect that

$$k(T)U'(c(T))e^{-\theta T} = 0.$$

Our transversality condition can be thought of as the limit of this condition as T becomes very large.

Returning to the equation $\mu = U'(c)$, differentiating both sides yields

$$\mu' = U''(c)c'$$

so we can rewrite (ii) as

$$c' = -\frac{U'(c)}{U''(c)}[\phi'(k) - (n + \delta + \theta)].$$

Ignoring the transversality condition for the moment, we are left with two autonomous differential equations in c and k

$$c' = -\frac{U'(c)}{U''(c)}[\phi'(k) - (n + \delta + \theta)] \tag{11.17}$$

$$k' = \phi(k) - c - (n + \delta)k \tag{11.18}$$

Equations (11.17) and (11.18) have received a lot of attention from economists. The first of these can be rewritten in terms of the **elasticity of marginal utility** which is defined as

$$\eta(c) = \frac{U''(c)c}{U'(c)}.$$

Using this concept we can rewrite equation (11.17) as

$$\frac{c'}{c} = \sigma(c)[(\phi'(k) - n - \delta) - \theta] \tag{11.19}$$

where $\sigma(c) = -\eta^{-1}(c)$,[8] which give us the optimal growth rate of consumption. Equation (11.19) says this growth rate is directly proportional to the difference between the net marginal product of capital, (accounting for population growth and depreciation), $\phi'(k) - n - \delta$, and the rate of time preference θ. The higher the marginal product of capital relative to the rate of time preference, the more it pays to reduce the current level of consumption in order to enjoy higher consumption in the future which is made possible by the additional investment entailed. Hence the growth rate of consumption is positive.

Equation (11.18) is called the **Keynes Ramsey** rule.

Equation (11.18) implies that in the **steady state** where our variables have settled down and $k' = 0$ optimum consumption is given by

$$c^* = \phi(k^*) - (n + \delta)k^*.$$

If we maximize c^* with respect to k^* we get as a necessary condition

$$\phi'(k^*) = n + \delta$$

which is often called the **golden rule**.

To maximize consumption the marginal product of capital $\phi'(k^*)$ should equal the sum of the growth rate of the labor force and the depreciation rate.

Phase diagram analysis

As equations (11.17) and (11.18) represent an autonomous system of first order differential equations, we can analyze their solution using the phase diagram techniques discussed in Section 9.8 of Chapter 9. Recall that a phase diagram plots the loci of points in the c, k space where $c' = 0$ and $k' = 0$.

---

[8] $\sigma(c)$ is sometimes called the **instantaneous elasticity of substitution**.

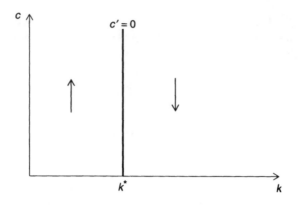

Figure 11.1   Dynamics of c

Consider $c' = 0$ first. From equation (11.19) we have

$$c' = \sigma(c)[(\phi'(k) - n - \delta) - \theta]c$$

Provided $\sigma(c)$ is finite for all values of c in the control region (including $c = 0$) then $c' = 0$ when

$$\phi'(k) = n + \delta + \theta \quad \text{or} \quad c = 0.$$

If the case $c = 0$ gives rise to the optimal solution then our calculus techniques have led us to a solution which is at the boundary of the control region. Mathematically this is possible though admittedly not likely with $c^* = 0$. Shortly we shall see that this possibility violates other necessary conditions.

The other case $\phi'(k) = n + \delta + \theta$ has a unique solution for k say k^* and is represented by a vertical line in Figure 11.1.

From equation (11.17)

$$\frac{\partial c'}{\partial k} = -\frac{U'(c)}{U''(c)}\phi''(k) < 0$$

so c' and k move in opposite directions. As we increase k, c' must decrease. Hence $c' > 0$ to the left of the vertical line $c' < 0$ to the right of the vertical line, giving the directional arrows as shown in Figure 11.1.

Next the locus for $k' = 0$, represents points where $c = \phi(k) - (n + \delta)k$. As we have assumed that $\phi(k)$ is strictly concave, this gives a strictly concave function in k. This locus is portrayed in Figure 11.2.

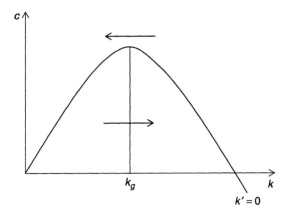

Figure 11.2   Dynamics of k.

Recall that the golden rule level of capital leads to the maximum level of consumption so this level is k_g in Figure 11.2, a fact that we will use later on in our analysis.

From equation (11.18)

$$\frac{\partial k'}{\partial c} = -1$$

so k' and c move in opposite directions. As we increase c, k' must decrease, implying that $k' > 0$ below the $k' = 0$ curve and $k' < 0$ above this curve giving the directional arrows as shown in Figure 11.2.

Combining Figures 11.1 and 11.2 we obtain our phase diagram as shown in Figure 11.3.

The steady state solution

A dynamic equilibrium is defined as a point where our economic variables settled down. From this phase diagram we see that three points A, B, and E present themselves, at least mathematically, as candidates for the dynamic equilibria. In this section we wish to show that only E represents the dynamic equilibrium, the other points A and B violating our necessary conditions.

Suppose the initial capital k_0 is such that $0 < k_0 < k^*$. Consider a streamline that leads to point A such as CD in Figure 11.4.

The initial consumption level behind this streamline is too high and consumption continues to rise until the economy reaches zero capital at point D. Consumption then falls to zero at point A. Thus c has jumped from a positive

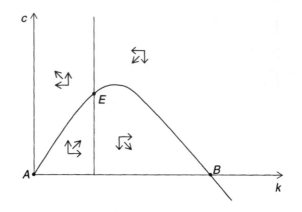

Figure 11.3   Phase diagram of the model.

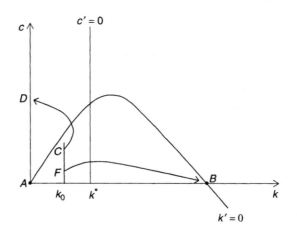

Figure 11.4   Streamlines for various initial consumptions.

value to zero. But this conflicts with Keynes-Ramsey rule for the growth rate of optimal consumption given by equation (11.18). Such a streamline cannot represent the optimal solution. Next consider a streamline that leads to point B such as FB in Figure 11.4. As this trajectory approaches B, k is approximately a constant which from Figure 11.2 is greater than the golden rule level of capital k_g, so near B.

$$n + \delta - \phi'(k) > 0. \tag{11.20}$$

Now consider equation (11.17) again which we rewrite as

$$\frac{dU'(c)dt}{U'(c)} = n + \delta - \phi'(k) + \theta > \theta$$

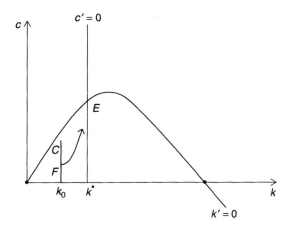

Figure 11.5   The convergent streamline.

by virtue of equation (11.20). It follows that near B, $U'(c) = ae^{bt}$, where a and b are constants and $b > \theta$. It follows that close to B

$$k(T)U'(c(T))e^{-\theta t} = \bar{k}a\,e^{bt}e^{-\theta t} = \bar{k}a\,e^{(b-\theta)t}.$$

But with $b - \theta > 0$ this violates the transversality condition

$$\lim_{T \to \infty} k(T)U'(c(T))e^{-\theta t} = 0.$$

So any streamline that leads to B cannot represent the optimal solution.

The optimal solution must then start off with a level of consumption between C and F with a streamline that leads us to point E, as shown in Figure 11.5. This point we know is called the **steady state**.

A similar analysis can be conducted for the case where the initial capital stock k_0 is greater than k^*.

Exercises for 11.5

Consider an economy where production function is

$$Y = K^{3/4}L^{1/4}$$

and whose social welfare function is

$$U(c) = \log c$$

where $c = C/L$. Suppose the growth rate of the population L is 1%, the depreciating rate is 10%, and the social discount rate is 5%.

(i) Show that the elasticity of marginal utility and instantaneous elasticity of substitution are constants.

(ii) Write the production function in per capita terms and formulate the problem given to the economy by the Solow/Ramsey model studied in Section 11.5.

(iii) Write down the current value Hamiltonian. What are the necessary conditions for an optimal solution?

(iv) Show that the necessary conditions imply the following differential equations:

$$k'(t) = k(t)^{3/4} - c(t) - 0.11k(t)$$
$$c'(t) = \left(\tfrac{3}{4}k(t)^{-1/4} - 0.16\right)c(t).$$

By considering $c'(t) = 0$ with $c(t) \neq 0$ find the steady state level of per capita capital stock. Hence find the steady state level of per capita consumption.

(v) Show that the transversality condition as given by equation (11.16) is satisfied at the steady state.

Answers to Exercises

Exercises for Chapter 1

1.1

1. (i)

$$A + B = \begin{pmatrix} 4 & -2 \\ 4 & 8 \end{pmatrix}, \quad -3A = \begin{pmatrix} -6 & 15 \\ -18 & -3 \end{pmatrix},$$

$$C(A + B) = CA + CB = \begin{pmatrix} 4 & 8 \\ 52 & 54 \end{pmatrix},$$

$$(A + B)C = \begin{pmatrix} -10 & -12 \\ 40 & 68 \end{pmatrix}.$$

(ii)

$$AB = \begin{pmatrix} 14 & -29 \\ 10 & 25 \end{pmatrix}, \quad BA = \begin{pmatrix} 22 & -7 \\ 28 & 17 \end{pmatrix},$$

$$ABC = \begin{pmatrix} -145 & -218 \\ 125 & 210 \end{pmatrix},$$

$$BCA = \begin{pmatrix} 186 & -49 \\ 394 & -121 \end{pmatrix}, \quad CAB = \begin{pmatrix} 10 & 25 \\ 150 & 55 \end{pmatrix}.$$

AB and BA are not the same.

(iii) $\operatorname{tr} AB = \operatorname{tr} BA = 39$, $\operatorname{tr} ABC = \operatorname{tr} BCA = \operatorname{tr} CAB = 65$.

2. (i)

$$AB = \begin{pmatrix} 16 & 12 & 41 \\ 29 & 12 & 58 \end{pmatrix}.$$

BA does not exist.

(ii)

$$(AB)' = B'A' = \begin{pmatrix} 16 & 29 \\ 12 & 12 \\ 41 & 58 \end{pmatrix}.$$

(iii)

$$AA' = \begin{pmatrix} 59 & 61 \\ 61 & 89 \end{pmatrix}$$

which is symmetric.

3. (i)

$$AB = BA = \begin{pmatrix} 0 & 0 & 0 \\ 0 & 0 & 0 \\ 0 & 0 & 0 \end{pmatrix},$$

the 3×3 null matrix.

4. A square matrix A is symmetric idempotent if $A' = A$ and $A^2 = A$.
   (i) $\operatorname{tr} A = 1$, $\operatorname{tr} B = n - 1$.
   (ii) Ax is an $n \times 1$ vector whose elements are all $\bar{x} = \sum_{i=1}^{n} x_i/n$. Bx is an $n \times 1$ vector whose jth element is $x_j - \bar{x}$.

1.2

1. $|A| = -6$, $|B| = 22$, $|AB| = |BA| = -132$, $|A'| = -6$, $|B'| = 22$.
2. $|A| = -1$, $|A'| = -1$.
3. $|A| = 0$, $|B| = 0$.

1.3

1.

$$A^{-1} = \frac{1}{6} \begin{pmatrix} 4 & 1 \\ -2 & 1 \end{pmatrix}, \quad B^{-1} = -\frac{1}{16} \begin{pmatrix} 8 & 0 \\ -5 & -2 \end{pmatrix},$$

$$(AB)^{-1} = -\frac{1}{96} \begin{pmatrix} 32 & 8 \\ -16 & -7 \end{pmatrix}.$$

2. *A* is nonsingular,

$$A^{-1} = -\frac{1}{6} \begin{pmatrix} 36 & -9 & 6 \\ -78 & 18 & -12 \\ -10 & 2 & -2 \end{pmatrix},$$

B is nonsingular,

$$B^{-1} = \begin{pmatrix} 7 & -3 & -3 \\ -1 & 0 & 1 \\ -1 & 1 & 0 \end{pmatrix}.$$

3.

$$A^{-1} = \frac{1}{9} \begin{pmatrix} -3 & 4 & 15 \\ 0 & 3 & 0 \\ 3 & -4 & -6 \end{pmatrix}, \quad B^{-1} = \begin{pmatrix} -5 & -7 & 3 \\ 2 & 2 & -1 \\ 2 & 3 & -1 \end{pmatrix}.$$

4. $|A| = 2$ so *A* is nonsingular,

$$A^{-1} = \frac{1}{2} \begin{pmatrix} 1 & 1 & -1 \\ -1 & 1 & -1 \\ -1 & -3 & 5 \end{pmatrix}.$$

1.4

1. (i) A set of m vectors $a_1, \ldots, a_m$ are linearly dependent if there exists scalars $\lambda_1, \ldots, \lambda_m$ not all of which are zero such that

$$\lambda_1 a_1 + \cdots + \lambda_m a_m = \mathbf{0}.$$

2. (i)

$$A \cong \begin{pmatrix} 1 & -3 & -2 & 11 \\ 0 & 1 & 11 & -33 \\ 0 & 0 & 6 & -18 \\ 0 & 0 & 0 & 0 \end{pmatrix},$$

hence $r(A) = 3$.
   (ii) $|B| = 1$, hence $r(B) = 4$.
3. $r(A) = 2$ for $x = 0$, 1 or 6. $r(A) = 3$ for all other values of x.
4. (ii) $r(N) = \operatorname{tr} N = K$, $r(M) = \operatorname{tr} M = n - K$.

1.5

1. (i)

$$A \otimes B = \begin{pmatrix} 0 & -7 & 0 & 14 \\ -8 & -5 & 16 & 10 \\ 0 & 21 & 0 & 28 \\ 24 & 15 & 32 & 20 \end{pmatrix}, \quad B \otimes A = \begin{pmatrix} 0 & 0 & -7 & 14 \\ 0 & 0 & 21 & 28 \\ -8 & 16 & -5 & 10 \\ 24 & 32 & 15 & 20 \end{pmatrix}$$

$$(A \otimes B)' = A' \otimes B' = \begin{pmatrix} 0 & -8 & 0 & 24 \\ -7 & -5 & 21 & 15 \\ 0 & 16 & 0 & 32 \\ 14 & 10 & 28 & 20 \end{pmatrix},$$

$$\text{tr} (A \otimes B) = \text{tr} A \, \text{tr} B = 15.$$

(ii)

$$\text{vec} \, ABC = (C' \otimes A) \text{vec} \, B = \begin{pmatrix} 54 \\ 178 \\ 61 \\ 87 \end{pmatrix}.$$

(iii) $\text{tr} \, AB = (\text{vec} \, A')' \text{vec} \, B = 57.$
(iv) $\text{tr} \, ABC = (\text{vec} \, A')'(C' \otimes I_2) \text{vec} \, B = 141.$

Exercises for Chapter 2

2.2

1. (i) Trivial solution for all values of α other than $\alpha = 0.75$.
   (ii) If $\alpha = 0.75$ system has an infinite number of solutions and our general solution can be written as

$$x^* = \begin{pmatrix} -2\lambda \\ \lambda/2 \\ \lambda \end{pmatrix}, \ \lambda \text{ being any real number.}$$

2. In matrix notation $Ax = 0$, A is 3×4 so we must have $r(A) < 4$, the number of variables. Hence if a nontrivial solution exists an infinite number

of solutions exist. The general solution can be written as

$$x^* = \begin{pmatrix} 2\lambda \\ -2\lambda \\ \lambda \\ 0 \end{pmatrix}, \ \lambda \text{ being any real number.}$$

3. If $k \neq 32/2$, then $r(A) = 3$ and the only solution is the trivial solution. For $k = 32/2$ the general solution can be written as

$$\begin{pmatrix} x^* \\ y^* \\ z^* \end{pmatrix} = \begin{pmatrix} -15\lambda/2 \\ -3\lambda \\ \lambda \end{pmatrix}, \ \lambda \text{ being any real number.}$$

2.3

1. If $c = 9$ the system of equations is consistent, and the general solution can be written as

$$x^* = \begin{pmatrix} 3 - \lambda \\ -1 \\ \lambda \end{pmatrix}, \ \lambda \text{ being any real number.}$$

2. $r(A) = 2 < 3$, the number of variables, so no unique solution exists. If $c \neq 38$ then the equations are inconsistent and have no solution. If $c = 38$ the system of equations have an infinite number of solutions and the general solution can be written as

$$x^* = \begin{pmatrix} 85/7 + 5\lambda/13 \\ 7\lambda/13 \\ 11/7 + \lambda \end{pmatrix}, \ \lambda \text{ being any real number.}$$

3. (i) In matrix notation $Ax = b$ and as A is 3×4, $r(A) < 4$, the number of variables. Hence if the system is consistent it has an infinite number of solutions.
   (ii) The general solution can be written as

$$x^* = \begin{pmatrix} 10 - 5\lambda \\ 4 - 3\lambda \\ \lambda \\ 3 \end{pmatrix}, \ \lambda \text{ being any real number.}$$

2.4

1. (i) The equations have an unique solution

$$x^* = \frac{1}{8} \begin{pmatrix} 42 \\ 5 \\ 22 \end{pmatrix}.$$

(ii) Equations do not have an unique solution, as $|A| = 0$, and the first equation is inconsistent with the third equation; so no solution exists.

(iii) Equations do not have a unique solution as $|A| = 0$, and the general solution can be written as

$$x^* = \begin{pmatrix} 3 + 2\lambda \\ 0 \\ \lambda \end{pmatrix}, \quad \lambda \text{ being any real number.}$$

2. Consider a system of n linear equations in n variables which we write as

$$Ax = b.$$

If A is nonsingular then the solution for x_i can be written as

$$x_i^* = \begin{vmatrix} a_{11} & \cdots & b_1 & \cdots & a_{1n} \\ \vdots & & \vdots & & \vdots \\ a_{n1} & \cdots & b_n & \cdots & a_{nn} \end{vmatrix} \Big/ |A|,$$

where the numerator is obtained by replacing the ith column of A by the vector b and taking the determinant.

$$x_1^* = \begin{vmatrix} 1 & 2 & -2 \\ 4 & 2 & 1 \\ 8 & 0 & 1 \end{vmatrix} \Big/ |A| = 42/8, \quad x_2^* = \begin{vmatrix} 1 & 1 & -2 \\ 0 & 4 & 1 \\ 1 & 8 & 1 \end{vmatrix} \Big/ |A| = 5/8$$

$$x_3^* = \begin{vmatrix} 1 & 2 & 1 \\ 0 & 2 & 4 \\ 1 & 0 & 8 \end{vmatrix} \Big/ |A| = 22/8, \quad \text{where } |A| = \begin{vmatrix} 1 & 2 & -3 \\ 0 & 2 & 1 \\ 1 & 0 & 1 \end{vmatrix}.$$

Exercises for Chapter 3

3.2

1. (i) The endogenous variables are the variables of interest to us in our economic analysis. The whole purpose of building the model in the first place is to get some insight into what determines the values of these variables. The exogenous variables are variables whose values are taken as fixed for the purposes of our analysis. They are noneconomic variables, economic variables determined by noneconomic forces, or economic variables determined by economic forces other than those at play in the model. Definitional equations represent relationships between the variables of the model which are true by definition. Behavioral equations purport to tell us something of the behavior of some economic entities. The structural form is the original form of the model as presented by economists. The reduced form is obtained by solving for the endogenous variables in terms of the exogenous variables. The solutions are called the equilibrium values of the endogenous variables. A model is complete when the number of linear equations in the model equals the number of endogenous variables and the model has a unique solution.

   (ii) Comparative static analysis concerns itself with how the equilibrium values of the endogenous variables change when we change the given values of the exogenous variables. If we write the structural form as

$$Ax = b$$

where x is a vector containing the endogenous variables and b is a vector containing the endogenous variables or linear combinations of the exogenous variables, then the reduced form is given by

$$x = A^{-1}b$$

and all our comparative static results are summarized by

$$\Delta x = A^{-1}\Delta b$$

where Δb is the vector of changes in the values of the exogenous variables. Often in our economic analysis we are not interested in finding the complete reduced form. Instead, all that we are interested in is the equilibrium value of one of the endogenous variables and our comparative static analysis is concerned with how this equilibrium value changes when there are changes in the values of the exogenous variables. In this case we can use Cramer's rule to solve for the equilibrium value of the endogenous variable in question.

2. (i) The reduced form of the model is

$$
\begin{pmatrix} Y^* \\ C^* \\ I^* \end{pmatrix} = \frac{1}{1-b-d} \begin{pmatrix} 1 & 1 & 1 \\ b & 1-d & b \\ d & d & 1-b \end{pmatrix} \begin{pmatrix} G \\ a \\ c \end{pmatrix}.
$$

(ii) The effects are

$$
\Delta Y^* = 1/(1 - b - d),
$$
$$
\Delta C^* = b/(1 - b - d),
$$
$$
\Delta I^* = d/(1 - b - d).
$$

(iii) In our answer to (i) we replace a by $a - bT$. In (ii) our results are obtained by adding the first column of A^{-1} to $-b$ times the second column. For example the change in equilibrium consumption is now given by

$$
\Delta C^* = \frac{b - b(1 - d)}{1 - b - d} = \frac{bd}{1 - b - d}.
$$

3. (i)

$$
\Delta Q^* = \frac{-b\beta \Delta T}{\beta - b} = -\text{ve}, \quad \Delta P^* = \frac{-\beta \Delta T}{\beta - b} = -\text{ve}.
$$

(ii)

$$
\Delta Q^* = \frac{\beta c \Delta R}{\beta - b} = -\text{ve}, \quad \Delta P^* = \frac{c \Delta R}{\beta - b} = -\text{ve}.
$$

4.

$$
Y^* = \frac{\lambda(\alpha + \gamma + G) + \delta M}{\lambda(1 - \beta) + \delta \tau}, \quad r^* = \frac{(1 - \beta)M - \tau(\alpha + \gamma + G)}{\lambda(1 - \beta) + \delta \tau}.
$$

Required increase in the money supply is given by $\Delta M = \tau \Delta G/(1 - \beta)$.

Exercises for Chapter 4

4.1

(i)

$$(x_1 \quad x_2) \begin{pmatrix} 1 & 0.5 \\ 0.5 & 0 \end{pmatrix} \begin{pmatrix} x_1 \\ x_2 \end{pmatrix}.$$

(ii)

$$(x \quad y) \begin{pmatrix} 13 & 16 \\ 16 & 17 \end{pmatrix} \begin{pmatrix} x \\ y \end{pmatrix}.$$

(iii)

$$(x_1 \quad x_2 \quad x_3) \begin{pmatrix} 3 & -1 & 1.5 \\ -1 & 1 & -2 \\ 1.5 & -2 & 3 \end{pmatrix} \begin{pmatrix} x_1 \\ x_2 \\ x_3 \end{pmatrix}.$$

(iv)

$$(x_1 \quad x_2 \quad x_3) \begin{pmatrix} -3 & 1 & 0 \\ 1 & -1 & 2 \\ 0 & 2 & -8 \end{pmatrix} \begin{pmatrix} x_1 \\ x_2 \\ x_3 \end{pmatrix}.$$

(v)

$$(x_1 \quad x_2 \quad x_3) \begin{pmatrix} 42 & 1.5 & 4 \\ 1.5 & ? & 3 \\ 4 & 3 & -7 \end{pmatrix} \begin{pmatrix} x_1 \\ x_2 \\ x_3 \end{pmatrix},$$

4.2

1. (i) $\lambda_1 = 0, \lambda_2 = 2$.
   (ii) $\lambda_1 = 1, \lambda_2 = 0, \lambda_3 = 6$.
   (iii) $\lambda_1 = 1, \lambda_2 = 0, \lambda_3 = 3$.
   (iv) $\lambda_1 = \lambda_2 = -5, \lambda_3 = -1$.

4.4

1. (i) The vectors $x_1, \ldots, x_m$ are orthogonal if $x_i' x_j = 0$ for $i \neq j$. They are orthonormal if they are orthogonal and

$$x_i' x_i = 1 \quad \text{for } i = 1, \ldots, n.$$

(ii) Three such vectors would be

$$\begin{pmatrix} 1 \\ 1 \\ 0 \end{pmatrix}, \begin{pmatrix} -1 \\ -1 \\ 0 \end{pmatrix}, \text{ and } \begin{pmatrix} -3 \\ 0 \\ 1 \end{pmatrix}.$$

(iii) Two such vectors are

$$x_2 = \frac{1}{\sqrt{2}} \begin{pmatrix} -1 \\ 1 \\ 0 \end{pmatrix} \quad \text{and} \quad x_3 = \frac{1}{\sqrt{2}} \begin{pmatrix} -1 \\ 0 \\ 1 \end{pmatrix}.$$

2. (i)

$$x_1 = \frac{1}{\sqrt{2}} \begin{pmatrix} 1 \\ 1 \end{pmatrix}, \quad x_2 = \frac{1}{\sqrt{2}} \begin{pmatrix} -1 \\ 1 \end{pmatrix}.$$

(ii)

$$x_1 = \frac{1}{\sqrt{5}} \begin{pmatrix} 1 \\ -2 \end{pmatrix}, \quad x_2 = \frac{1}{\sqrt{2}} \begin{pmatrix} 2 \\ 1 \end{pmatrix}.$$

(iii)

$$x_1 = \frac{1}{\sqrt{2}} \begin{pmatrix} 0 \\ 1 \\ -1 \end{pmatrix}, \quad x_2 = \frac{1}{\sqrt{3}} \begin{pmatrix} 1 \\ -1 \\ -1 \end{pmatrix}, \quad x_3 = \frac{1}{\sqrt{6}} \begin{pmatrix} 2 \\ 1 \\ 1 \end{pmatrix}.$$

4.5

3.

$$Q = \frac{1}{\sqrt{2}} \begin{pmatrix} 1 & 0 & 1 \\ -1 & 0 & 1 \\ 0 & \sqrt{2} & 0 \end{pmatrix}.$$

The main diagonal elements of $Q'AQ$ are the eigenvalues $-5, -5$, and -1.

4. (i) (a)

$$Q = \frac{1}{\sqrt{2}} \begin{pmatrix} 1 & 1 \\ 1 & -1 \end{pmatrix}.$$

The main diagonal elements are the eigenvalues 0 and 2.

(b)

$$Q = \frac{1}{\sqrt{30}} \begin{pmatrix} 0 & -\sqrt{5} & 5 \\ \sqrt{6} & 2\sqrt{5} & 2 \\ -2\sqrt{6} & \sqrt{5} & 1 \end{pmatrix}.$$

The main diagonal elements are the eigenvalues 1, 0, and 6.

(c)

$$Q = \frac{1}{\sqrt{6}} \begin{pmatrix} 0 & \sqrt{2} & 2 \\ \sqrt{3} & -\sqrt{2} & 1 \\ -\sqrt{3} & -\sqrt{2} & 1 \end{pmatrix}.$$

The main diagonal elements are the eigenvalues 1, 0, and 3.

(ii) (a), (b), (c). In each case A is positive semidefinite so $x'Ax \geq 0$ for all x.

4.6

1. (i)

$$y_1 = \frac{1}{\sqrt{3}}x_1 - \frac{\sqrt{2}x_2}{\sqrt{3}}$$

$$y_2 = x_1 + \frac{1}{\sqrt{2}}x_2$$

(ii)

$$y_1 = \frac{1}{\sqrt{2}}x_1 - \frac{1}{\sqrt{2}}x_2$$

$$y_2 = x_3$$

$$y_3 = \frac{1}{\sqrt{2}}x_1 + \frac{1}{\sqrt{2}}x_2.$$

2.

$$\begin{pmatrix} x \\ y \end{pmatrix} = \frac{1}{\sqrt{2}} \begin{pmatrix} 1 & 1 \\ 1 & -1 \end{pmatrix} \begin{pmatrix} v_1 \\ v_2 \end{pmatrix}.$$

The quadrative form is indefinite.

4.7

1. $r(A) = \operatorname{tr} A = 1$, $r(B) = \operatorname{tr} B = n - 1$. A has $n - 1$ eigen values of 0 and 1 eigen value of 1. B has $n - 1$ eigen values of 1 and 1 eigen value of 0. Both A and B are positive semidefinite and both have determinants of zero.
2. $r(N) = \operatorname{tr} N = K$, $r(M) = \operatorname{tr} M = n - K$. N has K eigen values of 1 and $n - K$ eigen values of zero. M has $n - K$ eigen values of 1 and K eigen values of zero. Both matrices have determinants of zero.
3. (i), (ii), (iii) All matrices have rank of 2.

4.8

1. (i) The leading principal minors are -3, 5, and -25.
   (ii) The leading principal minors are -3, 2, and -4.
2. The first order principal minors are 2, 1, and 2, the second order principal minors are 1, 1, and 1, and the determinant of the matrix is 0.
3. The first order principal minors are 1, 3, and 8 but a second order principal minor is -1.

Exercises for Chapter 5

5.2

1. Let $y = f(x)$ be a differentiable function of many variables. The gradient vector is

$$\nabla f(x) = \begin{pmatrix} f_1(x) \\ \vdots \\ f_n(x) \end{pmatrix},$$

and the Hessian matrix is

$$H(x) = \begin{pmatrix} f_{11}(x) & \cdots & f_{1n}(x) \\ \vdots & & \vdots \\ f_{n1}(x) & \cdots & f_{nn}(x) \end{pmatrix}.$$

(i)

$$\nabla y(x) = \begin{pmatrix} 3x_1^2 x_2^2 \\ 2x_1^3 x_2 \end{pmatrix}, \quad H(x) = \begin{pmatrix} 6x_1 x_2^2 & 6x_1^2 x_2 \\ 6x_1^2 x_2 & 2x_1^3 \end{pmatrix}.$$

(ii)

$$\nabla y(\boldsymbol{x}) = \begin{pmatrix} 5x_1^4 - 6x_1x_2 \\ -3x_1^2 + 2x_2 \end{pmatrix}, \quad H(\boldsymbol{x}) = \begin{pmatrix} 20x_1^3 - 6x_2 & -6x_1 \\ -6x_1 & 2 \end{pmatrix}.$$

(iii)

$$\nabla y(\boldsymbol{x}) = \begin{pmatrix} 1/x_2 \\ -x_1/x_2^2 \end{pmatrix}, \quad H(\boldsymbol{x}) = \begin{pmatrix} 0 & -1/x_2^2 \\ -1/x_2^2 & 2x_1/x_2^3 \end{pmatrix}.$$

(iv)

$$\nabla y(\boldsymbol{x}) = \frac{1}{(x_1 + x_2)^2} \begin{pmatrix} 2x_2 \\ -2x_1 \end{pmatrix},$$

$$H(\boldsymbol{x}) = \frac{1}{(x_1 + x_2)^3} \begin{pmatrix} -4x_2 & 2(x_1 - x_2) \\ 2(x_1 - x_2) & 4x_1 \end{pmatrix}.$$

(v)

$$\nabla y(\boldsymbol{x}) = (x_1^2 - 2x_2^2)^4 \begin{pmatrix} 10x_1 \\ -20x_2 \end{pmatrix},$$

$$H(\boldsymbol{x}) = (x_1^2 - 2x_2^2)^2 \begin{pmatrix} 90x_1^2 - 20x_2^2 & -320x_1x_2 \\ -320x_1x_2 & 360x_2^2 - 20x_1^2 \end{pmatrix}.$$

(vi)

$$\nabla y(\boldsymbol{x}) = \frac{1}{x_1^{-2} + x_2^{-3}} \begin{pmatrix} -2x_1^{-3} \\ -3x_2^{-4} \end{pmatrix},$$

$$H(\boldsymbol{x}) = \frac{1}{(x_1^{-2} + x_2^{-3})^2} \begin{pmatrix} 2x_1^4(x_1^{-6} + 3x_2^{-3}) & -6x_1^{-3}x_2^{-4} \\ -6x_1^{-3}x_2^{-4} & 3x_2^{-5}(4x_2^{-2} + x_2^{-3}) \end{pmatrix}.$$

(vii)

$$\nabla y(\boldsymbol{x}) = e^{2x_1 + 3x_2} \begin{pmatrix} 2 \\ 3 \end{pmatrix}, \quad H(\boldsymbol{x}) = e^{2x_1 + 3x_2} \begin{pmatrix} 4 & 6 \\ 6 & 9 \end{pmatrix}.$$

(viii)

$$\nabla y(x) = \begin{pmatrix} 6x_1x_2 - 7\sqrt{x_2} \\ 3x_1^2 - 7x_1/2\sqrt{x_2} \end{pmatrix},$$

$$H(x) = \begin{pmatrix} 6x_1 & 6x_1 - 7/2\sqrt{x_2} \\ 6x_1 - 7/2\sqrt{x_2} & 7x_1/4x_2^{3/2} \end{pmatrix}.$$

5.3

1. (i) (a) $A \cap B$

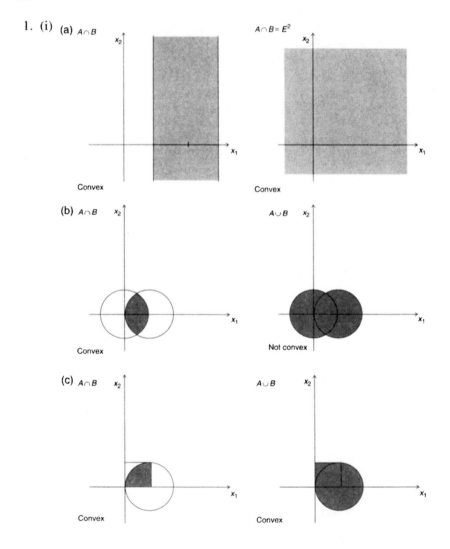

2. S has one element.

3. (ii)

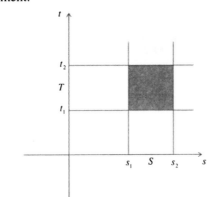

4. $X_1 \cup X_2$ need not be convex. Counter example:

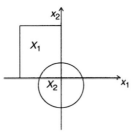

5. (i) Let $y = f(x_1, \ldots, x_n) = f(\boldsymbol{x})$ be a function of many variables. This function is homogeneous of degree r if

$$f(\lambda x_1, \ldots, \lambda x_n) = \lambda^r f(x_1, \ldots, x_n).$$

Euler's theorem

If $y = f(\boldsymbol{x})$ is homogeneous of degree r and differentiable then

$$x_1 \frac{\partial f}{\partial x_1} + \cdots + x_n \frac{\partial f}{\partial x_n} = rf(\boldsymbol{x}).$$

6. (i) The Cobb-Douglas function is homogeneous of degree $\alpha + \beta$, the CES production function is homogeneous of degree 1.

(ii) For the Cobb-Douglas function the marginal products are homogeneous of degree $\alpha + \beta - 1$ and for the CES production function they are homogeneous of degree 0.

8. A set X is convex if $u, v \in X \Rightarrow \lambda u + (1 - \lambda)v \in X$ for all $0 \leq \lambda \leq 1$. A function $f(x)$ is convex on a convex set X if

$$\lambda f(u) + (1 - \lambda)f(v) \geq f(\lambda u + (1 - \lambda)v), \quad 0 \leq \lambda \leq 1,$$

and for all $u, v \in X$.
   (i) Neither convex nor concave.
   (ii) Convex.
   (iii) Concave.
   (iv) Convex.
   (v) Concave.
   (vi) Concave.
9. The largest convex domain in E^2 for which the function is convex is

$$D = \left\{ \binom{x}{y} \Big/ x \geq \frac{5}{12} \right\}.$$

10. (i) Strictly concave.
    (ii) Strictly convex.
    (iii) Strictly concave.
    (iv) Strictly convex.
13. If $f(x)$ is a concave function then $S^{\geq} = \{x / f(x) \geq k\}$ is a convex set.

5.4

1. Consider a nonlinear equation

$$F(y, x_1, \ldots, x_n) = 0. \tag{1.1}$$

The implicit function theorem addresses the question when it is possible to solve this equation for y as a differentiable function of $x_1, \ldots, x_n$.

In nonlinear economic models, equilibrium conditions often give rise to an equation like (1.1). In this equation the y is the endogenous variable and $x_1, \ldots, x_n$ are the exogenous variables. Before any comparative static analysis can be conducted we need to know the condition required to ensure that we can solve the equilibrium equation for y as a differentiable function of $x_1, \ldots, x_n$.

2. (i) An implicit function is defined and

$$\frac{dy}{dx} = \frac{7y^2 - 3x^2 - 8xy}{4x^2 - 14xy}.$$

(ii) An implicit function is defined and

$$\frac{dy}{dx} = -\frac{2x + 8y}{4y^3 + 8x}.$$

3. An implicit function is defined and

$$\frac{\partial y}{\partial x_1} = -\frac{1 + 3x_2}{2(x_2 + y)} = -2$$

at the point,

$$\frac{\partial y}{\partial x_2} = -\frac{3x_1 + 2y + 2x_2}{2(x_2 + y)} = -\frac{5}{2}$$

at the point.

4. The condition we require is $F_Y = 1 - C' - I' + M' \neq 0$, and $\partial Y / \partial G = 1/(1 - C' - I' + M)$.

5. Implicit functions are defined with

$$\frac{dy}{dx_1} = (3y_2^2 - 2x)/(15y_1^4 y_2^2 - 2y_1) = 1 \text{ at the point,}$$

$$\frac{dy}{dx_2} = (10y_1^4 x - 2y_1)/(15y_1^4 y_2^2 - 2y_1) = -4 \text{ at the point.}$$

6. The condition is $L_r(1 - C') + I' L_Y \neq 0$

$$\partial Y / \partial_1 M = \frac{I'}{L_r(1 - C') + I' L_Y} = +\text{ve},$$

$$\frac{\partial r}{\partial M} - \frac{I - C'}{L_r(1 - C') + I' L_Y} = -\text{ve}.$$

5.5

1. (i) $f(x) \approx x_0^{1/2} + \frac{1}{2}x_0^{-1/2} dx - \frac{1}{8}x_0^{-3/2} dx^2 + \frac{1}{16}x_0^{-5/2}$. Evaluating this at $x_0 = 4$, $x = 4.05$ and $dx = 0.05$ we get $f(4.05) \approx 2.012461$.

   (ii) (a) $(x + 1)^{1/2} \approx 1 + \frac{1}{2}dx - \frac{1}{8}dx^2 + \frac{3}{48}dx^3$. For $dx = 0.2$, we get $(1.02)^{1/2} \approx 1.0955$.

   (b) $e^x \approx 1 + dx + \frac{1}{2}dx^2 + \frac{1}{6}dx^3$ so $e^{0.2} \approx 1.22133$.

   (c) $\log x \approx dx - \frac{1}{2}dx^2 + \frac{1}{3}dx^3$ so $\log 1.2 \approx 0.18266$.

2. (i) $f(x) \approx f(x_0) + \nabla f(x_0)' dx + \frac{1}{2}dx' H(x_0) dx$.

   (ii) $f(x_1, x_2) \approx 1 + \frac{1}{4}dx_1 + \frac{3}{4}dx_2 - \frac{3}{32}dx_1^2 + \frac{3}{16}dx_1 dx_2 - \frac{3}{32}dx_2^2$.

   With $dx_1 = 0.1$, $dx_2 = -0.1$ we get $(1.1)^{1/4}(0.9)^{3/4} \approx 0.94625$.

   (iii) $dy = \frac{1}{4}x_1^{-3/4} x_2^{3/4} dx_1 + \frac{3}{4}x_1^{1/4} x_2^{-1/4} dx_2$, $dy \approx -0.05$.

3. The total derivative is defined by

$$\frac{dy}{dx_1} = \frac{\partial y}{\partial x_1} + \frac{\partial y}{\partial x_2}\frac{dx_2}{dx_1}.$$

The total derivative differs from the partial derivative $\partial y/\partial x_1$, when x_2 is itself a function of x_1.

$$\frac{\partial y}{\partial x_1} = 3x_1^2, \quad \frac{dy}{dx_1} = 3x_1^2 + 14x_2/x_1.$$

Exercises for Chapter 6

6.1

1. (i) $\binom{0}{0}$ is a saddle point, $\binom{3}{-3}$ is a strict local minimum.

(ii) $\frac{1}{3}\binom{-2}{1}$ is a strict local minimum, $\frac{1}{4}\binom{2}{-1}$ is a saddle point.

(iii) $\binom{0}{0}$ is a saddle point, $\binom{1}{1}$ is a strict local minimum, $\binom{-1}{-1}$ is a strict local minimum.

(iv) $\begin{pmatrix} 0 \\ 0 \\ 0 \end{pmatrix}$ is a strict local minimum.

(v) $\frac{1}{20}\begin{pmatrix} 1 \\ 11 \\ -2 \end{pmatrix}$ strict local minimum.

(vi) $\frac{1}{137}\begin{pmatrix} -14 \\ 29 \\ -369 \end{pmatrix}$ a saddle point.

2. The six critical points are

$$\binom{0}{0}, \binom{0}{1}, \binom{1}{0}, \binom{-1}{0}, \binom{1/\sqrt{5}}{2/5}, \binom{-1/\sqrt{5}}{2/5}.$$

$\binom{1/\sqrt{5}}{2/\sqrt{5}}$ is a strict local minimum

$\binom{-1/\sqrt{5}}{2/\sqrt{5}}$ is a strict local minimum.

6.2

1. (i) Total profit $\Pi = p(L^{1/2} + K^{1/2}) - wL - rK$.

(ii) $L^* = p^2/4w^2, K^* = p^2/4r^2$.

(iii) The Hessian matrix is negative semidefinite in the nonnegative orthant so the function is concave on its domain and any local maximum will be a global maximum.

(iv) Both functions are homogeneous of degree zero.
(v)

$$\frac{\partial L^*}{\partial w} = -\frac{p^2}{2w^3}, \quad \frac{\partial K^*}{\partial r} = -\frac{p^3}{2r^3}.$$

(vi) Profit function is $M = p^2/4w + p^2/4r$ with

$$\frac{\partial M}{\partial p} = p/2w + p/2r, \quad \frac{\partial M}{\partial w} = \frac{-p^2}{4w^2}, \quad \frac{\partial M}{\partial r} = -\frac{p^2}{4r^2}.$$

2. (i) Total profit is $\Pi = 4pL^{1/4}K^{1/2} - wL - rK$.
   (ii) $L^* = 4p^4/r^2w^2, K^* = 8p^4/r^3w$.
   (iii) Π is concave on its domain.
   (iv) Homogeneous of degree 0.
   (v)

$$\frac{\partial L^*}{\partial w} = -\frac{8p^4}{rw^3}, \quad \frac{\partial K^*}{\partial r} = -\frac{24p^4}{r^4w}.$$

   (vi) Profit function is $M = 4p^4/r^2w$ with $\partial M/\partial p = 16p^3/r^2w$, $\partial M/\partial w = -4p^4/r^2w^2$, $\partial M/\partial r = -8p^4/r^3w$.

6.3

1. $x_1^* = 3/2, x_2^* = 9/2, |H| = 16$.
2. (i) $Z = x_1x_2 + \lambda(Y - p_1x_1 - p_2x_2)$.
   (ii) $Z_\lambda = Y - p_1x_1 - p_2x_2 = 0, Z_1 = x_2 - \lambda p_1 = 0, Z_2 = x_1 - \lambda p_2 = 0$.
   (iii) $|\bar{H}| = 2p_1p_2 > 0$.
   (iv) $x_1^* = Y/2p_1, x_2^* = Y/2p_2$.
   (v)

$$M = Y^2/4p_1p_2, \quad \frac{\partial M}{\partial p_1} = -\frac{Y^2}{4p_1^2p_2}, \quad \frac{\partial M}{\partial Y} = \frac{Y}{2p_1p_2}.$$

   (vi) $\lambda^* = Y/2p_1p_2$.
3. (i) $Z = wL + rK + \lambda(Q_0 - 4K^{1/4}L^{1/4})$.
   (ii) $Z_\lambda = Q_0 - 4K^{1/4}L^{1/4} = 0, Z_L = w - \lambda K^{1/4}L^{-3/4} = 0, Z_K = r - \lambda K^{-3/4}L^{1/4} = 0$.

(iii)

$$\bar{H}(L, K, \lambda) = \frac{L^{-7/4}K^{-7/4}}{4} \begin{pmatrix} 0 & 4K^2L & 4KL^2 \\ 4K^2L & 3\lambda K^2 & -\lambda KL \\ 4KL^2 & -\lambda KL & 3\lambda L^2 \end{pmatrix}.$$

Require $|\bar{H}| < 0$ at K^*, L^*, λ^*.

(iv)

$$L^* = \left(\frac{Q_0}{4}\right)^2 \left(\frac{r}{w}\right)^{1/2}, \quad K^* = \left(\frac{Q_0}{4}\right)^2 \left(\frac{w}{r}\right)^{1/2}.$$

(v) $M = Q_0^2(rw)^{1/2}/8$.

(vi) $\partial M/\partial w = Q_0 r^{1/2} w^{-1/2}/16$, $\partial M/\partial Q_0 = Q_0(rw)^{1/2}/4$.

(vii) $\lambda^* = \partial M/\partial Q_0 = Q_0(rw)^{1/2}/4$.

4. (i) $Z_\lambda = u_0 - x_1^a x_2^b = 0$, $Z_1 = p_1 - a\lambda x_1^{a-1} x_2^b = 0$, $Z_2 = p_2 - b\lambda x_1^a x_2^{b-1} = 0$.

(ii)

$$\bar{H} = x_1^{a-2} x_2^{b-2} \begin{pmatrix} 0 & ax_1x_2^2 & bx_1^2x_2 \\ ax_1x_2^2 & -a(a-1)\lambda x_2^2 & -ab\lambda x_1 x_2 \\ bx_1^2x_2 & -ab\lambda x_1 x_2 & -b(b-1)\lambda x_1^2 \end{pmatrix}.$$

(iii) $|\bar{H}| < 0$ at the critical point.

(iv)

$$\bar{x}_1 = u_0 \left(\frac{ap_2}{bp_1}\right)^b, \quad \bar{x}_2 = u_0 \left(\frac{bp_1}{ap_2}\right)^a.$$

(v)

$$\frac{\partial M}{\partial p_1} = a^{-a+1} b^{-b} p_1^{a-1} p_2^b u_0.$$

6.4

The set of feasible solutions is a hyperplane so it is convex and closed. The objective function is strictly concave. So there will be a unique local maximum which is also a global maximum.

(i) $Z = -1/x_1 - 1/x_2 + \lambda(Y - p_1x_1 - p_2x_2)$.

(ii) $Z_\lambda = Y - p_1x_1 - p_2x_2 = 0$, $Z_1 = 1/x_1^2 - \lambda p_1 = 0$, $Z_2 = 1/x_2^2 - \lambda p_2 = 0$.

(iii) $|\bar{H}| = 2p_1^2/x_2^3 + 2p_2^2/x_1^3 > 0$ for all positive x_1 and x_2.

(iv) $x_1^* = Y/(p_1 + \sqrt{p_1 p_2}), x_2^* = Y/(p_2 + \sqrt{p_1 p_2})$.

(v) $M = -(\sqrt{p_1} + \sqrt{p_2})^2/Y, \partial M/\partial p_1 = -p_1^{-1/2}(\sqrt{p_1} + \sqrt{p_2})Y, \partial M/\partial Y = (\sqrt{p_1} + \sqrt{p_2})^2/Y^2$.

(vi) $\lambda^* = (\sqrt{p_1} + \sqrt{p_2})^2/Y^2 = \partial M/\partial Y$.

Exercises for Chapter 7

7.2

1. (i) $\dfrac{\partial M}{\partial w} = -L^*$, (ii) $\dfrac{\partial M}{\partial r} = -K^*$, (iii) $\dfrac{\partial M}{\partial p} = L^{*1/2} + K^{*1/2}$.

2. (i) $\dfrac{\partial M}{\partial w} = -L^*$, (ii) $\dfrac{\partial M}{\partial r} = -K^*$, (iii) $\dfrac{\partial M}{\partial p} = 4L^{*1/4} K^{*1/2}$.

7.3

1. (i) $\dfrac{\partial M}{\partial p_1} = -\lambda^* x_1^*$, (ii) $\dfrac{\partial M}{\partial p_2} = -\lambda^* x_2^*$, (iii) $\dfrac{\partial M}{\partial Y} = \lambda^*$.

2. $\dfrac{\partial M}{\partial w} = L^*$, $\dfrac{\partial M}{\partial r} = K^*$, $\dfrac{\partial M}{\partial Q_0} = \lambda^*$.

3. (i) $\dfrac{\partial M}{\partial p_2} = \bar{x}_2$, (ii) $\dfrac{\partial M}{\partial u_o} = \bar{\lambda}$.

7.4

1. (i) $Z_\lambda = p_1 x_1 + p_2 x_2 - Y, Z_1 = U_1 + \lambda p_1 = 0, Z_2 = U_2 + \lambda p_2 = 0$

   (ii)

$$|\bar{H}| = \begin{vmatrix} 0 & p_1 & p_2 \\ p_1 & U_{11} & U_2 \\ p_2 & U_{21} & U_{22} \end{vmatrix} > 0$$

at the critical point.

   (iii)

$$\bar{H} \begin{pmatrix} d\lambda \\ dx_1 \\ dx_2 \end{pmatrix} = \begin{pmatrix} dY - x_1 dp_1 - x_2 dp_2 \\ -\lambda dp_1 \\ -\lambda dp_2 \end{pmatrix}.$$

   (iv) $\dfrac{\partial x_1}{\partial p_2} = -x_2 \dfrac{\bar{H}_{12}}{|\bar{H}|} - \lambda \dfrac{\bar{H}_{32}}{|\bar{H}|}$.

(v)

$$\left(\frac{\partial x_1}{\partial Y}\right)_{\substack{\text{Prices}\\\text{constant}}} = \frac{\bar{H}_{12}}{|\bar{H}|}.$$

(vi) $dY - x_1 dp_1 - x_2 dp_2 = 0$.

2. (i) $e_{12} = \varepsilon_{12} - \alpha_2\eta_1$, where e_{12} is the cross elasticity of demand, α_2 is the proportion of income Y spent on good 2, and η_1 is the income elasticity of demand for good 1.

7.5

1. (i) $x_1^* = \alpha Y/(\alpha + \beta)p_1,\ x_2^* = \beta Y/(\alpha + \beta)p_2$.
   (ii)

$$V = \left(\frac{\alpha}{p_1}\right)^\alpha \left(\frac{\beta}{p_2}\right)^\beta \left(\frac{Y}{\alpha + \beta}\right)^{\alpha+\beta}.$$

(iii)

$$e = (\alpha + \beta)\left[u\left(\frac{p_1}{\alpha}\right)^\alpha \left(\frac{p_2}{\beta}\right)^\beta\right]^{1/\alpha+\beta}.$$

(iv)

$$\bar{x}_1 = u^{1/(\alpha+\beta)}\left(\frac{\alpha p_2}{\beta p_1}\right)^{\beta/(\alpha+\beta)}, \quad \bar{x}_2 = u^{1/(\alpha+\beta)}\left(\frac{\beta p_1}{\alpha p_2}\right)^{\alpha/(\alpha+\beta)}.$$

2. (i) $\bar{x}_1 = up_1^{1/(\rho-1)}/(p_1^\sigma + p_2^\sigma)^{1/\rho},\ \bar{x}_2 = up_2^{1/(\rho-1)}/(p_1^\sigma + p_2^\sigma)^{1/\rho}$, where $\sigma = \rho/(\rho - 1)$.

   (ii) $e = u(p_1^\sigma + p_2^\sigma)^{1/\sigma}$.

   (iii) $V = y(p_1^\sigma + p_2^\sigma)^{-1/\sigma}$.

   (iv) $x_1^* = yp_1^{\sigma-1}/(p_1^\sigma + p_2^\sigma),\ x_2^* = yp_2^{\sigma-1}/(p_1^\sigma + p_2^\sigma)$.

3. (i) $\bar{x}_1 = w_1^{\sigma/\rho}y/(w_1^\sigma + w_2^\sigma)^{1/\rho},\ \bar{x}_2 = w_2^{\sigma/\rho}y/(w_1^\sigma + w_2^\sigma)^{1/\rho}$ where $\sigma = \rho/(\rho - 1)$.
   (ii) $C = y(w_1^\sigma + w_2^\sigma)^{1/\sigma}$.

4. (i)

$$\bar{x}_1 = \left(\frac{y}{100}\right)^{4/3}\left(\frac{2w_2}{w_1}\right)^{1/3}, \quad \bar{x}_2 = \left(\frac{y}{100}\right)^{4/3}\left(\frac{w_1}{2w_2}\right)^{2/3}.$$

(ii)

$$C = \frac{3}{2}\left(\frac{y}{100}\right)^{4/3} w_1^{2/3}(2w_2)^{1/3}.$$

(iv) $x_1^* = (50p)^4/2w_1^3 w_2$, $x_2^* = (50p)^4/4w_1^2 w_2^2$, $\Pi^* = (50p)^4/4w_1^2 w_2$.

(v) $y^* = 50^4 p^3/w_1^2 w_2$.

Exercises for Chapter 8

8.2
1. (i) $S_R = \frac{1}{2}(1 + 1/n) \to \frac{1}{2}$ (ii) $S_R = \frac{1}{6}(2 + 3/n + 1/n^2) \to \frac{1}{3}$

(iii) $S_R = \frac{1}{4}(1 + 2/n + 1/n^2) \to \frac{1}{4}$

8.3
1. $\dfrac{256}{3}$

2. (i) $\dfrac{52}{3}$,   (ii) $7\dfrac{1}{5}$,

(iii) $\dfrac{2}{5}$,   (iv) 5796.375,

(v) $\dfrac{2}{3}$.

8.4
1. (i) $-9x^{-4}/4 - 7x^3/3 + c$ (ii) $2(1 + x)^{1/2} + c$

(iii) $\dfrac{3}{2}e^{x^2} + c$ (iv) $-x^2/2 - 2x^{-5}/5 + c$

(v) $\dfrac{2}{3}x^{3/2} - 2x^{1/2} + c$ (vi) $\dfrac{1}{5}(x^2 + 2x + 7)^{5/2} + c$

(vii) $4(x^{5/2} - x^{3/2})^{-1} + c$ (viii) $-\dfrac{2}{5}(1 - x^5)^{1/2} + c$

c is an arbitrary constant.

2. (i) $2[(x+1)^{7/2}/7 - 2(x+1)^{5/2}/5 + (x+1)^{3/2}/3] + c$

   (ii) $\frac{2}{27}\left(\frac{1}{5}(3x+2)^{5/2} - \frac{4}{3}(3x+2)^{3/2} + 4(3x+2)^{1/2}\right) + c$

   (iii) 0.4566

3. When x ranges from -1 to 1, u remains fixed at 2.

4. (i) $x \sin x + \cos x + c$ (ii) $x^2/2 \log 3x - x^2/6 + c$

   (iii) $xe^x - e^x + c$ (iv) $\frac{2}{3}(1+x)^{3/2}x - \frac{4}{15}(1+x)^{5/2} + c$

   (v) $x \log x - x + c$ (vi) $\frac{1}{3}e^{3x}\left(x^3 - x^2 + \frac{2}{3}x - \frac{2}{9}\right) + c$

   (vii) $e^{ax}(a \sin bx - b \cos bx)/(a^2 + b^2) + c$

8.5

1. (i) divergent   (ii) convergent
   (iii) convergent   (iv) divergent
   (v) divergent

2. (i) $\dfrac{13}{12}$ (ii) $\dfrac{8}{3}$

   (iii) $\dfrac{1}{3}$ (iv) $\dfrac{121}{70}$

8.6

1. (i) $x_1^* = Y/2p_1, x_2^* = Y/2p_2$
   (ii) $V = Y^2/4p_1p_2$
   (iii) $CS = 0.09116Y, C = 0.09544Y, E = 0.08713Y$

2. (i) $x_j^* = \gamma_j(1 - \beta_j) + \beta_j(y - \sum_{i \neq j} \gamma_i p_i)/p_j$.
   (ii) $CS = (0.1)\gamma_1 p_1^o(1 - \beta_1) + h \log 1.1, h = \beta_1(y - \sum_{i \neq j} \gamma_i p_i)$.
   (iii) $C = (0.1)\gamma_1 p_1^o + [(1.1)\beta_1 - 1](y - \sum_i \gamma_i p_i^o), E = C/(1.1)^\beta$.

Exercises for Chapter 9

9.4

1. (i) $y(x) = 2e^{-4x} + (e^{2x} - e^{-4x})/6$.
   (ii) $y(x) = (5e^{-7x} + e^{-x})/6$.
   (iii) $y(x) = x^2 + 2(x + 1) - 4e^{x-1}$.

2. (i) $dY/dt + aY = -\bar{I}/v, a = (\gamma - 1)/v$.

(ii) $(\gamma - 1)/v > 0$.

(iii) As $0 < \gamma < 1$ and $v > 0$, this condition will not hold and the time path for Y will be explosive.

3. (i) Consumers when faced with rising prices may buy now to avoid higher prices in the future in which case $c > 0$. Alternatively they may hold off buying now expecting prices to fall in the future in which case $c < 0$.

(ii) $P(t) = (\alpha - a)/(b - \beta) + P(0)e^{-dt}$, with $d = (b - \beta)/c$.

(iii) $c < 0, \bar{P} = (\alpha - a)/(b - \beta)$.

4. (ii) $\phi(k) = k^\alpha$,

(iv)

$$k^* = \left(\frac{s}{n + \delta}\right)^{1/(1-\alpha)},$$

(v)

$$c^* = \left(\frac{s}{n + \delta}\right)^{\alpha/(1-\alpha)} - (n - \delta)\left(\frac{s}{n + \delta}\right)^{1/(1-\alpha)},$$

$$k_g^* = \left(\frac{n + \delta}{\alpha}\right)^{1/(\alpha-1)}, \quad s_g^* = \alpha.$$

9.6

1. (i) $y = 2e^{2x} + xe^{2x}$.

(ii) $y = -4e^{2x}/3 + 7e^{-x}/3$.

(iii) $y = -14/3 + 4x - 3x^2 + c_1e^{3x} + c_2e^{-x}$.

(iv) $y = -2xe^{-x} + c_1e^{3x} + c_2e^{-x}$

(v) $y = (12xe^{2x} + 14e^{2x} + 31e^{-x})/9$.

(vi) $y = 2 + e^{x/2}(2\cos x/2 + 2\sin x/2)$.

(vii) $y = -x + x^2/2 + 2 - e^{-x}$.

(viii) $y = x^2e^{-x}/2 + c_1e^{-x} + c_2xe^{-x}$.

2. (i) $y = -2x + xe^{3x} + c_1 + c_2e^{3x}$.

(ii) $y = -6 + 3x + x^2e^{-x}/2 + c_1e^{-x} + c_2xe^{-x}$.

(iii) $y = \frac{3}{2} - 3x - \frac{4}{3}xe^{-x} + c_1e^{2x} + c_2e^{-x}$.

9.7

1. The real roots and the real parts of imaginary roots of the nth degree polynominal equation

$$a_0m^n + a_1m^{n-1} + \cdots + a_{n-1}m + a_n = 0$$

are negative if and only if the first n determinants of

$$a_1, \begin{vmatrix} a_1 & a_3 \\ a_0 & a_2 \end{vmatrix}, \begin{vmatrix} a_1 & a_3 & a_5 \\ a_0 & a_2 & a_4 \\ 0 & a_1 & a_3 \end{vmatrix}, \begin{vmatrix} a_1 & a_3 & a_5 & a_7 \\ a_0 & a_2 & a_4 & a_6 \\ 0 & a_1 & a_3 & a_5 \\ 0 & a_0 & a_2 & a_4 \end{vmatrix} \cdots$$

are all positive, where it is understood that in these determinants we set $a_r = 0$ for all $r > n$ needed to obtain these determinants.

2. (i) Divergent.
   (ii) Convergent.
   (iii) Divergent.

9.8

1. (i)

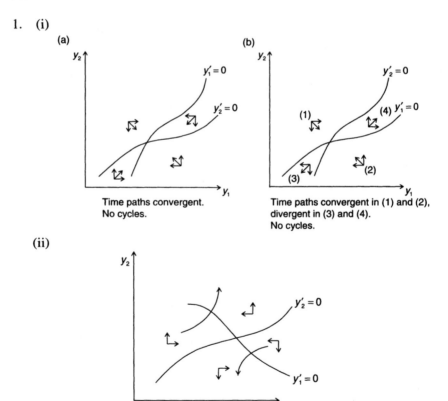

(a) Time paths convergent.
No cycles.

(b) Time paths convergent in (1) and (2),
divergent in (3) and (4).
No cycles.

(ii)

Divergent time paths without oscillations.

(iii)

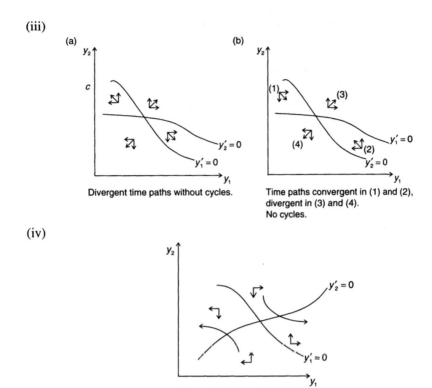

Divergent time paths without cycles.

Time paths convergent in (1) and (2),
divergent in (3) and (4).
No cycles.

(iv)

Time paths divergent without cycles.

Exercises for Chapter 10

10.2

1. (i) $0 < f' < 1$.
   (ii) $-1 < f' < 0$.
   (iii) $f' > 1$.
   (iv) $f' < -1$.

(a) Divergent without cycles.
(b) $0.0399\pi < y_t < 0.9601\pi$, divergent without cycles, otherwise convergent without cycles.
(c) Divergent without cycles.

10.3

1. (i) $y = c_1 + c_2 e^{3x}$.
   (ii) $y = 20 + 8x + x^2 + (c_1 + c_2 x)2^x$.

(iii) $y = -2 + 6x + x^2 + 2^{x/2}(c_1 \cos \pi x/4 + c_2 \sin \pi x/4)$.

(iv) $y = x^2 2^{x-1} + 32 + 8x + c_1 2^x + c_2 x 2^x$.

(v) $y = 3.2^x - 3 - 5x/2 + x 2^{x-2}$.

2.　(i) $(2 + \alpha)^2 \beta^2 > 4(1 + \alpha)$.

　(ii) $(2 + \alpha)^2 \beta = 4(1 + \alpha)$.

　(iii) $(2 + \alpha)^2 \beta < 4(1 + \alpha)$. Convergent $\beta(1 + \alpha) < 1$, divergent $\beta(1 + \alpha) > 1$.

　(iv)

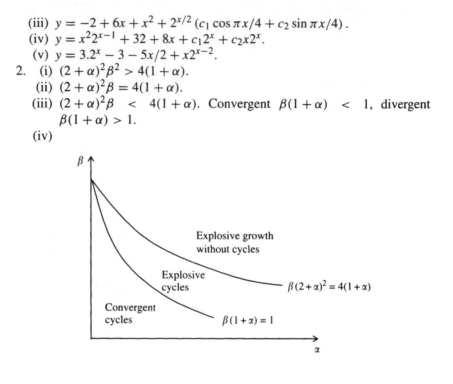

3.　When time is treated as a discrete variable, we regard our economic variables as changing only after the passage of discrete intervals of time. If $y(x)$ is our economic variable then $y(x)$ is defined for $x = 0, 1, 2, \ldots$.

　For continuous time the economic variables are regarded as changing continuously.

　In a second order linear differential equation with constant coefficients, cycles can only occur in the case where the roots of the auxiliary equation are conjugate complex numbers. In a second order linear difference equation with constant coefficients, cycles can occur in all three cases: where the roots of the auxiliary equation are real and distinct, real and equal, and conjugate complex. For example in the first case if m_1 and m_2 are the distinct roots and $|m_1| > |m_2|$ with m_1 negative then eventually m_1 dominates and we have cycles. This means that for difference equations unlike differential equations we must look at the conditions on the parameters of our model that ensure

　(i) m_1 and m_2 are both positive

　(ii) m_1 and m_2 are both negative

　(iii) m_1 negative, m_2 positive but $|m_1| > m_2$.

10.5

(i) $Y_t - cY_{t-1} + cY_{t-2} = a/(1-b), c = v/(1-b), m^2 - cm + c = 0,$
$\bar{Y} = a/(1-b).$

(ii) $c > 4$. No oscillations.

(iii) $c = 4$. Explosive growth, no oscillations.

(iv) $c < 4. c < 1$ convergent cycles, $c > 1$ divergent cycles.

(v) $c > 4$ implies that the accelerator is greater than 4 times the marginal propensity to save etc.

10.6

1. (i) divergent
   (ii) divergent
   (iii) convergent

2.

$$\Delta_1 = \begin{vmatrix} 1 & a_1 + a_3 - a_2 - 1 \\ a_1 + a_3 - a_2 - 1 & 1 \end{vmatrix}$$

$$\Delta_2 = \left| \begin{array}{cc:cc} 1 & 0 & a_1 + a_3 - a_2 - 1 & 3 - 2a_1 + a_2 \\ a_1 - 3 & 1 & 0 & a_1 + a_3 - a_2 - 1 \\ \hdashline a_1 + a_3 - a_2 - 1 & 0 & 1 & a_1 - 3 \\ 3 - 2a_1 + a_2 & a_1 + a_3 - a_2 - 1 & 0 & 1 \end{array} \right|$$

$$\Delta_3 = \left| \begin{array}{ccc:} 1 & 0 & 0 \\ a_1 - 3 & 1 & 0 \\ 3 - 2a_1 + a_2 & a_1 - 3 & 1 \\ \hdashline a_1 + a_3 - a_2 - 1 & 0 & 0 \\ 3 - 2a_1 + a_2 & a_1 + a_3 - a_2 - 1 & 0 \\ a_1 - 3 & 3 - 2a_1 + a_2 & a_1 + a_3 - a_2 - 1 \end{array} \right.$$

$$\left. \begin{array}{ccc} a_1 + a_3 - a_2 - 1 & 3 - 2a_1 + a_2 & a_1 - 3 \\ 0 & a_1 + a_3 - a_2 - 1 & 3 - 2a_1 + a_2 \\ 0 & 0 & a_1 + a_3 - a_2 - 1 \\ \hdashline 1 & a_1 - 3 & 3 - 2a_1 + a_2 \\ 0 & 1 & a_1 - 3 \\ 0 & 0 & 1 \end{array} \right|$$

Exercises for Chapter 11

11.3
1.   (i)

$$x^*(t) = 4 - 2t$$
$$u^*(t) = -2$$
$$\lambda^*(t) = -5.$$

   (ii)

$$x^*(t) = -4 + 0.9827e^{-t} + 5.0173e^t$$
$$\lambda^*(t) = -0.9827e^{-t}$$
$$u^*(t) = -2 + 0.9827e^{-t}.$$

   (iii)

$$x^*(t) = 0.7499e^{-3t} + 0.1945e^{3t} + 0.0556$$
$$\lambda^*(t) = 0.3333 + 2.3343e^{3t}$$
$$u^*(t) = 0.1667 + 1.1672e^{3t}.$$

2.   (i) The problem facing the consumer is

$$\max \int_0^{40} \log C(t)e^{-0.02t}dt$$

subject to

$$W'(t) = 0.05\,W(t) - C(t)$$
$$W(0) = 1, W(40) = 0.5,$$

The control variable is consumption $C(t)$, the state variable is wealth $W(t)$.

   (ii) The necessary conditions are

$$\frac{e^{-0.02t}}{C} - \lambda = 0$$
$$\lambda' = -0.05\lambda$$
$$W' = 0.05\,W - C$$
$$W(0) = 1, W(40) = 0.5$$

These conditions are also sufficient.

$$C^*(t) = 0.03386e^{0.03t}$$
$$W^*(t) = 1.693e^{0.03t} - 0.693e^{0.05t}.$$

3. (i) The reformulate problem is

$$\text{Maximize} \quad \int_a^b f(u(t), x(t), t)dt$$

subject to $\quad x'(t) = u(t)$

$$x(a) = x_a, \ x(b) = x_b.$$

(ii) The Hamiltonian is

$$H = f(u(t), x(t), t) + \lambda u(t).$$

The necessary conditions are

$$\frac{\partial f(u, x, t)}{\partial u} + \lambda = 0$$

$$\lambda' = -\frac{\partial f(u, x, t)}{\partial x}$$

$$x' = u$$

$$x(a) = x_a, x(b) = x_b$$

11.4

1. (i)

$$x^*(t) = 4e^t + e^{t+10} - e^{10-t} + 1$$
$$\lambda^*(t) = -2 + 2e^{10-t}$$
$$u^*(t) = 1 - 2e^{10-t}.$$

(ii)

$$x^*(t) = \tfrac{1}{4}e^t + \tfrac{1}{2}e^{t+1} - \tfrac{1}{2}e^{1-t} + \tfrac{7}{4}$$
$$\lambda^*(t) = -4 + 4e^{1-t}$$
$$u^*(t) = -\tfrac{7}{4} + e^{1-t}.$$

(iii)

$$x^*(t) = 0.7998e^{-3t} + 0.1446e^{3t} + 0.0556$$
$$\lambda^*(t) = 0.3333 + 1.7354e^{3t}$$
$$u^*(t) = 0.1667 + 0.8677e^{3t}.$$

(iv)

$$x^*(t) = 1.6796e^t - \frac{e^{1-t}}{4} - \frac{t}{2}$$
$$\lambda^*(t) = -1 + e^{1-t}$$
$$u^*(t) = (t - 1 + e^{1-t})/2.$$

(v)

$$x^*(t) = 2e^t$$
$$\lambda^*(t) = -10 + 27.1828e^{-t}$$
$$u^*(t) = 0.$$

(vi)

$$\lambda^*(t) = -10 + 73.8904e^{-t}$$
$$u^* = 4 \quad 0 \le t \le 0.2082$$
$$u^* = 2 \quad 0.2082 < t \le 2$$
$$x^*(t) = -4 + 5e^t \quad 0 \le t \le 0.2082$$
$$x^*(t) = -2 + 9.8723e^t \quad 0.208 < t < 2.$$

2. (i) The consumer's problem is

$$\text{maximize} \quad \int_0^T \log C(t)e^{-\delta t}\,dt$$
$$\text{subject to} \quad W' = rW - C$$
$$W(0) = W_0, \ W(T) \ge 0.$$

(iii) The necessary conditions are

$$\frac{e^{-\delta t}}{C} - \lambda = 0$$

$$\lambda' = -\lambda r$$

$$W' = rW - C$$

$$W(0) = W_0, \ W(T) \geq 0, \ \lambda(T) \geq 0, \ \lambda(T)W(T) = 0.$$

The conditions are also sufficient.

(vi) Optimal consumption rises over time if $r > \delta$. If not it will fall over time.

3. (i) The problem facing the community is

$$\text{maximize} \quad \int_0^{100} \log au^\alpha \, dt$$

$$\text{subject to} \quad x' = -u$$

$$x(0) = 1000, \ x(100) \geq 0.$$

(ii) The Hamiltonian is

$$H = \log a + \alpha \log u - \lambda u.$$

A set of necessary and sufficient conditions are

$$\frac{\alpha}{u} - \lambda = 0$$

$$\lambda' = 0$$

$$x' = -u$$

$$x(0) = 1000, \ x(100) \geq 0, \ \lambda(100) \geq 0, \ x(100)\lambda(100) = 0.$$

(iii) The optimal rate of extraction is

$$u^* = 10$$

with the accompanying time path for the resource given by

$$x^*(t) = 1000 - 10t.$$

11.5

(i) The elasticity of marginal utility is $\eta(c) = -1$. The instantaneous elasticity of substitution is $\sigma(c) = 1$.

(ii) The production function in per capita is

$$y = k^{3/4}.$$

The problem facing the economy is

$$\text{Maximize} \quad \int_0^\infty e^{-0.05t} \log c \, dt$$

$$\text{subject to} \quad k' = k^{3/4} - c - 0.11k$$

$$k(0) = k_0, \ k(\infty) \geq 0, \ 0 \leq c(t) \leq \phi(k).$$

(iii) The current value Hameltonian is

$$H_c = He^{0.05t} = \log c + \mu(k^{3/4} - c - 0.11k)$$

(iv) The necessary conditions for an optimal solution are

$$\frac{1}{c} - \mu = 0$$

$$\mu' = -\mu\left(\frac{3}{4}k^{-1/4} - 0.16\right)$$

$$k' = k^{3/4} - c - 0.11k$$

$$k(0) = k_0, \ \lim_{T\to\infty} \lambda(T) \geq 0, \ \lim_{T\to\infty} k(T) \geq 0, \ \lim_{T\to\infty} \lambda(T)k(T) = 0.$$

(vi) The steady state level of per capita stock is

$$k^* = 482.7976.$$

and the steady state level of per capita consumption is

$$c^{**} = 49.8891.$$

Further Reading

Books Set at a More Elementary Level

Bradley, T. and Patton, P., 2002. *Essential Mathematics for Economics and Business*, 2nd Ed. Wiley, New York.
Glaister, S., 1984. *Mathematical Methods for Economists*, 3rd Ed. Blackwell, New York.
Renshaw, G., 2005. *Maths for Economics*. Oxford University Press, New York.
Wisniewski, M., 1997. *Introductory Mathematical Methods in Economics*, 2nd Ed. McGraw-Hill, New York.

Books Set at a Similar Level

Black, J. and Bradley, J.F., 1993. *Essential Mathematics for Economists*, 2nd Ed. Wiley, New York.
Birchenhall, C. and Grout, P., 1984. *Mathematics for Modern Economists*. Philip Allen, Oxford.
Chiang, A.C., and Wainwright, K., 2005. *Fundamental Methods of Mathematical Economics*, McGraw-Hill, New York.
Klein, M.W. 1998. *Mathematical Methods for Economics*. Addison Wesley, New York.
Sydsaeter, K. and Hammond, P.J., 2005. *Mathematics for Economic Analysis*. Prentice Hall, New Jersey.

Books at a More Advanced Level

Intrilligator, M., 1971. *Mathematical Optimization and Economic Theory*. Prentice Hall, New Jersey.
Lambert, P.J., 1985. *Advanced Mathematics for Economists, Static and Dynamic Optimization*. Blackwell, New York.
Silberberg, E., 1990. *The Structure of Economics: A Mathematical Analysis*. McGraw-Hill, New York.

Simon, C.P. and Blume, L., 1994. *Mathematics for Economists*. Norton and Co, New York.

Sydsaeter, K., Hammond, P., Seierstad, A., and Strom, A., 2005. *Further Mathematics for Economic Analysis*. Prentice Hall, New Jersey.

Wade Hands, D., 1991. *Introductory Mathematical Economics*. D.C. Heath and Co, New York.

Books of a More Specialised Nature

Chiang, A.C., 1992. *Dynamic Optimization*. McGraw-Hill, New York.

Dhrymes, P.J., 2000. *Mathematics for Econometrics*, 3rd Ed. Springer, New York.

Hadley, G., 1964. *Linear Algebra*. Addison-Wesley, New York.

Kamien, M., and Schwartz, N., 1981. *Dynamic Optimization: The Calculus of Variations and Optimal Control in Economics and Management*. North-Holland, New York.

Leonard, D. and Van Long, N., 1992. *Optimal Control Theory and Static Optimization in Economics*. Cambridge University Press, New York.

Seierstad, A., and Sydsaeter, K., 1987. *Optimal Control Theory with Economic Applications*. North-Holland, New York.

Turkington, D.A., 2002. *Matrix Calculus and Zero-One Matrices*. Cambridge University Press, Cambridge.

Varian, H., 1992. *Microeconomic Analysis*, 3rd Ed. Norton, New York.

Index

Lightning Source UK Ltd.
Milton Keynes UK

175872UK00001B/82/P